Overleaf: June Garden Border with Pink and White Gumpo Azaleas in Flower

Virginia Bluebells

Chinese Evergreens

Harvest of Fall Vegetables

Spring Garden Border of Tulips and Pansies

Southern Living®
Garden Guide
Houseplants, Vegetables, Trees, Shrubs and More

by the Garden and Landscape Staff
Southern Living® Magazine

John Alex Floyd, Jr.	Senior Horticulturist
Lois B. Trigg	Associate Garden Editor
Linda C. Askey	Assistant Garden Editor
Vicki Ingham	Editorial Assistant
Beth Maynor	Photographer
Van Chaplin	Photographer
Sylvia Martin	Photographer
Yukie McLean	Illustrator

Copyright© 1981 by Oxmoor House, Inc.
Book Division of Southern Progress Corporation
P.O. Box 2463, Birmingham, Alabama 35201

Eugene Butler	Chairman of the Board
Emory Cunningham	President and Publisher
Vernon Owens	Executive Vice President
Don Logan	Vice President and General Manager
Gary McCalla	Editor, *Southern Living*
John Logue	Editor-in-Chief
Jerry Higdon	Production Manager

Southern Living® Garden Guide

Editor: Karen Phillips Irons
Book Design Concept: Robert G. Herr, Charles Crone
    Associates, Inc.
Design Adaptation: James R. Weldon
Editorial Assistants: Cecilia Robinson, Rebecca Gilliland

Library of Congress Catalog Number: 80-84409
ISBN: 0-8487-0518-1
Manufactured in the United States of America
Third Printing 1983

Contents

Preface

Almost from the first issue of *Southern Living* magazine, our readers have been asking us gardening questions. Of course, we have always tried to answer them with good information to help solve their problems. So in September, 1966, we started a "Letters to Our Garden Editors" column in *Southern Living*.

Over the years its popularity has grown, and today many people look upon this page as the "Dear Abby" of gardening. During these 15 years, one person has been responsible for its success: Beth Carlson, who was our Assistant Garden Editor until she retired in 1978. She still comes to the office regularly to prepare the monthly feature. Therefore, the authors of *Garden Guide* feel it is only fitting to dedicate this book to her.

Acknowledgments must also be made to the many people who have contributed to the preparation of this book. Mr. Fred Thode of the Department of Horticulture, Clemson University, Clemson, South Carolina, was the senior reviewer for *Garden Guide*. Other reviewers include Dr. Dan Ezell of the Horticulture Department of Clemson University and Mr. David Chambers of Callaway Gardens in Pine Mountain, Georgia, who reviewed the vegetables section; Dr. J. E. Fairey of the Department of Botany, Clemson University, and Mrs. Lindsay Smith and Mrs. Hugh Kaul, members of the Birmingham Botanical Society, who reviewed the wildflowers section; and Marc Reynolds of the Netherlands Flower Bulb Institute, who reviewed the bulbs section.

We also appreciate the help of many of our coworkers at *Southern Living*, especially Susan Denman, Editorial Assistant; Cathy Boozer, Assistant Copy Chief; Lori Davis, Editorial Assistant for the Garden and Landscape Department; Rebecca Scoggins, Editorial Assistant to Philip Morris and me; and finally, the other editors who had to tolerate all of us during the writing and editing.

We hope that *Garden Guide* will help each of you solve many of the problems that you may be having with your gardens, as well as stimulate many new gardening ideas and projects.

John Alex Floyd, Jr.
January 1981

Introduction

Whether you want to grow the perfect petunia, the juiciest tomato, the healthiest houseplant, the stateliest tree, or the rarest wildflower, there is usually a question that has to be answered. The information in *Garden Guide* is designed to help you answer many of the typical questions that arise. While intended mainly for use by Southern gardeners, much of the information in *Garden Guide* is also adaptable to other regions. Remember, the lowest average temperature in the South generally ranges from −5 degrees F. in the Upper South to above freezing year-round in Florida. If you live outside the South and wish to know whether one of the outdoor plants included in *Garden Guide* will grow in your area, check with your local nurseryman or county Extension agent as to its adaptability to your area.

Garden Guide is divided into eight sections according to subject matter for easy use. The questions are printed in boldface type to help you quickly find subjects of particular interest to you.

"Annuals and Perennials" not only gives the reader guidance for growing and cultivating the flowering plants in the South, but it also suggests basic ways to blend these plants into garden borders for continuous bloom throughout the spring, summer, and fall.

"Bulbs" provides cultural information on all of the common types of bulbs as well as the time of planting and the planting depths. Included, too, are a few unusual species that do exceptionally well in the South. In addition to discussing bulbs for outdoor use, this section provides tips on selected types that grow well indoors.

"Vegetables, Herbs, and Small Fruits" comprises one of the most extensive sections of the book. Everything from planting to harvesting your vegetable garden is covered. A chart of good vegetable selections for the South is also given. Culinary herbs are featured,

Bulbs, page 40

Trees & Shrubs, page 176

as well as easy-to-grow fruits suitable for home culture.

"Houseplants" provides answers to tough questions on how to care for plants and which plants to select. Selecting the right houseplants for your interior and using them effectively as bold indoor accents are also discussed.

"Pests and Diseases" is a working chapter that identifies the insects and diseases of the plants discussed in the other chapters of the book. Questions and answers on how to control and correct your problems are covered.

"Lawns and Ground Covers" explains how to grow most of the popular Southern turf grasses suitable for the home. Ground cover choices and uses are discussed in relation to how turf can be used or eliminated in the residential grounds.

"Trees and Shrubs" describes how to grow woody ornamental plants successfully. Proper planting techniques and proper care are stressed to help you keep your trees and shrubs actively growing.

"Wildflowers" familiarizes you with the growing of these plants in the home landscape. Basic planting, culture, and identification features are included.

The authors have attempted to present each plant discussed in this book with an acceptable common name and an accurate botanical name. *Hortus Third* was the basis of the plant identification system, in addition to help from the United States National Arboretum and Southern botanical gardens as well as colleges and universities that are active in horticulture throughout the South. Botanical names are important when evaluating plants because the shapes and growth rates are so diverse. To eliminate confusion, only the term selection or type is used to denote a variation within a species. *Garden Guide* is completely indexed and cross-referenced for easy use.

Vegetables, Herbs, & Small Fruits, page 68

Houseplants, page 116

Lawns & Ground Covers, page 164

Annuals & Perennials

Hybrid Coneflowers

Annuals and perennials are the gardener's palette with which to paint the landscape in spring, summer, and fall. In garden borders or in massed plantings, annuals and perennials can provide anything from a riot of brilliant color to a subdued range of delicate hues. Different types of flowers may be blended for an interplay of color as the seasons change. Or, a single type may be used for consistent, season-long color. Whether you plant ten flowers or a hundred, you will enjoy the most effective flower display if you use these basic tips.

—Plan your garden carefully to achieve harmonious color blends. Complementary

Impatiens

Marigolds

Pansy

Daylilies

Wax Begonias

Cascading Petunias

colors (violet and yellow, blue and orange, red and green) tend to intensify each other. Neutral or subdued hues planted between brilliant colors will prevent clashes and make the brighter colors more prominent.

—Keep in mind that perennials will remain in place for years, while annuals must be replaced every year. This allows you to experiment every year with different color schemes and planting designs. Use the perennials as the framework around which to plan the annuals. But be sure to blend the colors and blooming times carefully.

—Give annuals and perennials a neutral background, such as a fence, wall, hedge, or screen planting. An appropriate background enhances the effect and allows you to create your own personal design.

—Frame a small or narrow lawn with a colorful annual or perennial border. Or, use a border as the edging for one side of a wide expanse of lawn. This will define the open lawn and give the garden a sense of enclosure. The foreground of green turf also intensifies the interplay of color in the garden border.

—Try planting annuals and perennials in containers for portable seasonal color.

—Bring intensity of color and pattern into a small space with annuals and perennials. The color of annuals and perennials can be warm or cool, depending upon the hue. Vibrant reds and yellows create an exciting, bold sweep of color or a dramatic accent.

Cottage Pinks

Zinnias

Plantain Lily (Hosta)

13

Portulaca

Canna

White, blues, and violets tend to be cooler. A color scheme that combines warm and cool colors or intense hues and paler tints will create visual movement in the garden. In small gardens, every square inch of planting area is important. When you place annuals or perennials into such a setting, they almost always become an accent. Thus, annuals and perennials can bring a bright seasonal look to the garden while requiring a very limited amount of space. Colorful annuals and perennials may also enhance the lines of small formal gardens or provide spots of color to accentuate a free form curve in an informal garden.

Planting annuals and perennials properly is an important factor in growing them successfully. Prepare planting beds by digging the soil to a depth of 12 to 18 inches. Work in plenty of peat moss, leaf mold, or compost to ensure good drainage. Space plants properly, as crowded plants grow less vigorously. If you sow seed directly in the beds, thin seedlings to give them adequate spacing.

When transplanting seedlings grown in pressed peat pots, make sure the pot is completely covered in the ground. If not, the exposed edges may act as a wick, drawing water away from the roots.

If plants are received with bare roots, soak the roots overnight before planting. If the plants are in containers, be sure to set the plant at the same depth as it grew in the container. Remember to press the soil firmly around each plant, then water well to make sure the roots can grow into the surrounding soil to receive nutrients and water. Air pockets around the plant's roots prevent this and allow the roots to dry out.

Mulching promotes better growth by deterring weeds and conserving moisture. Fertilize your annuals and perennials lightly at plantingtime with a formulation such as 5-10-10 to get them off to a good start.

Four O'Clocks

Coleus

Shasta Daisies

Annuals

What is the difference between annuals, biennials, and perennials?

Annuals germinate from seed, produce flowers and seeds, and die, all in one year. Generally, seeds are started indoors before the last frost or sown outdoors after the last frost for bloom in spring, summer, or fall. Biennials start from seeds but spend the first year growing and producing foliage. In the second year, they bloom, set seeds, and die. Perennials grow and produce flowers for three years or more. Each year the foliage and flowers die and the roots go dormant, storing energy for new growth in the next growing season. Perennial seeds are generally sown in spring or summer for bloom the following year. Some perennials, such as butterfly weed (*Asclepias tuberosa*) and Shasta daisy (*Chrysanthemum* x *superbum*), require two years to produce flowering plants. Perennials may also be started from dormant root stock, which are generally set out in fall for bloom the following spring or summer.

Please give me some guidelines for preparing planting beds for annuals.

In the Upper and Middle South, where the ground freezes in the winter, begin preparing the soil in the spring. In the Lower South, you can begin working the soil anytime. Planting beds for annuals should be raised slightly above ground level to allow for settling and to promote good drainage. (*See Figure 1.*)

Dig the soil to a depth of 12 to 18 inches. Work in a generous amount of organic material, such as peat moss, leaf mold, or compost. If the beds are prepared at least two weeks prior to planting, you may also work in fertilizer; the recommended rate is about ½ cup fertilizer, such as 5-10-10, per square yard of bed area. If you plant within two weeks after preparing the beds, wait until plants are well established before applying fertilizer; otherwise, the fertilizer may burn tender roots.

Fig. 1 *Plant annuals in raised beds to promote good drainage.*

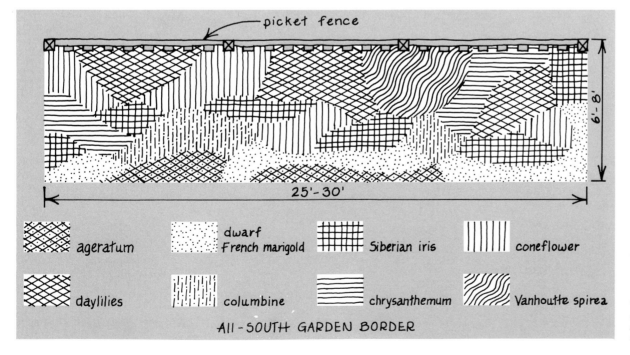

picket fence

6'-8'

25'-30'

ageratum

dwarf French marigold

Siberian iris

coneflower

daylilies

columbine

chrysanthemum

Vanhoutte spirea

All-SOUTH GARDEN BORDER

Garden borders form the floral edge of a garden. An effective garden border makes use of the rich variety of form, texture, and color in plant materials available to Southern gardeners. Plant selections in interlocking patterns to help create visual movement throughout the border. This sketch suggests a border design using plants that will work anywhere in the South. On the following pages are designs using plants particularly well suited to two of the major regions of the South.

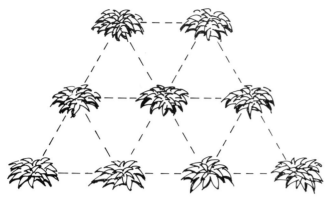

Fig. 2 *Plant annuals in a grid pattern to space them properly. Check seed packets or transplant tags for the correct distance for each selection.*

Can you give me any tips for planting annuals from seeds?

Proper spacing is important for annuals. Before planting, make a grid by pressing your hoe handle into the soil. Space indentations according to the distance specified for mature plants; distance will vary according to plant selection. (*See Figure 2.*)

Next, plant the seeds at the intersections of the grid lines. Seeds sown in early spring need ⅛- to ¼-inch soil covering; seeds planted later in the season require a ¼- to ½-inch soil covering. (The exception is fine seeds, which never need to be covered.)

Firmly press the soil over the seeds to make a shallow depression. This acts as a reservoir to collect water for the seeds. Water them gently but thoroughly with a fine spray, and keep them moist until they have sprouted. When the plants are 2 to 4 inches tall and have several sets of leaves, pinch off the tip of each stem to encourage branching and more profuse flowering.

Taller-growing annuals like cosmos (*Cosmos bipinnatus*) and larkspur (*Delphinium sp.*) may need to be staked to protect them from breaking in wind and heavy rain. Place the stakes 8 to 10 inches into the ground at plantingtime to avoid damaging the annuals' shallow roots later. Stakes should be 4 to 8 inches shorter than the plants' height at maturity.

How should I care for my summer annuals?

The most critical time for summer annuals is the first few weeks after transplanting.

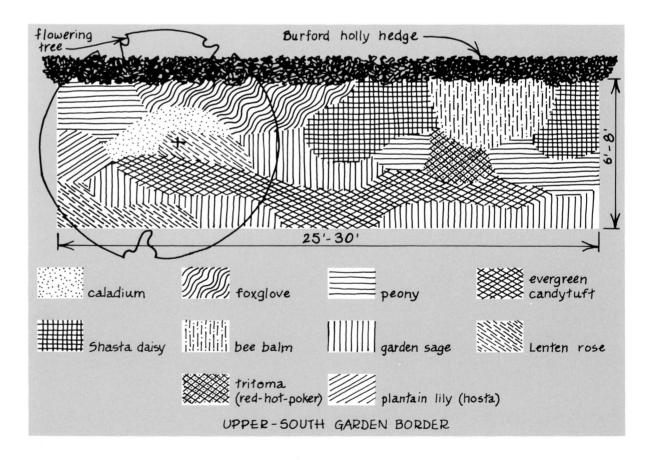

To increase the likelihood of your success with bedding plants, give careful attention to the following points.

—Feeding: Light monthly applications of fertilizer are better than one heavy application. This allows a steady rate of growth and good flower production. Too much fertilizer results in heavy foliage growth and few flowers. (*See Figure 3.*)

—Inspecting: Check plants every few days for pests and diseases.

—Mulching: An organic mulch can decrease water loss through evaporation, reduce weed competition, and stabilize the soil temperature. Pine straw, ground bark, sawdust, and peanut hulls are all useful for this purpose.

—Pruning: Many annual flowers benefit from pinching out the terminal growth of the plant. This results in more compact growth that is more resistant to wind and storm damage. Each time a new shoot develops four sets of leaves, pinch out the top two pairs. New shoots will grow from the base of the remaining leaves.

—Watering: Young plants need frequent waterings until their root systems are well established. After the first few waterings, reduce the frequency and soak the soil deeper each time. Allow the soil surface to become dry between waterings once plants are established.

Is it possible to collect seeds from my annuals to use for next year's garden?

Some of the best bargains in the garden are your annual flowers. To collect seeds, just pull off the dried flowers, open them, and remove the seeds. (*See Figure 4.*) Wait until two or three days after a rainfall to collect seeds. If you collect them while they are wet,

Fig. 3 *Frequent, light applications of fertilizer will encourage annuals to produce an abundance of flowers.*

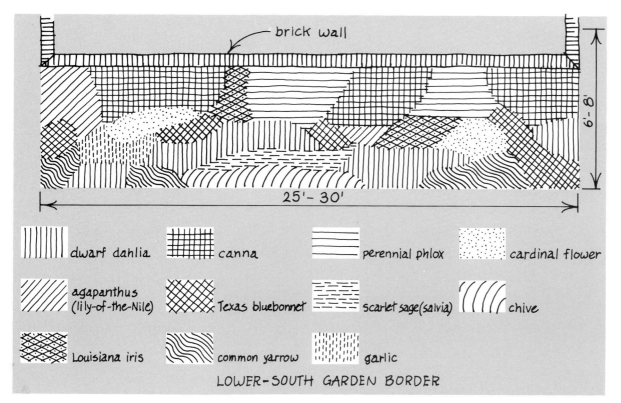

brick wall

6'-8'

25'-30'

|||||| dwarf dahlia   canna   perennial phlox   cardinal flower

agapanthus (lily-of-the-Nile)   Texas bluebonnet   scarlet sage (salvia)   chive

Louisiana iris   common yarrow   garlic

LOWER-SOUTH GARDEN BORDER

Fig. 4 *Pick off spent flowers, open them, and remove the seeds.*

they may rot in storage. To ensure that seeds are sufficiently dry, spread them on a paper towel on a sunny windowsill for a few days; then store them in sealed envelopes, and keep them in any cool, dry place until plantingtime next spring.

From which annuals do you suggest I try to collect seeds?

Collecting seeds is particularly easy on marigolds (*Tagetes sp.*), ageratum (*Ageratum sp.*), zinnias (*Zinnia elegans*), garden balsam (*Impatiens balsamina*), scarlet sage (*Salvia splendens*), and sunflowers (*Helianthus annuus*). Do not attempt to collect very small seeds, such as those of petunias (*Petunia* x *hybrida*) or pansies (*Viola* x *wittrockiana*). They are difficult to handle and may not germinate satisfactorily. Remember, plants from collected seeds are highly variable in size, color, and form.

Please suggest some low-growing, compact flowering annuals to use in a long, sunny border.

Sweet alyssum (*Lobularia maritima*), ageratum, dwarf marigold, dwarf zinnia, Madagascar periwinkle (*Catharanthus roseus*), and dwarf scarlet sage would be good choices. These annuals have a long blooming season and are available in a variety of colors.

What kinds of flowers can be planted in planters that are exposed to full sun?

Many flowers will do well in full sun if they get enough water. Petunias are an old-time favorite, but marigolds, zinnias, portulacas (*Portulaca grandiflora*), and verbena (*Verbena* x *hybrida*) should also thrive in your planters.

Please suggest some annuals to fill in flower beds where bulbs have finished blooming.

For early color, start seeds of ageratum, petunia, snapdragon (*Antirrhinum majus*), and verbena in flats indoors in March to set out between the bulbs in late May. If you prefer late-flowering annuals, you can transplant marigold and zinnia in April, or you can sow seeds where you wish them to flower. Other seeds to sow in early spring include California poppy (*Eschscholzia californica*), candytuft (*Iberis sempervirens*), coreopsis

One of the best low-growing annuals for sunny locations in Southern gardens is dwarf marigold.

Verbena's long blooming season and brightly colored flowers make it an excellent choice for flower beds after bulbs finish blooming.

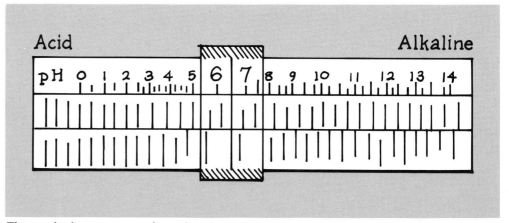

The standard measurement for soil acidity is pH. Soil with a pH of 7.0 is neutral; a pH below 7.0 indicates acid soil and above 7.0, an alkaline soil. Correct pH is critical to the success of your gardening, whether you are growing annuals and perennials, vegetables, or trees and shrubs. The best way to determine the pH of your soil is to have a soil test made.

(*Coreopsis sp.*), nigella (*Nigella damascena*), portulaca, sweet alyssum, and annual baby's breath (*Gypsophila elegans*).

What annuals would look good in a foliage border?

Annuals which are planted for their foliage include coleus (*Coleus blumei*), copperleaf (*Acalypha wilkesiana*), and amaranth (*Amaranthus sp.*). Coleus makes an especially good border in combination with caladiums ((*Caladium sp.*). Coleus also works well with other shade-loving annuals such as impatiens (*Impatiens sp.*), browallia (*Browallia sp.*), or bedding begonias (*Begonia* x *semperflorens* Cultorum).

Copperleaf and amaranth are actually tropical shrubs that can be grown as annuals in Southern gardens. Copperleaf grows to 3 feet in height, with dull bronze to reddish brown leaves. Tolerant of most soils, it needs full sun for best results. Amaranth may reach a height of 3 to 4 feet, so give it plenty of room. Since its colors are generally overpowering, use it by itself in a sunny border or as a small specimen planting.

Are bachelor's-buttons hard to grow? How should I plant them?

Bachelor's-buttons or cornflowers (*Centaurea cyanus*) are hardy, prolific, and easy to grow. Early-spring bloomers, bachelor's-buttons open their flowers at the end of the tulip season. They are often interplanted with spring-flowering bulbs to help conceal the browning foliage of spent daffodils and tulips. Plant seeds over the bed as soon as the bulbs are planted.

Plant bachelor's-buttons anytime from September through March. They grow best in full sun and fertile, well-drained soil but will tolerate dry soil. They can also be grown successfully in a seashore garden. Sow seeds on top of prepared soil; then cover them with about ¼ inch of finely pulverized soil. In open ground, germination should take place within 10 to 15 days. To prolong flowering, water regularly when rainfall is sparse, and pinch faded blooms.

Do you recommend wax begonias for planters? How long will they bloom?

Wax begonias are an excellent choice for containers or planters. Plants set out in early spring in partial sun or shade and moist, rich soil will bloom prolifically through the summer and fall. In the Lower South, they will continue flowering through most of the

Their colorful foliage makes coleus and caladiums two of the most popular foliage plants for the shady border.

Wax begonias can provide a colorful display all summer and into the fall.

Fig. 5

Fig. 6 *Sow geranium seeds over the medium as if you were sprinkling a pinch of salt.*

Fig. 7 *To avoid disturbing the seeds when watering, cover the container with a single layer of newspaper and pour water on it, allowing the moisture to seep through. Or, you may simply mist the surface of the soil.*

winter. In the Middle and Upper South, you can enjoy their blooms during the winter by potting wax begonias before the first frost and bringing them indoors. In the spring, take cuttings from these plants to start new begonias for the next summer's garden.

How can I keep my coleus from looking so leggy?

Coleus grow fast, but pinching them back will keep them low and dense. (*See Figure 5.*) When the major stalk of a seedling or transplant becomes 5 or 6 inches long, pinch it back about 1 inch. Pinch the tips of all developing lateral shoots when they are about 4 inches long. Later, pinch all of the growing tips back about every two weeks to keep the plant low and dense.

The leaves of my geraniums are turning brown and falling off. I water, then I do not water; I put the plants in partial shade, then in open sunshine; I fertilize, then I starve the plants; I have some in pots and some in the ground. Nothing I try seems to work.

It is natural for some geranium (*Pelargonium* x *hortorum*) leaves to turn brown as new leaves are developing; remove brown leaves as you remove spent blooms. Your basic problem is the on-again, off-again approach. Try this procedure.

Cluster three healthy rooted cuttings in a pot or in a bed outdoors in fertile, well-drained soil where they will receive semishade. Fertilize weekly, using a mild solution of houseplant fertilizer for potted plants and a general fertilizer for those in the ground. Do not overwater, but water when the soil dries out. If you put the plants on a specified program and stick with it, you should produce healthy, flowering plants.

We have never been able to root geranium cuttings and carry them over the winter. Please give us some ground rules.

Before the first frost, dig up geraniums, leaving some soil on the roots, and let the plants dry for several days. Then place each plant in a separate mesh bag (like those used to sack citrus or potatoes in supermarkets), and store in a cool, dry place (above freezing). Next spring, make 2- to 3-inch cuttings; root in vermiculite.

What is the best way to start greenhouse geraniums for use indoors this winter?

To have blooming greenhouse geraniums for indoor use in January and February, start seeds in November. Fill seed flats with a moistened medium of equal parts perlite and peat moss. Space seeds about 4 inches apart, or sow seeds individually in bedding plant flats. Sow seeds on top of the soil, and cover with about ¼ inch of soil. Water with a mister to avoid disturbing the seeds. (*See Figures 6, 7.*)

Most common geranium types, such as the Sprinter hybrids or selections, will germinate in the greenhouse in 5 to 15 days when the temperature is maintained at 75 degrees. Germination of scented geraniums takes longer, from 20 to 50 days. Germination rate is high, usually about 90 percent under good conditions.

When seedlings are about 1 inch tall, begin fertilizing with liquid 18-18-18 according to label recommendations. Apply fertilizer every two weeks until plants reach a height of about 4 inches, then transplant into 4-inch pots. Withhold fertilizer for about two weeks while the 4-inch plants are becoming established in their new containers, and then resume the biweekly feedings. Maintain the greenhouse temperature between 68 and 75 degrees.

When should I plant impatiens?

You can set nursery plants out after the last frost. Plant them in well-prepared, well-drained soil in light to deep shade. Do not fertilize the bed at plantingtime. Allow plants to become established (about 2 weeks in the ground); then fertilize sparingly every six weeks at the rate of about ¼ cup of 5-10-10 per square yard of planted area (about ½ teaspoon per plant) and water thoroughly. Keep faded flowers removed to prolong the colorful display. As plants become leggy, you can increase your planting by rooting tip cuttings of healthy stems. (*See Figure 8.*)

Can I use impatiens indoors in a hanging basket?

Impatiens make superb container plants and are at their best in hanging baskets. In the fall, dig the healthiest plants and pot them for indoor display. Locate potted impatiens in bright, indirect light and allow the soil to dry partially between waterings.

Can you recommend some selections of impatiens?

Among the best selections are Futura (red), Elfin Scarlet (red), Elfin Blue (bluish purple), Twinkles (red and white), Scarlet Ripple (red and white), Tangeglow (reddish orange), Tangerine (salmon), and Pink Baby (pink).

There are so many selections of marigolds available that I do not know how to choose the best ones for my garden. Can you help me?

The way to choose is on the basis of plant size, as this determines landscape use. The tall types are best used as cut flowers and as a background for other annuals and perennials. The dwarf types are particularly suitable for low edgings, or they can be interplanted in the vegetable garden. The following classification may help you.

Extra-Dwarf types reach 6 to 8 inches in height; flowers are also small, the largest being about 2½ inches across.

Super-French types are dwarf plants (12 inches tall), but the flowers may be 3 inches or more across.

Nugget marigolds are dwarfish, about 10 inches tall, with 2-inch flowers. They bloom quickly, in five weeks from seeds, and are also noted for their continuous bloom.

Indoors or outdoors, impatiens make good hanging basket plants for shaded areas.

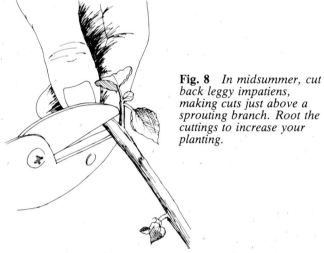

Fig. 8 *In midsummer, cut back leggy impatiens, making cuts just above a sprouting branch. Root the cuttings to increase your planting.*

In this formal planting, a tall type of marigold provides a sweep of color behind the dark-green clipped hedge.

Triple Orange is a triploid hybrid marigold with carnation-type flowers 2½ inches across.

Red Wheels, a dwarf-gigantea marigold, has single flowers 3 inches across on plants 14 inches tall.

Marigolds are spectacular in masses. Space transplants of dwarf selections 6 inches apart and taller types 12 inches apart.

For best flowering, nasturtiums should be grown in full sun and fertilized with a low-nitrogen fertilizer.

Dwarf Double-French types are double-flowered hybrids with 2-inch flowers covering the 8- to 12-inch plants.

Super-Petite marigolds are slightly taller (8 to 10 inches) than the Extra-Dwarf types, with large double flowers.

Triploid hybrids are noted for low-seed production. Plant energy is therefore channeled into flower production, resulting in continuous bloom. Plants are 14 to 15 inches tall, with 2½-inch double flowers.

Semidwarf hybrids produce 3- to 3½-inch double flowers on 14- to 16-inch plants. Although not truly dwarf compared to smaller types, semidwarfs produce compact, mounded plants.

Dwarf Gigantea types also feature large flowers (to 4 inches) on compact plants 10 to 14 inches tall. Flowers may be carnationlike or single.

Dwarf French-crested marigolds produce medium to large flowers (1½ to 3 inches) on 12-inch plants. They are noted for early bloom.

Chrysanthemum-flowered plants vary in height from 12 inches to over 30 inches. Flowers are large (up to 4¼ inches) and mumlike.

Jubilee hybrids are 18 to 24 inches tall, bearing flowers up to 4 inches across. Their sturdy, compact form makes these marigolds resistant to wind and rain damage.

Gigantea types are noted for early bloom, bearing 5-inch double flowers on 30-inch-tall plants.

Hedge marigolds are medium tall (16 to 24 inches), bushy plants, with flowers up to 5 inches across. As the name implies, they may be used for temporary hedges or as background plants in the flower border.

Super hybrids produce the largest plants and flowers of all hybrid marigolds. Mature plants reach 2½ to 3 feet tall; flowers often measure up to 5 inches across and nearly as deep, with deeply ruffled petals.

Grow marigolds in full sun, if possible. They may do quite well in a location that receives direct sun only part of the day, four or five hours, but they will not flower well in shade. Plants also become leggy and sparse without adequate light.

I understand marigolds are easy to grow. Can you tell me how to do it?

After danger of late-spring frost is past, sow seeds directly in the ground or set out transplants. If you choose to start seeds early in a cold frame, sow seeds at least six weeks before the last expected frost. Space transplants about 6 inches apart for dwarf selections, about 12 inches apart for taller types. Plants grown from seeds sown directly in the ground should be thinned to this spacing when 2 to 3 inches tall.

Mulch transplants when set out. If you sow seeds directly in the ground, apply mulch when seedlings are about 4 inches tall.

Begin fertilizing when seedlings reach 4 to 6 inches in height or after nursery transplants have been in the ground about a month. Use 5-10-10 or similar analysis fertilizer at the rate of ½ cup per square yard of planted area. Repeat the application every six weeks until about a month before the first frost is expected in your area.

My nasturtiums have produced abundant foliage but almost no flowers. I planted them in well-prepared soil. What is wrong?

Nasturtiums (*Tropaeolum majus*) thrive on drought and neglect. Fast growing and tolerant of the worst garden soils, they grow best in full sun and average to poor soil. As you have found, nasturtiums planted in good soil tend to produce abundant foliage but few flowers.

Try planting nasturtiums in any garden soil. Sow seeds after danger of frost has passed. Keep faded blossoms and yellowed foliage removed to prolong the life and good looks of your plants. Feed them monthly with ½ cup of 5-10-10 or other general purpose fertilizer per square yard of planted area. Water plants when they appear wilted and the soil is dry.

I have been told that pansies are heavy feeders. What is the best fertilizer? Also, what pests are attracted to pansies?

Feed pansies with a high-nitrogen fertilizer, such as 12-6-6, either in liquid or dry form; apply about every two weeks in the fall until the weather turns cold. Start fertilizing again in early spring when the plants begin growing.

Pests to watch for include pill bugs, snails, and slugs. Control snails and slugs with methiocarb pellets; control pill bugs with diazinon. With either pesticide, apply according to label directions and use caution when applying.

We like the fall color of ornamental peppers. Can we plant them in July to enjoy them this fall?

Yes, but plant seeds of ornamental pepper (*Capsicum annuum*) as early in July as possible. Keep the seedbed constantly moist until the seeds germinate; then shade the young seedlings for several days. The plants should begin to provide color in four to six weeks and continue until the first freeze.

What can I do when my petunias get leggy?

You can keep petunias bushy by pinching out the topmost blossoms and trimming the foliage freely three or four times during the summer. (*See Figure 9.*) If the plants are healthy, you can also rejuvenate them in late summer by shearing them back to about half their height. Fertilize petunias with 5-10-10 or similar complete fertilizer at the rate of ½ cup per square yard of planted area. Keep them well watered, and mulch with pine straw or ground bark to conserve soil moisture. Container-grown petunias will also respond well to shearing and an application of concentrated liquid houseplant fertilizer, such as 18-18-18.

To obtain maximum flower production, feed pansies in fall and spring.

Ornamental peppers are a good replacement for spent summer annuals.

Masses of colorful petunias will work well in a variety of landscape combinations, provided they have plenty of space to grow.

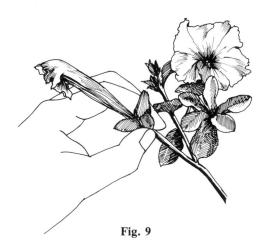

Fig. 9

Annuals & Perennials   23

Drifts of white petunias create a backdrop for a colorful display of calendulas in early spring or fall. In summer, petunias could be combined with marigolds or zinnias for a similar effect.

These giant cactus-flowered zinnias hold their large, frilly blooms several inches above the foliage. The long stems are perfect for cutting.

Can you give me some suggestions on using petunias?

In a border planting, petunias can be used alone or in combination with other annuals. When using petunias alone, mass the plantings for greatest impact. Using a single color can make the effect even more pleasing. If you are using two colors of petunias together, use one color to dominate and the other to accent and highlight. If you use petunias in combination with other bedding plants, be cautious when mixing colors. Use companion colors with such annuals as calendulas (*Calendula officinalis*), marigolds, zinnias, ageratum, and salvia. In borders, remember that petunias are low to medium in height and should be used in the foreground.

A lesser-known but equally spectacular class of petunias is the cascading petunias. These work well in hanging baskets or along retaining walls, where their cascading form can be displayed to best advantage.

What conditions does portulaca need to give the best flower display?

Portulaca requires full sun for its inch-wide blossoms to open every morning. Plant it in poor soil in any hot, dry location, such as a rock garden or a bank, or use it as a ground cover or container plant. Start plants from seeds sown indoors four to six weeks before the last frost; or broadcast the fine seeds outdoors after the danger of frost is past. Portulaca is an annual, but it may reseed itself year after year.

I have never had success with annual sweet peas. Please tell me the right way to grow them.

Plant annual sweet pea seeds (*Lathyrus odoratus*) in October or November. Annual sweet peas do not fare well during summer heat. The earlier you plant them, the more bloom you can expect prior to hot summer days. Plant in well-drained soil in full sun, and plan to support the vines with wires or a trellis. Work the soil well before planting, and add ½ pound of lime to a 25-foot row, mixing it well into the surface soil. Before planting, soak the seeds in water; or spread a moistened paper towel on a saucer. Scatter the seeds on the towel; then roll the seeds gently so that most of their surfaces contact the moist towel. Place the saucer of seeds (still in the moist towel) in a plastic bag, seal it, and put it in a warm place. Check the seeds daily for signs of sprouting, which should start in about three days.

How should I choose zinnias?

A good way to choose zinnias is to decide what height plant you want, then choose colors and flower forms from selections in that size group. Extra dwarf zinnias bloom the earliest of all zinnias and include the Thumbelina and Mini series. Plants are about 6 to 8 inches tall with mounded form. Blooms are 1¼ to 2 inches wide, double or semidouble. Use these small zinnias in borders or in pots.

Dwarf zinnias, growing from 7 to 14 inches tall, include narrowleaf zinnias (*Zinnia angustifolia*), the Cupids, the Button series, and the All-America award-winning Peter Pan series. This size is popular for borders, containers, and mass plantings.

Narrowleaf zinnias are a low-growing species with small, single gold blooms that cover the ground like wildflowers. Because of the growth habit, these zinnias are suitable for adding color to a naturalistic landscape.

The Cupid and Button types are mounding plants with 1- to 1½-inch round blooms, which are often used in small arrangements and bouquets.

The Peter Pan zinnias produce 3- to 4-inch double flowers. Selections are named by color and include cream, orange, gold, pink, plum, and scarlet.

Half tall zinnias are comprised of the Lilliput (pompon) selections, which grow 18 to 24 inches tall. The plants are bushy and rounded, heavily covered with 1½- to 3-inch round flowers. They are popular for cutting.

The Ruffles series and Pumila zinnias fall into the tall category, reaching a height of 24 to 30 inches. The Ruffles hybrids produce ruffled double blooms about 2 to 4 inches wide on an upright, uniform-size plant. Cherry Ruffles, Yellow Ruffles, and Scarlet Ruffles are All-America Selections winners. Pumila zinnias are often listed as "Cut and Come Again" because of their prolific flowering. Blooms are round double flowers 2 to 3 inches across. They are quite popular for cutting.

Giant zinnias are 30 inches or more tall and include the dahlia-flowered selections, the State Fair series, and the giant cactus-flowered types. Dahlia-flowered types have very large, fully symmetrical flowers that resemble huge dahlia blooms; the broad petals layer to form a flower about 4 inches thick. Among these types are the California Giants and the All-America award-winning Giant Sun hybrids.

The State Fair series is a group of heavy-stemmed, mildew-resistant zinnias. Growing 30 to 36 inches tall, they are well suited for use as a background in the flower border and for cut flowers.

Giant cactus-flowered selections include several new types with flowers 5 to 7 inches in diameter. Cactus-flowered blooms have long, thin petals that curl under like a strip of crepe paper. The plants begin to bloom when about 18 inches tall and continue all summer, growing to a height of 2½ to 3 feet. All-America winners are Wild Cherry, Carved Ivory, and the following mildew-resistant Zenith hybrids: Rosy Future, Torch, Firecracker, and Yellow Zenith.

Grow zinnias in full sun and well-prepared soil. You can begin sowing seeds directly in the ground as soon as the danger of frost is past, and continue sowing them every two weeks through July, for a summer-long supply of fresh color in the garden.

For a medium-tall single-flowered selection, try Sombrero.

Gold Sun is a dahlia-flowered zinnia selection that grows 18 to 24 inches tall.

Perennials

What are some hardy perennials and biennials that I can plant in the fall?

Most perennials, if purchased as dormant bare-root plants, should be planted in the fall. They will develop root systems over the winter and bloom the following year. (Some perennials may not bloom until the second year; check mail-order or seed catalogs for this information.) Perennials that you can plant as late as November include daylily (*Hemerocallis sp.*), coneflower (*Rudbeckia fulgida*), columbine (*Aquilegia sp.*), larkspur, bleeding-heart (*Dicentra spectabilis*), candytuft, phlox (*Phlox sp.*), sweet violet (*Viola odorata*), coralbell (*Heuchera sanguinea*), plantain lily (*Hosta sp.*), and lily of the valley (*Convallaria majalis*).

Biennials that can be planted in the fall include foxglove (*Digitalis sp.*), Canterbury-bell (*Campanula medium*), and sweet William (*Dianthus barbatus*).

Planted in the fall, candytuft blooms in March and April across the South.

Sweet William provides a colorful addition to the garden border in spring. Plant it in well-drained soil and a sunny location.

Thrift is one of the best heat- and drought-tolerant perennials.

Asters thrive in full sun. The bushy plants are covered with blooms in late summer and fall.

What is the best way to grow biennials like foxglove and sweet William?

These biennials can be grown from seeds sown in early summer for bloom the following year. Set plants 12 to 18 inches apart in well-drained soil. Most biennials do well in full sun or light shade; but in the Lower South, foxglove requires partial to full shade. Sweet William flowers best in full sun and light, sandy soil. Never bury the stems and be sure to keep the top of the root structure level with the soil surface, since root tops and stems need good air circulation.

Are there any perennials that are heat and drought tolerant?

Moss pink or thrift (*Phlox subulata*), yarrow (*Achillea sp.*), and stokesia (*Stokesia laevis*) are heat and drought tolerant. Moss pink is a durable ground cover which forms a thick carpet, bearing tiny red, blue, or white blooms in the spring. Old clumps may die out after several years, so divide them every two to three years, leaving the youngest clumps.

Yarrow blooms in summer and fall; its height varies from 6 inches to more than 4 feet. Yarrow heads are composed of tiny yellow, pink, or white flowers, depending on the selection. Plant this perennial in full sun and well-drained soil. In windy areas, stake the taller selections. Divide yarrow about every three years.

Stokesia is a dependable plant for summer and fall bloom. Plants reach from 12 to 18 inches high, and flowers are blue, pink, or white, depending on the selection. Clumps should be divided every three years.

I would like to plant some perennials in a shady spot. What would you suggest?

Hosta or plantain lily, bleeding-heart, and hardy geranium (*Geranium sp.*) would be good choices.

Hosta needs moist, rich soil and should be grown in a shady spot. The foliage is green or variegated, and the flowers are pale lavender.

Bleeding-heart needs a rich, well-drained, moist soil. The species *Dicentra spectabilis* produces red to pink blooms for about four weeks in the spring. The foliage will die back after a month, so interplant them with annuals. The hybrid Luxuriant blooms a few weeks later than *D. spectabilis* and continues blooming sporadically until frost; foliage remains until fall. Plants range in height from 10 inches to 2 feet.

Hardy geranium (*Geranium sp.*), unlike the large-flowered florist geranium, forms a small, mounding plant and produces 1- to 2-inch flowers in pink, blue, or violet. Blooming through the summer, this plant will reach heights of 4 to 14 inches, depending on the selection. Unlike most other perennials, hardy geranium grows better if it is left undivided.

I have a large, open area I would like to plant with perennials. Can you tell me about some that will grow well in full sun?

Many familiar perennials will grow well in full sun. Hardy asters (*Aster sp.*) bloom in late summer and fall, producing white, pink, red, yellow, purple, or blue flowers. Depending on the selection, height ranges from 2 to 4 feet. Dwarf selections only reach a height of about 10 inches.

Coreopsis produce yellow, daisylike flowers through summer on plants which range from 1 to 3 feet tall, depending on the selection. Because coreopsis reseed easily, plants may need to be divided after two or three years.

Daisies (*Chrysanthemum sp.*) will grow best in rich soil, although they will tolerate poorer soils. Depending on the selection, daisies flower in the spring, summer, and fall and produce single, double, or anemone-type blooms. Painted daisies (*C. coccineum*) flower in spring. Flower colors include shades of red, white, and pink. Painted daisies reach about 2 feet in height and should be cut back after flowering to encourage a second blooming in summer. Divide crowded clumps every two or three years in the spring. Shasta daisies flower in spring and summer, producing white blooms with brilliant yellow centers.

Transvaal daisies (*Gerbera jamesonii*) are low-growing plants that produce delicate single or double flowers. The flower colors include pink, crimson, orange, white, and yellow. Flowers are borne on 12- to 18-inch-long stems rising from a basal rosette of leaves. Plant them in rich, well-drained soil. In the Upper and Middle South, they must be protected with a layer of mulch during the winter.

Heat and drought resistant perennials, such as yarrow, thrift, and stokesia, would also be good choices for planting in a sunny, open area.

How does one grow and use cannas successfully?

To grow cannas (*Canna generalis*) successfully, plant them in moist soil to which you have added compost or cow manure. These showy hybrids of Central and South American species like hot weather and full sun but will tolerate partial shade.

Plant the rhizomes in the spring, spacing them 15 to 18 inches apart and covering them with 1 to 2 inches of soil. During the growing season, give them plenty of water, but be sure to provide good drainage. Feed the plants every two to four weeks with 5-10-10 fertilizer. To prolong flowering, pick off faded blossoms. After frost, cut the stalks back to the ground. In the spring, divide crowded clumps if necessary, and replant root stocks.

Cannas are used most effectively massed in single colors against a plain background, such as evergreens or a stone wall, or beside a pool. Low-growing cannas make an attractive planting beside large rocks or stone steps. A group of three rhizomes can make an effective foliage accent as well as producing flowers.

Massed daisies create a striking effect against an evergreen background.

For lush, green foliage and large, showy flowers, plant canna lilies in full sun and moist soil. Space the plants 1 foot apart or less for a dense, massed effect, and 3 feet apart to showcase individual flowers.

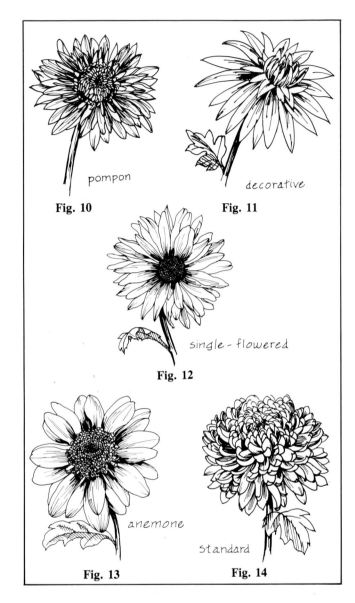

pompon

decorative

Fig. 10   Fig. 11

single-flowered

Fig. 12

anemone

Standard

Fig. 13   Fig. 14

How are mums classified? Can you tell me something about the different types?

Garden chrysanthemums may be classified by plant shape (cushion or upright) but are more often divided according to flower form. Although there are more than a dozen types, the following are the most popular and readily available.

Pompons have profuse clusters of blossoms. The disc of each flower is yellow or at least distinct from the surrounding petals. Flowers average 1 to 2 inches across. Plants are compact, ranging from 15 to 24 inches tall. (*See Figure 10.*)

Spoon mums are named for their spoon-shaped petals. Flowers range from 3 to 5 inches in diameter, and plants are 18 to 24 inches tall.

Decorative types produce both larger plants and flowers than the pompon; flower form is variable and may be 2 to 4 inches across. Plants are upright, growing to 3 feet tall. (*See Figure 11.*)

Single-flowered mums have daisylike blossoms, a single row of petals surrounding a prominent flat or slightly rounded center. Petals are long and slender, and the flowers may be 2 to 3 inches across. (*See Figure 12.*)

Anemone types, like the single-flowered, have a disc center with petals arranged in rows around it; however, the center of anemone mums tends to be larger and more rounded and the petals shorter than those of the single-flowered types. (*See Figure 13.*)

Standards, also known as football or exhibition mums, are large-flowered types; blooms may be 5 to 7 inches across. Plants are upright and single-stemmed, often reaching a height of as much as 3 feet. (*See Figure 14.*)

What is the difference between disbudding and pinching, in reference to mums?

Disbudding and pinching as applied to mums are as different as pruning and shearing as applied to woody plants. Disbudding, like pruning, involves the selective removal of plant parts. It is used primarily when growing large exhibition mums. The practice involves removing most of the flower buds in order to channel the plant's energy into the production of fewer, larger blooms.

The first step in disbudding is to remove all side shoots (not leaves) as soon as they form, leaving only the terminal buds at the top of the plant; keep all side shoots removed throughout the growing season. (*See Figure 15.*) As flower buds form in the terminal cluster, remove all but one or two. (*See Figure 16.*) Disbudding results in larger flowers on all but cushion-type mums.

Since disbudded chrysanthemums grow tall and tend to be top heavy because of the

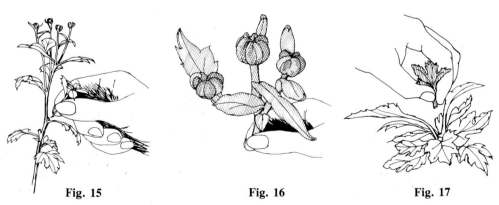

Fig. 15   Fig. 16   Fig. 17

large flowers, they generally need to be staked. Erect stakes at plantingtime to avoid damaging the roots later on.

Pinching is akin to shearing—much more drastic than disbudding. On mums, it involves pinching out the tips of all shoots (not leaves) several times during the growing season. (*See Figure 17.*) It stimulates branching and results in a compact plant and more, but smaller, flowers.

Begin pinching at plantingtime. Snip off the tips of all shoots when you set plants out. During the summer, continue to pinch out the tips of all new shoots every three or four weeks until mid-August, or about ten weeks before the intended time of bloom.

Can you tell me the easiest way to propagate chrysanthemums?

The easiest way to start new plants is from root divisions of established plants. Dig up the clumps, and break them apart through the root ball where a healthy new stem arises.(*See Figure 18.*) Be sure each division contains a healthy stem and root system. Replant in well-prepared soil. While dividing clumps is the easiest method of propagating mums, it increases the possibility of disease organisms infecting your new plants. A better way to establish new plants is to root cuttings from new growth. (*See Figure 19.*)

I received some potted mums as a gift this winter. Should I throw them away when the flowers die, or will they bloom again?

Potted gift mums may have spent their flowers by February, but this does not mean the plants are dead. They will not bloom again in their pots, but they can be planted outdoors and brought into bloom again next fall.

First, cut the tops of the plants back to about 3 inches. (*See Figure 20.*) Remove the plants from the container and divide the root ball to separate the plants (there are usually four to five plants in a pot). (*See Figure 21.*) To facilitate the separation of the roots, use a sharp knife to cut lightly through those roots that may have already become matted around the soil ball. Next, pull the plants apart carefully (*see Figure 22*) and plant in sunny, well-drained soil at the same depth they grew previously.

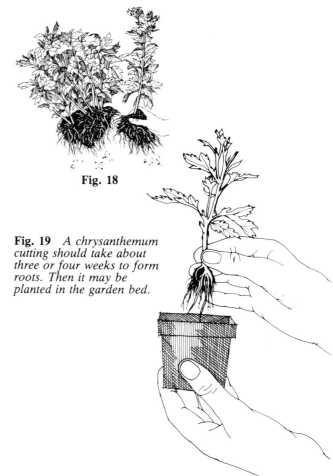

Fig. 18

Fig. 19 *A chrysanthemum cutting should take about three or four weeks to form roots. Then it may be planted in the garden bed.*

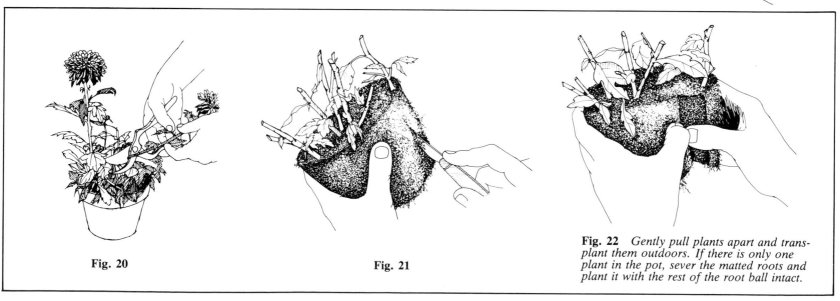

Fig. 20

Fig. 21

Fig. 22 *Gently pull plants apart and transplant them outdoors. If there is only one plant in the pot, sever the matted roots and plant it with the rest of the root ball intact.*

Coneflowers are popular in perennial gardens because they resist drought and bloom prolifically.

Echinacea is often referred to as pink coneflower.

Cottage pinks are both colorful and highly fragrant in a sunny garden border.

In parts of the Middle and Lower South, gerberas may overwinter.

What are the different selections of coneflower? Do all selections require full sun?

Coneflower is the common name for flowers in two different genera. Selections in the genus *Echinacea* are drought-resistant perennials that produce sunflower-shaped blooms in a variety of colors. Selections include The King (coral with maroon center), Bright Star (rosy red with maroon center), Robert Bloom (purple with orange center), and White Lustre or White King (white with bronze center). *Echinacea* should be planted 18 to 24 inches apart. Divide the clumps every three years.

Rudbeckia fulgida is also called coneflower, but its blossoms are always yellow with dark centers. Easy-to-grow selections of this perennial include Goldquelle and Goldsturm. *Rudbeckia fulgida* should be spaced 12 to 15 inches apart and the clumps divided every other year.

Both *Echinacea* and *Rudbeckia* thrive in full sun but will tolerate light shade. Soil should be well drained, particularly in winter.

What is the best way to propagate cottage pinks?

Cottage pinks (*Dianthus plumarius*) are easily propagated by layering in the fall or from seeds in the spring. Select lower branches with bare stems. On each stem, make an inch-long diagonal cut halfway through the stem and secure the stem to the soil, cut side down. After roots form, separate the stem and new roots from the parent plant. Set the new plants 12 to 18 inches apart in well-drained, lime-enriched soil and full sun. Be sure to keep the crowns, or tops of the root structures, level with the soil surface. Stems and root tops need good air circulation, so do not mulch cottage pinks until after the ground freezes.

Cottage pinks grow in the Middle and Upper South, blooming in spring and early summer. These perennials grow to about 12 inches tall and bear fragrant rose-colored, purple, white, or variegated flowers. The selection Helen produces salmon-colored blooms all summer. Old flowers can be sheared off to attain the best effect from the evergreen foliage.

Can you give me some tips for growing shasta daisies successfully?

Shasta daisies may be grown throughout the South if planted in full sun and well-tilled soil amended with compost or leaf mold. From spring through fall, plants require plenty of water; but during dormancy in winter, they need good drainage. Seeds sown in spring will bloom the second year. Depending on the selection, Shasta daisies will flower from early summer through fall. To prolong flowering, remove faded blossoms. Every two years, divide and reset established plants in the fall. Crowded clumps tend to develop crown rot.

Our bed of red gerberas (transvaal daisies) gets three to four hours of afternoon sun and we fertilized three times last year, but they have stopped blooming. What can we do?

Discontinue fertilizing for the rest of this year. In early fall, they will probably cycle into bloom again. Heavy fertilization stimulates the growth of foliage and inhibits blooming.

When should I plant daylilies?

In the Upper and Middle South, you can set out daylilies anytime from spring through fall; but it is best to plant early in the growing season to give the root system time to become well established before winter. In the Lower South and Florida, you can plant them anytime.

There are so many selections of daylilies. Are there any criteria for choosing which selections to plant?

In addition to flower color, height, bud count, and size, you will want to consider time of bloom and whether the foliage is evergreen. June is considered midseason for daylily bloom in the South. Some selections bloom early, April to June; others are late, July to August. Daylily foliage may be evergreen or dormant (dies back in winter), depending on the selection. Besides appearance, this is important in regional adaptation; gardeners in the Lower South may have trouble growing the dormant type.

What soil and light requirements do daylilies have?

Although daylilies are at their best in full sun, they will tolerate partial shade. The soil tolerance of daylilies is also broad; however, they will have better quality blooms if grown in fertile, friable soil.

My daylilies have become quite crowded and flower quality has been declining. Will dividing them help? When and how should I do it?

Dividing should help your daylilies. In fact, vigorous selections may need to be dug up and divided every four or five years. Divide and transplant daylilies as soon as possible after flowering. After digging, knock what soil you can off the clumps; hose off remaining soil to expose the crown. Without soil around the roots, you will be able to see where to divide them. If plants do not easily pull apart by hand, use a sharp knife to cut them apart. Replant the divisions immediately. (*See Figures 23–27.*)

Whether you choose an evergreen or a dormant type for a mass planting of daylilies, plant a single color for the strongest impact.

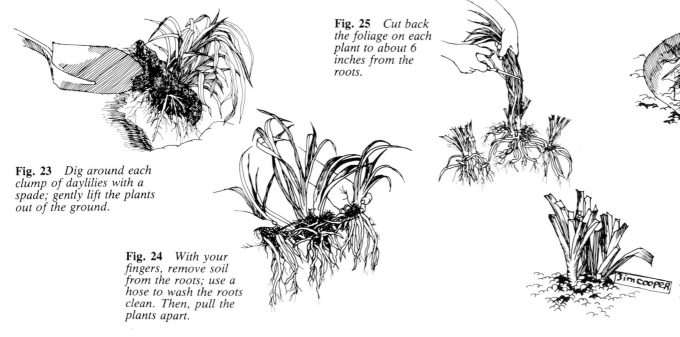

Fig. 23 *Dig around each clump of daylilies with a spade; gently lift the plants out of the ground.*

Fig. 24 *With your fingers, remove soil from the roots; use a hose to wash the roots clean. Then, pull the plants apart.*

Fig. 25 *Cut back the foliage on each plant to about 6 inches from the roots.*

Fig. 26 *Mound soil in the bottom of each hole; spread roots over the mound. To keep the plant identified, attach a tag with the selection name.*

Fig. 27 *Refill the hole, adjusting the soil under the plant to hold the bottom of the stalk at ground level. Firm the soil around each plant.*

Dusty miller makes an excellent edging plant, but it can also be grown in containers.

Is dusty miller easy to grow in alkaline soil?

Yes. Dusty miller (*Centaurea cineraria, C. ragusina,* or *C. gymnocarpa*) does best in sandy, well-drained soil in a sunny location. However, it will tolerate almost any soil that is relatively dry. Grown as an annual in the Upper and Middle South, dusty miller should be treated as a perennial in the Lower South. It is valued mostly for its silvery white foliage and makes a good edging plant or ground cover for hot, dry sites.

What is the best way to propagate four-o'clocks?

Four-o'clocks (*Mirabilis jalapa*) may be started from seeds sown indoors four to six weeks before the last frost, or outside after the last frost. However, to obtain large, prolific plants quickly, propagate four-o'clocks from the tubers produced by mature plants. Dig up the dahlialike tubers and store them in a cool, dry place over the winter. In the spring, plant them in full sun and well-drained soil, spacing the plants about 12 inches apart. Four-o'clocks blossom every afternoon, occasionally bearing several colors on one plant.

Are there any dwarf selections of hollyhocks?

Although many hollyhocks (*Alcea rosea*) grow as tall as 9 feet, dwarf selections have been developed that will grow no taller than 24 inches. They bloom earlier than the taller hollyhocks. Some gardeners treat them like annuals rather than perennials because they will flower during the first growing season. Two selections to try are Majorette (mixed colors) and Silver Puffs (rosy pink). Both grow easily from seeds. Silver Puffs has rust-resistant foliage.

Will Lenten rose do well in mass plantings?

Yes, exceptionally well. Try planting Lenten rose (*Helleborus orientalis*) in masses under trees, in a shady border, or as a ground cover planting near the entrance of the house. Mass plantings protect the plants and help reduce maintenance. Once they are in

Dwarf hollyhocks are good spike flowers for summer flowering.

The nodding, bell-like flowers of Lenten rose are carried on slender stems that display the blossoms above the mass of foliage.

place, mulch plantings with leaf mold, pine bark, or compost. This helps control weeds and adds organic matter to the soil.

Another advantage of mass plantings of Lenten rose is the production of seedling plants. When allowed to grow for several years in an undisturbed location, Lenten rose will produce an abundance of young plants within the mass.

When and how do you prune pampas grass?

Prune pampas grass (*Cortaderia selloana*) in the winter. Remove all dead foliage and cut the stalks back to about 4 or 5 inches in height. New growth will come out in spring, with feathery plumes appearing in early summer.

What kinds of peonies will grow in the South?

Contrary to popular belief, a number of peony selections will grow in the South. Peonies (*Paeonia lactiflora*) are classified by flower structure into five types: single, Japanese, double, semidouble, and anemone. Although the single and Japanese types are generally considered best for the Southern garden, many double-flowering types and a few anemone and semidouble types can also be successfully grown.

Among the single types, selections recommended for the South include Imperial Red, Le Jour (white), Seashell (pink), and Sparkling Star (dark pink).

Recommended selections of the Japanese types include Ama-No-Sode (dark pink); Largo and Do Tell (pink); Isani-Gidui and Shaylor's Sunburst (white); Comanche, Mikado, Dignity, and Nippon Brilliant (red).

Double-flowering types to try include Edulis Superba, Martha Bulloch, Mons. Jules Elie, Therese, Walter Faxon (pink); Elsa Sass, Festiva Maxima, Florence Nicholls, Gardenia, Kelway's Glorious (white); Felix Crousse, Big Bend, Karl Rosenfield, and Philippe Rivoire (red).

The Primevere (white) selection of the anemone type is a good choice for the Southern garden. If you want to try semidouble peonies, choose Minnie Shaylor (pink fading to white) or Phyllis Kelway (pink).

Never prune pampas grass until winter. Spring pruning may hurt the production of the feathery plumes.

Peonies are particularly effective in the Southern garden when combined with such strongly vertical plants as iris.

Japanese Peony

Semidouble Peony

Anemone Peony

Single Peony

Annuals & Perennials 33

Nodding blossoms are evidence of the peony's size and weight. To keep peony stems erect, stake before foliage fills out.

If properly cared for, peonies may live and bloom 15 to 25 years or longer.

Peonies are at their most spectacular when planted in large groups to create masses of color.

How are peonies sold?

Peonies are sold as root divisions and are available from nurseries and mail-order catalogs for fall planting. Be sure to buy a standard division. This is one with three to five eyes (buds) and at least three good roots that are 4 to 6 inches long. Small divisions offered at reduced prices usually give poor results. Many nurseries start shipping peony root divisions in late August or early September. If you receive yours this early, pack them in dry peat moss and place in a paper bag; refrigerate until later in the fall.

We want to purchase some peonies for our garden but know nothing about how to plant them. Can you help us?

Since peonies do not transplant well, select a permanent location initially. Keep in mind that plants live 15 to 25 years or longer. Peonies need full sun but will do well in partial shade as long as they get about 6 to 8 hours of sunlight daily. Afternoon shade is desirable, as it protects flowers from fading during the warmest part of the day.

Peonies need plenty of space to grow, so allow 3 to 4 feet between plants. Choose a site far enough from other plants to avoid competition for nutrients and space.

Prepare the planting hole about two weeks before planting so the soil can settle; otherwise, the roots will settle with the soil and may end up too deep, which can result in no blooms. Dig the hole 2 to 3 feet in diameter and 2 to 3 feet deep. Work organic matter into the soil, as for most perennials. With all types of soil, incorporate 1 pound of bone meal or superphosphate with two-thirds of the backfill soil, and fill the planting hole to within 8 to 10 inches from the top; then finish filling with the remaining backfill to which no bone meal or superphosphate has been added.

Plant the root divisions so the eyes are only 1 inch below the soil surface, being careful to place them so the eyes will grow upward. Firm the soil around the root division, and water well. If planted correctly, peonies will not require fertilizer for two or three years. After this time, a trowel full of 5-10-10 applied each spring before bloom will be sufficient. Broadcast the fertilizer in a band 6 to 18 inches from the plant crown; work it into the soil, being careful to avoid disturbing the roots.

Peonies require plenty of moisture, so keep the plants well watered during dry periods; to conserve moisture, mulch with a 2- to 4-inch layer of organic matter. Staking is necessary to support the large double flowers. To prevent damaging the foliage, be sure to erect stakes early before the plant fills out.

In September, cut the foliage to the ground and discard it. Also rake leaves and mulch away from the plant crown to expose it to as much cold as possible.

Can I successfully grow peonies in southern Florida? I am particularly interested in tree peonies.

Peonies are not usually successful in southern Florida. They bloom well only where they undergo a winter chilling period.

We have several old peony plants that we want to move. Please tell us how to replant them.

Peonies do not transplant well. However, if you must move them, do so in late September, October, or November. If the peonies have been growing in the same spot for more than two years, divide them when you move them. Carefully dig up the entire plant and shake or wash the soil from the roots. Expose the plants to air for a few hours so the roots will become less brittle; then you can divide the roots without breaking them too badly. Be sure that each division has 3 or more eyes (buds).

I planted a peony eight years ago. Each year it has produced beautiful foliage but never a flower. Why has it not bloomed?

Peonies require plenty of moisture, annual fertilizing with bone meal or superphosphate, and full sun for 6 to 8 hours a day. They also need plenty of space free from competition from trees and shrubs. Other possible reasons for your peony's failure to bloom are listed here.

—Incorrect soil pH: For best growth, peonies require a pH between 6 and 6.5. In overly acid or alkaline soils they may not receive the nutrients necessary to remain healthy and bloom.

—Planted too deeply: The eyes must be set no deeper than 1 inch for it to bloom.

—Insufficient winter-chilling period: Since cold requirements vary for different selections, you might replace your plant with one known to bloom well in your area.

Several years ago I planted an assortment of brilliantly colored hybrid perennial phlox. Now all the blooms are a dirty purple. What could have caused this change?

When hybrid perennial phlox are allowed to go to seed, the seeds scatter over the ground and germinate the next season. Usually these seedlings are very hardy growers and often revert to the flower color of one of their parents. Such seedlings can crowd out the hybrids, especially if the more desirable clumps of hybrids have not been well fertilized and watered and if they have not been separated every two or three years.

I would like to use plantain lilies both as ground cover under some trees and as a border for a sunny flower bed. Can you recommend some selections?

Any of the miniature plantain lilies (hosta) may be used as edging plants for flower beds as well as an effective ground cover in small beds beneath a tree canopy. The wavyleaf plantain lily (*Hosta undulata*) is more tolerant of sun than most other species. Plants form clumps 12 to 18 inches across. Leaves are variegated, with wavy margins, and flowers are pale lavender.

The blue plantain lily (*H. ventricosa*), on the other hand, is particularly sensitive to sunlight and must be grown in deep shade. It forms mounds about 2 feet across. Leaves are green; flowers are bluish lavender and very large.

Another miniature, the narrow-leaved or Japanese plantain lily (*H. lancifolia*), could probably be grown in either spot in your garden. It forms clumps 1½ to 2 feet wide. Leaves are green and slender, about 6 inches long and 1½ to 2 inches wide. Flowers are pale lavender.

I would like to use some plantain lilies in my woodland garden. Do you have any recommendations?

The large species of plantain lilies would be particularly suitable for your woodland garden. They are best displayed as specimens; but if they are in scale with their companions, the large plantain lilies can also be used as border plants and accents. Try Fortunes plantain lily (*H. fortunei*), Siebold or blue-leaved plantain lily (*H. sieboldiana*), or fragrant plantain lily (*H. plantaginea*).

Plantain lilies are particularly suitable for the woodland garden. The bold variegation of the selection Francee provides a touch of contrast in an all-green setting.

August Moon is a hybrid plantain lily, noted for its light-green, ribbed leaves.

What kind of care do plantain lilies require?

Plantain lilies require a rich, well-drained soil in a shady spot. In clay soil, you will need to raise the planting bed 10 to 12 inches above surrounding soil to ensure adequate drainage. Dig packaged cow manure into the planting bed at the rate of 2 to 3 gallons per square yard. Once established, plantain lilies should not require subsequent fertilizer and should thrive in the same location for many years. To maintain their distinctive appearance, space plants so they do not touch. And be sure to keep them mulched and watered in dry climates. You can propagate plantain lilies in spring and summer, either from division of clumps or from nursery-grown plants.

I have a row of fragrant plantain lilies that needs to be moved. When is the best time to move the plants, how large should the divided clumps be, and how far apart should they be planted?

The fragrant plantain lily, the only hosta species with scented flowers, may be divided anytime between early spring and early fall; the best time, however, is immediately after flowering, usually during late summer and early fall. Replanted in early fall, the plants can become established over the winter and will produce some blooms the following year. Divide them into clumps as small as you wish, as long as each clump has a crown. Fist-size pieces will produce blooms more quickly. Space clumps at least 2 feet apart. (*See Figures 28–30.*)

Please tell me something about Oriental poppies. Would they be easy to grow in the Upper South?

Yes. Oriental poppies (*Papaver orientale*) perform well for years in areas with cold winters. But unless they are planted very early in the spring, container-grown poppies may be dormant and fail to flower the first season. Give them a sunny spot with deep loamy soil rich in organic matter, and provide plenty of moisture during the growing season. Space plants 15 to 20 inches apart. Be careful not to break the brittle roots. Cover the root ball with 2 inches of soil, and mulch with 2 to 3 inches of organic material. Feed lightly with a balanced fertilizer early each spring. To increase the number of plants, divide the clumps of roots during late summer or fall.

Oriental poppies perform best in a sunny spot, planted in a deep, rich, well-drained soil.

Fig. 28 *Use a sharp knife to cut a clump of plantain lilies into smaller sections. Be sure each section has healthy roots and a crown.*

Fig. 29 *Fist-size clumps will produce blooms more quickly than smaller-size divisions.*

Fig. 30 *Replant divisions at the same depth the plant was growing previously, spacing clumps at least 2 feet apart.*

Is there a primula that overwinters well outside in the Middle and Upper South?

Cowslip primrose (*Primula veris*), an import from the meadows of England, will overwinter outside in the Middle and Upper South. For best growth, plant it in partial shade in moist, fertile, slightly acid soil. It may be difficult to grow in the Lower South because it cannot tolerate high summer temperatures.

Plants can be started either from divisions or from seeds, but obtaining divisions in late spring from a gardening friend is the most popular way of starting a new planting. For bright-yellow flowers in spring, sow seeds the preceding May. Start them in flats and transplant to the garden when true leaves have formed.

Some time ago I read that the American Rose Society will help a person get in touch with local Rosarians who can give good advice on growing roses successfully. Is this still being done? If so, please give me the address of the American Rose Society.

Yes, there are Consulting Rosarians who will come to your home, diagnose your rose problems, and advise you on combating pests and diseases and on feeding, watering, and other cultural practices. For names and addresses of Consulting Rosarians near you, write to the American Rose Society, Box 30,000, Shreveport, Louisiana 71130. Enclose a self-addressed, stamped envelope.

We are going to plant a few climbing roses on the fence across our backyard. Please suggest some selections that bloom well.

Some climbing roses produce showy displays during the spring months; outstanding red types are Paul's Scarlet and Blaze. These usually produce only a few flowers during summer and fall.

Many hybrid teas now come in climbing forms that often are more vigorous than their bush counterparts. When established, climbing hybrid teas often produce 75 to 125 large blooms borne on strong stems in spring. But they do not bloom as continuously as their bush parents.

Climbing forms of hybrid teas are as good for cut flowers as the bush types. Some of the more popular selections are Climbing Peace (yellow blend), Climbing Talisman (yellow blend), Climbing Crimson Glory (dark red), and Climbing Etoile de Hollande (dark red). Climbing Crimson Glory and Climbing Etoile de Hollande have long blooming seasons and grow rapidly. A climbing rose requires a few years to become established and produce a heavy crop, as plants bloom on last year's growth.

Cowslip primrose is the best primula for Southern gardens.

You will have to be patient with climbing roses, as they may require several years to begin heavy flower production.

Hybrid tea roses are evaluated yearly by the American Rose Society.

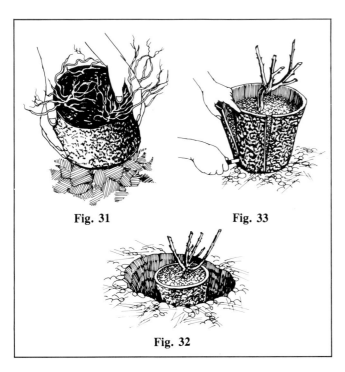

Fig. 31 **Fig. 33**

Fig. 32

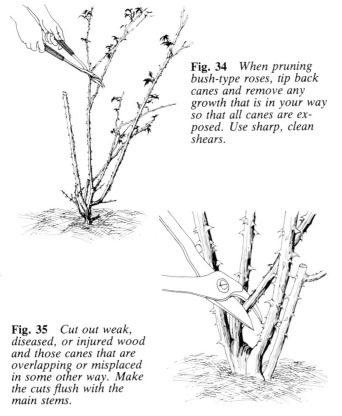

Fig. 34 *When pruning bush-type roses, tip back canes and remove any growth that is in your way so that all canes are exposed. Use sharp, clean shears.*

Fig. 35 *Cut out weak, diseased, or injured wood and those canes that are overlapping or misplaced in some other way. Make the cuts flush with the main stems.*

I just bought some roses grown in containers of pressed peat. What is the proper way to plant them?

If you are planting only a few roses, dig individual planting holes. If you are setting out more than a half-dozen roses, spade or till the entire bed; then dig individual holes. After the initial soil breaking, work compost, leaf mold, or similar organic matter into the soil. This improves soil structure for root growth and ensures adequate drainage. Organic matter also improves sandy soil by giving it substance in which roots may become more firmly anchored.

In clay or extremely sandy soil, where extensive rebuilding of soil is necessary, begin soil preparation at least two to four weeks in advance. In addition to organic matter, work rotted manure into the bottom of each hole at a rate of about 4 cups per hole. Peat pots need not be removed when you plant the roses. The container will protect the roots during planting, and then it will gradually decompose. (*See Figure 31.*) Planting holes should be twice as deep and wide as the containers, and even larger in clay soils. (*See Figure 32.*) After digging a hole, pack backfill soil under the container to elevate it a few inches above surrounding soil. The soil will settle after it has been watered.

Once the plant has been adjusted to the correct height, slit the sides of the container and fold them down so that no part of the pot protrudes above the soil. (*See Figure 33.*) Any part of the pot that is above the soil will act as a wick, drawing moisture away from the roots.

Fill in around the exposed root ball with soil, and pack it with your foot. Use excess soil to fashion a basin around the base of the plant to aid moisture collection in the root zone. Water newly set plants thoroughly, allowing the basin around the plant to fill completely with water.

How often should roses be fertilized, and how much should each bush receive at each feeding?

Roses are heavy feeders and require regular applications of fertilizer. When new growth starts in the spring, begin feeding roses every six to eight weeks. One-half cup of either a fertilizer especially formulated for roses or 5-10-10 or similar fertilizer should be adequate for each application. Water thoroughly after each feeding. Discontinue feeding in the late summer, as feeding too late will stimulate new growth that is susceptible to winter injury.

Roses are my favorite flower, but I have never been able to grow them successfully. Please give me some tips.

During the growing season, feed your roses once a month with about ¼ cup fertilizer, such as 5-10-10. Water them thoroughly every week when there is no rainfall. Spray or dust weekly with a fungicide to prevent or control diseases; apply an insecticide when pests become a problem.

Last spring, we planted a small rose garden, mainly hybrid teas. I need some guidance on pruning in late winter.

First, remove all dead or cold-damaged wood. Then select four to six healthy canes to become the main branches of each plant, and cut them back to 18 to 20 inches tall. Remove all other canes at ground level. (*See Figures 34–37.*) Do not prune climbing roses at this time; wait until after they have bloomed.

I have never pruned our 4-year-old climbing Blaze rose, but I think I should this spring. Please tell me how to prune it correctly.

Since most climbing roses produce a great abundance of flowers in early spring, they should receive their major pruning after the spring flush of blooms. On healthy, vigorous climbers, any cane over two years old should be removed or cut back severely. Thin last season's growth at least one-half, and cut back to within several feet of the base to encourage new growth. (*See Figure 38.*)

I have two rose trees that bloom well but have long, straggly branches and not much foliage. How much can I prune?

Frequent pruning is necessary to maintain attractive rose trees, and roses growing in tree form will endure a considerable amount. Cut back tall canes to achieve the shape you wish the plant to have. Cut wayward stems (those growing toward the center of the tree form and crisscrossing other stems) back to a main cane.

Quite a number of old rambler roses have grown thick over our back wall and into nearby trees and shrubs. I would like to cut the roses back this fall; what do you advise?

You can cut rambler roses back severely anytime of the year without killing the plants; but if you cut them in the fall, you will miss next year's flowers. Wait until they bloom next spring; then cut away as much as you wish.

I would like to try the old-fashioned method of growing roses from cuttings started under glass jars. How is it done?

This method, often referred to as "slipping," is still one of the best ways to propagate roses. Spring and summer are the best times to start cuttings. Take cuttings (slips) 3 to 4 inches long. Make each cut just below the point where a leaf stem emerges from the cane. Remove lower leaves of the cutting. To hasten rooting, dip the base of each cutting in a rooting hormone, and insert it in loose soil outdoors. Water well and cover with a glass jar. Keep the soil moist while roots are forming. (*See Figure 39.*)

Some rosarians put mud on top of the jar or smear the inside of the top with paint to prevent the hot sun from burning the tender cutting before it has formed roots. It takes from one to three months for a rose cutting to form roots.

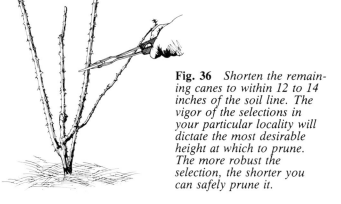

Fig. 36   *Shorten the remaining canes to within 12 to 14 inches of the soil line. The vigor of the selections in your particular locality will dictate the most desirable height at which to prune. The more robust the selection, the shorter you can safely prune it.*

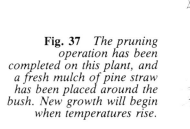

Fig. 37   *The pruning operation has been completed on this plant, and a fresh mulch of pine straw has been placed around the bush. New growth will begin when temperatures rise.*

Fig. 39

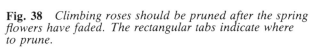

Fig. 38   *Climbing roses should be pruned after the spring flowers have faded. The rectangular tabs indicate where to prune.*

Bulbs

Dwarf Iris

There is something magical about bulbs. From tiny bulbs planted months before emerge colorful blossoms, sometimes as large as teacups. Then they fade into the landscape as quietly as they came. While tulips, daffodils, and hyacinths are the most popular and spring is their season of glory, bulbs can be enjoyed in every season.

Summer bulbs to grace your garden include amaryllis, caladiums, hardy begonias, lilies, gladiolus, and many more. One important factor to consider when planting summer-flowering bulbs is whether they require sun or shade. A shrewd gardener will also be aware of the successive flowering of different bulbs and harmonize them with the other plants in the landscape. Always make sure the sequence of bloom as well as the color combinations work well when adding bulbs to the garden. One special note about summer bulbs—some types, especially lilies, have very specific soil and drainage requirements. Be sure to check the answers to the questions regarding cultivation in *Garden Guide* for our recommendations.

Fall bulbs (except dahlias) are often rather exotic and very small, but that does not mean that they are not showy. Baby cyclamens, fall crocus, and spider lilies burst into the fall landscape with unexpected color. If you have ever enjoyed the azalea trails at Callaway Gardens in fall, you know the intense color that a mass of hardy cyclamens can provide. The flowers rarely grow over 12 inches tall; but each corm can produce 8 to 10 blossoms the first year, and flowering becomes denser with each successive season. Almost identical to spring crocus, fall-blooming crocus, in bright colors of pink, purple, and pure white, exhibit a sparkling, crisp quality when they pop through the fall leaves. The bulbs must be massed in groups of 12 or more and are at their best when displayed along walks or in rock gardens. Spider lilies, an old-fashioned choice but still popular around country homes, seem to say that cooler days are ahead. Delicate red spikes of

Tulips

Bearded Iris

Crocus

Rubrum Lily

R. O. Backhouse Daffodils

flowers seem to spring out of the ground into the landscape. They are hardy and come back year after year. Larger than other fall-blooming bulbs, dahlias tend to be more radiant during the weeks before the first frost than at any other time during their long blooming period. While many people regard dahlias as ordinary, the new hybrid types offer a wide array of colors, flower forms, and sizes (both in height and flower).

With the arrival of winter, bulbs outside go into hibernation, and indoor bulbs steal the show. The most popular spring bulbs may be forced indoors provided they have been programmed to flower (*see* the section on forcing bulbs indoors). With the traditional Christmas amaryllis and the scented hyacinths for your breakfast table, you can enjoy bulbs all through the winter.

Summer Snowflake

Bearded Iris

Fall Crocus

Imperial Strain Lily

Amaryllis

Baby Cyclamen

Hyacinth

Calla Lily

Scilla

Each season offers the opportunity not only to enjoy the beauty of your bulb display but also to learn how to enhance the display by studying and improving the planting design. Color and time of bloom are two elements to consider in planning. For example, if you want a long season of a single color, plant early-blooming bulbs such as crocus with later-blooming bulbs like tulips or hyacinths; or fill your flower bed with a single type of flower, choosing selections that bloom at different times.

If you prefer a color scheme that changes gradually with the season, plant early-, midseason-, and late-blooming bulbs of different but harmonious colors. Separate clashing or intense hues with pastels to make the brilliant colors more prominent.

Spacing of bulbs is a third design element. Consult the planting guidelines in this section for tips and ideas.

Spider Lilies

Hardy Amaryllis

Tulips

General Recommendations— Outdoor Use

When is the best time to plant spring-flowering bulbs such as daffodils, crocus, tulips, and hyacinths?

You can plant spring-blooming bulbs when soil temperatures drop to 60 degrees or below. Generally, this means that if you live in the Upper or Middle South, you can plant your bulbs after October 15. In the Lower South, wait until late December or even early January to put bulbs in the ground. Until plantingtime, keep the bulbs in a cool, dry, well-ventilated location (not in bags or sacks).

Most spring-blooming bulbs require a cold period for flowering. Although winters in the Upper and Middle South are usually cold enough to satisfy the chilling requirement, nature will need some assistance in the Lower South. To precool bulbs, place them in open paper bags in the refrigerator at 40 to 50 degrees for four to eight weeks before planting. Do not store bulbs with fruits or vegetables, as they emit ethylene gas and this can damage bulbs.

Can you give me some suggestions on how to display my bulbs?

You can organize your bulbs by time of bloom, selection, height, or color. Early-blooming crocus (*Crocus sp.*) can be planted with later-blooming tulips or hyacinths (*Hyacinthus orientalis*) for a varied and prolonged color show. Or you can plant all daffodils and stagger the blooming periods by choosing selections that flower at different times. Planting crocus, daffodils, and tulips of the same color offers a long season of color of different flower types.

Please tell me how to plant bulbs.

First, make sure your soil is friable, moderately fertile, and well drained. If the soil stays too wet, the bulbs will rot. In clay or otherwise poorly drained soil, improve

To enjoy the spring blooms of hyacinth and tulips, plant bulbs in the fall in the Upper and Middle South and in the winter in the Lower South.

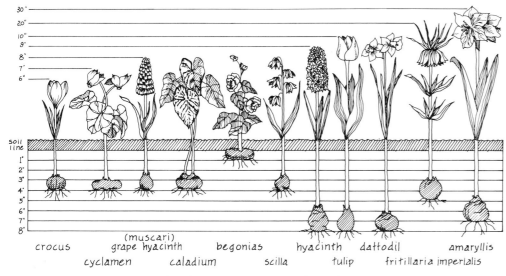

planting depths for popular bulbs

Fig. 1

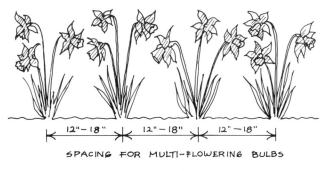

SPACING FOR MULTI-FLOWERING BULBS

Fig. 2

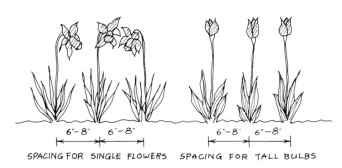

SPACING FOR SINGLE FLOWERS   SPACING FOR TALL BULBS

Fig. 3

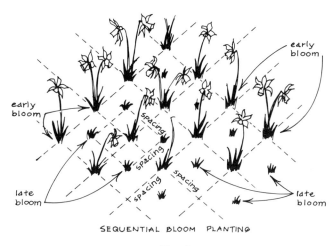

SEQUENTIAL BLOOM PLANTING

Fig. 4

drainage by adding sand or peat to a depth of 1 foot. In sandy soil, improve water retention by working in peat moss.

To prepare for planting, dig beds 8 to 10 inches deep and work in compost, ground pine bark, peat moss, or other organic matter at a rate of ½ bushel per square yard of planted area. Also incorporate bone meal or superphosphate at the rate of ½ pound per 8 square feet to promote good root development and best flower production.

Depth of planting for bulbs depends on their size. Small bulbs, 1 inch or less in diameter, should be covered with 1 to 2 inches of soil. Large bulbs, such as daffodils, should be planted 8 inches deep. Measure from the bottom or base of the bulbs when planting. (For more specific information, *see Figure 1.*) In the Lower South, plant bulbs 2 inches shallower than the chart recommendations.

Can you give me some tips on spacing bulbs?

Unless you are naturalizing bulbs, the spacing of bulbs in a mass planting should be influenced by the flowering habit of the bulbs, the landscape effect desired, and the location of the planting on the lot. Here are some design tips for planting bulbs.

—Space bulbs according to flowering habit. Generally, bulbs that produce multiple stems (*see Figure 2*) with several blooms per stem (like paper-white or liberty bells narcissus) can be spaced slightly farther apart than single-stem, solitary-bloom bulbs, like hybrid tulips. Profusely flowering bulbs will look like a dense, full planting when spaced 12 to 18 inches apart, while willowy single-bloom plants sometimes need to be as close as 6 to 8 inches to look like a mass of bloom. (*See Figure 3.*)

—Space bulbs according to color. Generally, scrambled colors will not be as effective in the landscape as drifts of separate colors. Brilliantly colored bulbs will appear more vivid than pastel shades and can be spaced farther apart for mass effect.

If you combine drifts of brilliant and soft colors, plant the brilliantly colored flowers in the background and the softer color in the foreground. You may have to plant more of the softer colored flowers to balance visually with the brighter color, even though the brighter colored flowers may be spaced farther apart.

—Space bulbs according to height. Taller flowering bulbs should be planted farther apart than shorter stem selections. For example, tulips, hyacinths, and daffodils should be planted 6 to 8 inches apart (measuring from tip to tip), while crocus and grape hyacinths (*Muscari sp.*) should be spaced 2 to 3 inches apart. Large allium (*Allium sp.*) may be spaced 10 to 12 inches apart.

—Space bulbs according to the terrain. On steeply sloping land viewed from the bottom of the slope, bulbs may be spaced farther apart than the recommended distance, since the slope causes the planting to appear more concentrated. On slopes viewed from an elevated position (the middle of the slope is at eye level of the viewer), bulbs should be planted closer together to look like a filled-in planting.

—Let distance work for you in planting. If a planting is to be viewed from a distance (from the street or across a large lot), a widely spaced bulb planting is best for mass effect. The bulbs may be planted 12 to 18 inches apart, depending on the type. By contrast, planting adjacent to a walkway or living area must be tightly spaced to develop a mass effect.

—Plant the bulbs in a sequential-bloom pattern to prolong the effect. (*See Figure 4.*) Combine early- and late-flowering bulbs in diamond patterns within the bed, based on the spacing considerations mentioned here. Plant the early bulbs at the corners of the diamonds and the late bloomers at the center of the pattern. This way, the plants that bloom at the same time are staggered in separate rows adequately spaced and the season of bloom is extended.

What is the correct way to store bulbs after blooming?

When blooms begin to fade, cut off the flowers and half of the stems. Leave the foliage, however, as it will produce food to replenish the bulbs for next year.

In the Upper South, you may leave the bulbs in the ground over the winter. In the Middle and Lower South, wait until the stems and leaves turn yellow and dry out. Then dig up the bulbs, shake off the excess soil, and let them dry outdoors in a protected spot for a few days; then remove any clinging soil. The bulbs must be dry before you store them.

One way to store bulbs is to place them in dry sand, vermiculite, peat moss, or other dry material, spacing them so that they do not touch each other. Store them in a cool, dry location until time to replant.

An easier way to store bulbs is to hang them up in discarded nylon hose or mesh vegetable bags. (*See Figure 5.*) It will not be necessary to separate them if they are hung in a cool, dry location where they receive good ventilation. As a safety precaution, you may want to treat them with a fungicide such as captan.

We would like to try some new kinds of bulbs for this spring. Do you have any suggestions?

Add variety to your spring garden with Siberian squill, ranunculus (*Ranunculus sp.*), allium, and grape hyacinth. In the Upper and Middle South, add snowdrop (*Galanthus nivalis*) to these. In the Middle and Lower South, plant Dutch iris (*Iris* hybrida), as well as those generally recommended; and in the Lower South, add freesia (*Freesia sp.*) to your garden. Southern gardeners, except those in South Florida, can also plant anemone (*Anemone sp.*) and hardy cyclamen (*Cyclamen coum*).

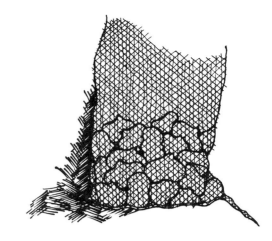

Fig. 5

Plant tiny cyclamen where you can enjoy them at close range.

Iris will make a graceful addition to spring gardens in the Middle and Lower South.

Allium provides unusual flower texture and form in a spring garden.

Popular Bulbs

Can I grow amaryllis outside in my flower bed? When should I set the bulbs out?

Popular throughout the South as potted plants for indoors, hardy amaryllis (*Hippeastrum sp.*) are also magnificent for flower borders. A large massed bed of amaryllis makes a dazzling border of summer color. Plants are large, averaging 2 to 3 feet tall.

If planted in early May, amaryllis should bloom in early summer. Plant bulbs in a sunny spot protected from winds. Amaryllis require good drainage. To plant the bulbs, dig the bed to a depth of 10 to 12 inches and spread a layer of crushed brick on the bottom. Set the bulbs on this layer so that the base of each bulb is 7 inches below soil level. Space bulbs 18 inches apart; then fill in with soil improved with compost, peat, or leaf mold.

During the growing season, keep beds well watered when rainfall is sparse. Fertilize established plants (one year or more in the ground) monthly with 5-10-10 or a similar fertilizer at the rate of ½ cup per square yard of bed.

Amaryllis bulbs that I dig in the fall for winter storage always seem to rot before I get them planted in the spring. Have you any suggestions?

Be sure the bulbs are thoroughly dry before storing and that they are kept completely dry during storage. In the Lower South, amaryllis can be left in the ground over the winter if mulched heavily with pine straw. Remove all but 1 to 2 inches of mulch as soon as the danger of frost is over.

I have tried unsuccessfully to grow anemones in my rock garden for the past two years. Please tell me what special treatment they require.

Anemones and other deep-rooted bulbs are often difficult to grow in a rock garden, as the soil is usually shallow and cannot be properly prepared. Anemones like a friable soil with good drainage; corms (bulbs) will decay if drainage is poor. If your soil has a high clay content, add processed manure, compost, or other organic matter. If the soil is naturally acid, work in 1 cup of lime per 10 square feet of planting area. Soak the corms overnight before planting for better sprouting. Set corms out in October and November in full sun, 1 to 2 inches deep and 4 inches apart.

Plant anemones in deep, well-drained soil and full sun.

Fig. 6 *Plant begonia tubers in damp peat moss; then cover with another inch of peat moss.*

Is there a begonia that will overwinter outside in the South?

Yes. The hardy begonia (*Begonia grandis*) may be left in the ground for years. It grows 2 to 3 feet tall, bearing spikes of small pink flowers and 3- to 6-inch leaves that are red underneath. The tubers enter a resting period when the plant dies back in winter. In the Upper South, protect the overwintering begonia with a mulch of pine straw or bark.

I have no idea what to do with the tubers of hybrid tuberous begonia that I received as a gift. Please give me some pointers.

Start tubers of tuberous begonia (*Begonia* x *tuberhybrida*), dented side up, in damp peat moss; the tops of the tubers should be about 1 inch below the surface. (*See Figure 6.*) When leaves appear, transfer the plants to a bed, or to pots or hanging baskets that are at least 8 inches deep. Plant in a mixture of equal parts peat moss, builder's sand, and potting soil. Set the base of each tuber 1 inch below the surface of the soil. Begonias like cool nights, plenty of moisture, and good ventilation. Hanging baskets provide the best ventilation; plant at least three to the basket.

If the leaves turn light green and become cupped, fertilize with 5-10-10 or 6-12-12. As long as the foliage is dark green and crimped downward, the begonias are in good condition.

I want to plant caladiums. Please advise me on buying bulbs.

Caladium bulbs (*Caladium hortulanum*) are available in different sizes. The larger bulbs generally produce more foliage. Mammoth-size bulbs, which are the largest, measure 3½ inches or more; jumbo-size bulbs measure 2½ to 3½ inches; size No. 1 bulbs are from 1½ to 2½ inches; and size No. 2 bulbs measure from 1 to 1½ inches. Larger bulbs are usually expensive, but the extra foliage can be worth it.

If you plan to use only a few caladiums, then the jumbo bulbs would be the best choice; but the smaller bulbs will perform satisfactorily when used in large quantities.

What kind of conditions and care do caladiums require?

Caladiums prefer moderately rich, porous, well-drained soil in a semishaded location (from 40 percent to 60 percent shade is ideal). Overwatering in poorly drained soil will cause the roots to decay. If the soil is allowed to dry out, caladium foliage wilts rapidly and will die if the plants stay dry too long. To keep the plants in good condition, keep them moist. Mulching will help retain soil moisture.

Can you give me some suggestions on the best way to use caladiums in my landscape?

Plant caladiums in annual beds or along walks, terraces, and borders. Use them in planting beds fronting shrubbery borders or along the base of evergreen hedges where the dark-green background makes the striking caladium foliage even more apparent.

In most cases, avoid salt-and-pepper mixtures of bulb types, because you will lose the beauty and impact of the colored foliage. By keeping bulb types together, each foliage type can retain its integrity.

How should I plant caladiums?

To plant caladiums in a plant bed, prepare the soil as for most bulbs (*see* page 45). Place the tubers on their side, setting them 4 inches deep and about 18 inches apart; pack

Hardy begonias are a good choice for a naturalized planting with ferns because the bulbs may be left in the ground undisturbed for years.

Caladiums provide color during the height of summer, provided they are planted in semishade and kept moist.

In this planting, caladiums provide a splash of color in their shady location and an interesting contrast to the finer-textured leaves of ivy.

Fig. 7

Calla lilies are prized for their ornamental, fragrant, and long-lasting blooms.

Plant calla lily where it will not have to compete with the roots of trees or large shrubs.

Crinum's delicate flowers may be white or shades of red.

the soil firmly around them. After the plants are established, apply 2 teaspoons of 5-10-10 per square foot of bed. Then apply 1 teaspoon per square foot each month thereafter during the growing season.

You can also plant caladiums in pots for use outdoors. Select large, firm bulbs with at least one well-developed sprout. A lightweight potting soil or sandy loam garden soil with a high content of organic matter will encourage vigorous growth.

Place 3 inches of soil in a 6-inch clay pot, carefully seat one large or several small bulbs (sprout side up) on top of the soil, and gently fill the pot with additional soil. (*See Figure 7.*) Be particularly careful not to damage the tender sprouts. Water generously, and set the pots where the plants will receive bright indirect light. In about three weeks, the reddish brown shoots of the young leaves should begin to appear above the soil. Planting bulbs in pots allows you to move the plants out of sight when the foliage begins to fade.

Calla lilies have such exotic flowers. Are they difficult to grow?

Calla lilies (*Zantedeschia sp.*) are fairly easy to grow if given slightly acid soil, moderate sunlight, and sufficient moisture. In addition, they must be planted where there is no competition from roots of trees and large shrubs. In southern Florida, callas may be grown outdoors year-round.

To grow calla lilies outdoors, plant the rhizomes in spring either in beds or containers. Plant them 4 to 6 inches deep and 8 to 12 inches apart in soil well amended with organic matter. The soil should never be permitted to become thoroughly dry. In the fall, dig the bulbs and store them in a cool, dry place. To use as houseplants, plant the rhizomes anytime and keep barely damp until shoots appear; then keep the soil moist and fertilize monthly.

Species to look for include *Z. aethiopica,* a spectacular white; *Z. elliottiana,* yellow; and *Z. rehmannii,* pink.

Can crinums be grown all over the South? If so, what are some tips for proper culture?

Crinums (*Crinum sp.*) grow best in the warm areas of the Middle and Lower South and require little attention. Flowers are produced primarily in the summer, in white or in shades of red.

Bulbs may be planted at any time, but spring or fall planting is preferred. Set bulbs about 6 inches deep in rich, somewhat moist soil with plenty of organic matter. Plant crinums in containers or in masses 3 feet apart in the flower border or in front of shrubbery.

Which spring crocus types produce the most outstanding flower display?

Try *Crocus chrysanthus* and *C. tomasinianus* for the best flower show in late winter. *C. chrysanthus* produces two to five blooms from each of three sets of sheathing leaves. This hardy crocus flowers from mid-January to late February each year and needs little care. Selections include Blue Giant (blue), Ladykiller (purple exterior, white interior), Cream Beauty (creamy yellow), and Snow Bunting (white). *C. tomasinianus,* also very hardy, blooms in early February. It spreads rapidly, producing in a few years a sheet of lavender in your garden. *C. aureus,* sold as Dutch Yellow Mammoth, makes a show at the same time.

Also recommended for the South are Remembrance, Dutch crocus, *C. vernus* selections, Joan of Arc, Queen of the Blues, and Striped Beauty. These will bloom in March and are larger and taller than the winter-flowering species.

Is there a fall-flowering crocus?

The popularity of crocus as early-spring flowers has almost overshadowed the autumn-blooming species. But you can add soft color to your autumn garden with any of these fall-flowering species: *Crocus cancellatus, C. longiflorus, C. medius, C. pulchellus, C. sativus, C. speciosus,* or *C. zonatus.* Flower colors range from lilac to blue to white.

Plant corms in full sun or light shade early in the fall. Space them 2 to 6 inches apart and cover with 2 to 4 inches of soil. For successive years of blooming, leave crocus in the ground all year and feed them every fall with bone meal or 5-10-5 fertilizer.

Another fall-flowering bulb is colchicum, sometimes called autumn crocus. Corms planted in August or September will produce pale rose to white crocuslike flowers in early fall. Foliage develops the following spring, then withers by early summer. Like crocus, colchicum will bloom year after year if left in the ground undisturbed. Plant them in full sun or light shade, spacing corms 6 to 9 inches apart and covering them with 3 to 4 inches of soil.

Use crocus selections with multiple blooms to create splashes of bright spring color in your garden.

Depending on the selection, crocus may bloom as early as mid-January.

What is the best way to start hardy cyclamens?

Hardy cyclamens (*Cyclamen coum*) can be started from either seeds or tubers, but plants grown from seeds take several years to begin blooming. Depending on size, tubers may begin to bloom the first year after planting; of course, foliage will be produced the first growing season.

Cyclamen tubers should be set in a well-tilled area that has been enriched with generous amounts of sand and organic matter; they should be covered with no more than 3 inches of soil and spaced from 6 to 18 inches apart. A light mulch of pine straw or finely ground pine bark is also recommended.

Both seeds and tubers should be planted in late summer or early fall. Cyclamens grown from seeds, however, should be started in a greenhouse and grown there for a full year. The following autumn, they can be set into the garden.

There are so many selections of daffodils. Are all of them equally well suited for growing in the South?

In most of the South, daffodils thrive in the garden for many years, especially the trumpet and large-cupped selections. However, not all daffodils will grow in all parts of the South. The Lower South is too hot and humid for many daffodils. Three species recommended for that climate are the Tazetta group, *Narcissus cyclamineus,* and jonquilla hybrids. The Tazetta group is not hardy and will not grow well north of Houston, Texas; Jackson, Mississippi; Montgomery, Alabama; Macon, Georgia; and Columbia, South Carolina. Flowers in this group are notably fragrant and cluster flowered. The Geranium selection is a late bloomer recommended for the South.

The hybrids of the species *N. cyclamineus* have nodding, narrow trumpets and petals that reflex. Excellent for naturalizing, these daffodils include many reliable selections famous in the South, such as February Gold and Peeping Tom.

Jonquilla hybrids bear from two to six flowers per stem and are noted for their fragrance. Most bloom later than the trumpet and large-cupped types. Dependable selections for the South include Baby Moon, Suzy, and Trevithian.

Crocus is usually thought of as a spring flower, but there are also a number of fall-flowering selections.

Bulbs 51

The informal look of daffodils makes them a good choice for a naturalized landscape.

Dahlias will thrive in a sunny spot and slightly acid, well-drained soil.

Daffodils recommended for the Upper and Middle South include trumpets, large-cupped, small-cupped, triandrus, cyclamineus, jonquilla, and double narcissi. All except trumpets may also be grown in the Lower South but should be treated as annuals.

Trumpets bloom early, bearing one flower per stem. Good selections include King Alfred, Mount Hood, Magnet, and Unsurpassable.

The large-cupped and small-cupped types also bear one flower per stem. Among the best large-cupped daffodils are Binkie, Professor Einstein, Fortune's Bowl, Fortune, Mrs. R. O. Backhouse, Flower Record, Ice Follies, and Carlton. Verger is a small-cupped daffodil recommended for the South.

Triandrus daffodils bear one to six flowers per stem. Thalia is an especially good selection for naturalizing in Southern gardens.

Double narcissi include any daffodil with more than one layer of petals. Stems may bear more than one flower. Selections for the South include Inglescombe, Mary Copland, Texas, and Yellow Cheerfulness.

Are daffodils easy to care for?

Daffodils are no more difficult to grow than any of the other bulbs. Over most of the South, they flower for many years with minimum care. Tolerant of either sun or shade, daffodils can add vibrant color almost anywhere in your garden.

Depth of planting depends on bulb size. Large daffodils should be planted 8 inches deep (4 inches deep in the Lower South); miniatures should be planted 4 inches deep (2 inches deep in the Lower South). Spacing between bulbs also depends on bulb size. As a rule, space large daffodils 6 inches apart and miniatures 4 inches apart.

The daffodils in a raised bed on the west side of our house get a lot of sun and heat, and the soil tends to dry out. For the second year, they have produced thick foliage but no blooms. What is the problem?

Divide the daffodils and replant them; they probably need more space. Rework and mulch the bed with 3 to 4 inches of pine bark, wood chips, or other available mulch to help stabilize soil moisture and temperature. During summer droughts, water thoroughly once a week, as raised beds dry out more quickly than those at ground level.

What kind of care should I give my dahlias?

Locate dahlias (*Dahlia* hybrida) in a spot that is protected from strong winds and receives at least six hours of sunlight daily. Plant in slightly acid, sandy loam that is well drained. If the soil is not naturally fertile, mix ¼ cup of 5-10-10 into the planting hole to a depth of 12 inches.

At plantingtime, drive a stake firmly into the ground about an inch from each tuberous root. When the plants are 12 inches tall, loosely tie them to the stakes with soft material. Continue to tie the plants periodically as they grow.

Mulch dahlias to aid in weed control and to conserve moisture. Feed each plant every three to four weeks during the growing season with ¼ cup of 5-10-10 or similar fertilizer formulation.

Why is it that some of our dahlias have large flowers and thin, weak stems? We have pinched out all side buds.

Excess nitrogen and too little phosphate can cause this condition. Some dahlia selections naturally have weak stems. Selections known for their strong stems include My Doris R. (large yellow), Emory Paul (large rose purple), and Lula Pattie (large white).

Can fritillaria be grown in the South?

Two species will grow in the Upper and Middle South: crown imperial (*Fritillaria imperialis*) and checkered fritillaria, also known as snake's-head or guinea-hen flower (*F. meleagris*). They are not dependable in the Lower South. Other species usually do not succeed outside their native habitats in the western part of the country.

Plant the bulbs in summer or fall in a somewhat alkaline soil (pH 6.0 to 7.5) and light shade. Set bulbs for *F. imperialis* 8 inches apart and 5 inches deep. Set *F. meleagris* 3 to 4 inches apart and cover with 3 to 4 inches of soil. When new growth appears in spring, dust with 5-10-5 fertilizer. Fritillaria bulbs may be left to overwinter in the ground.

Is there a way to keep gladiolus beds colorful for a longer period of time?

You can extend the period of gladiolus (*Gladiolus sp.*) blooms if you make a staggered planting in March. To do this, plant early-, middle-, and late-season selections each week until mid-March. Choose a sunny location, and plant the corms 4 to 6 inches deep and 6 to 8 inches apart in well-drained soil improved with organic matter.

After digging gladiolus, how long should I wait to separate the old ones from the new ones? Should I leave the foliage on to dry with the corms?

Cut off the foliage just before or immediately after digging. In about three weeks, test a few of the corms. The right time to separate the old from the new is when they come apart easily. Then check every few days; left together too long, the corms will become permanently fused. (*See Figure 8.*)

Would you advise planting hyacinth bulbs in outdoor planter boxes on a patio?

Hyacinths are not recommended for patio planters because they are so sensitive to temperature fluctuations, which are greater in containers than in the ground. Changes in temperature throw hyacinths off their flowering schedules and cause them to produce sparse blooms. Bulbs recommended for planters are crocus, daffodil, grape hyacinth, and tulip.

Crown imperial, a species of fritillaria, will grow and overwinter in the ground in the Upper South.

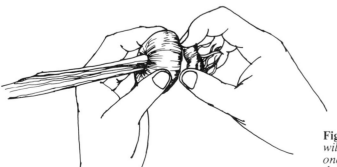

Fig. 8 *A new gladiolus cormel will form at the base of the old one. After they have dried, twist the old corm away from the new.*

A staggered planting of gladiolus in early spring will give an extended season of bloom in early summer.

The blossoms in the flower clusters of grape hyacinths open gradually, beginning with the lowest flowers and progressing upward.

Grape hyacinths naturalize well with common periwinkle and other spring-blooming flowers.

What is a good selection of grape hyacinth to use as ground cover under trees?

Armenian grape hyacinth (*Muscari armeniacum*) is a good choice for naturalizing in the setting. It bears a dense cluster of fragrant flowers atop an 8- to 10-inch stalk, with the mouth of each flower delicately edged in white. Selections include Heavenly Blue (deep-blue flowers) and Early Giant (earlier and slightly clearer blue). Blue Spike, another selection, resembles true hyacinths because it has tufts of double flowers on branched flower spikes.

The common grape hyacinth (*M. botryoides*), while less vigorous than the Armenian type, combines well with pansies, blue primroses, and other early-spring flowers. It is 6 to 12 inches in height and bears blue flowers rimmed with white teeth. Album is a pure white selection sometimes known as Pearls of Spain.

Please tell me how to plant grape hyacinths.

Plant grape hyacinths as soon as they become available in the fall, setting bulbs 4 inches deep (2 inches deep in the Lower South) and 3 inches apart. (For general instructions, *see* question on page 45 on planting bulbs.) To improve drainage, work sand into the area around the bulbs. (*See Figure 9.*)

Grape hyacinths tolerate either full sun or partial shade. Because of this adaptability to a range of lighting situations, grape hyacinths can be used in a variety of areas and in combination with many other plants.

Since the plants improve with age, it is best to let them remain undivided, provided they are not overcrowded. Grape hyacinths are not among the more expensive bulbs, so purchase new ones rather than disturb an existing planting.

Which kinds of iris will do well in the Southern garden?

Of the thousands of iris selections available, the ones of most interest to Southern gardeners may be divided into four major types (listed in order of bloom): bearded (*Iris hybrida*), Siberian (*I. sibirica*), Japanese (*I. hybrida*), and Louisiana (*Iris sp.*).

Bearded iris is the best-known type. Selections to try include Winter Olympics (white), Green Quest (chartreuse with yellow beard), Blue Sapphire (pale blue with yellow beard), and Watermelon (rose with yellow beard).

Fig. 9

Recommended selections of Siberian iris include Caesar's Brother (deep purple), Gatineau (light blue), Perry's Blue (medium to sky blue), and Snowcrest (white with ruffled petals).

The Japanese iris is not as well known to Southern gardeners, but you might try Great White Heron (white), Pink Frost (light pink), Mahogany (deep red), and Higo blend (a mix of purples, blues, whites, and yellows). All of these selections produce double flowers.

Louisiana iris is native to the swamplands of the lower Mississippi River Valley. This type is particularly suited to warm, moist areas where other iris types consistently fail. Selections to plant include Carolyn LaPoint (rose pink), Charley's Felicia (violet bi-tone), Charley's Michelle (rosy bi-tone), and Mrs. Ira Nelson (lavender).

Note: Most iris are rhizomatous and are planted and divided differently from bulbs. Dutch iris, however, is bulbous and handled like other spring-flowering bulbs.

When is the best time to plant iris?

Iris may be planted in spring or fall, but the best time is between mid-July and the end of September. Plants set out this early become established and bloom better the following spring than those set out in the fall, and they do not heave as badly if the ground freezes in winter.

What conditions do iris need to grow well?

Iris vary in their soil and light needs, but they require little care and will even tolerate neglect. Bearded iris require well-drained soil that is rich in organic matter, especially cow manure. They perform best in full sun in most of the South but require partial shade in the Lower South, as the summer sun may burn the foliage.

Siberian iris are less particular about soil than the bearded type, but they, too, require well-drained soil. Grow them in either full sun or partial shade.

Louisiana iris prefer moist, acid soil, as do Japanese iris. Without a rich, moisture-retentive soil, plants of these two types will do poorly. They can be grown successfully in either full sun or partial shade, provided the soil in sunny locations is capable of holding moisture during the warmest, driest summer months. Mulching will help.

How should I plant iris?

Prepare the soil as for annuals (*see* page 15), and mix in about ½ pint of 0-14-14 fertilizer for each 5- to 10-square-foot section of bed area. Dig a hole about 12 inches deep for each rhizome, then mound soil in the bottom of the hole and firm it. Set each rhizome on the mound, making sure the rhizome's top is even with the soil surface and the fan of leaves is above the ground. Then firm backfill soil around each plant. When planting in clay soil, plant rhizomes in raised beds to improve drainage and prevent crown rot.

In a massed planting, space rhizomes 8 to 14 inches apart, depending on how soon you want them to form a dense mass. But the closer you space them, the sooner you will need to dig up crowded clumps and divide them. Mulching is not advised, as it may lead to rotting of rhizomes in areas of high rainfall. If you live in the Upper South, however, a light mulch in winter will help protect the shallow-planted rhizomes.

Water plants during dry spells when they are actively growing. Keep iris beds free of weeds and grass, and topdress lightly with 5-10-10 in early spring.

Bearded iris are the most familiar to Southern gardeners.

This Spanish Gift bearded iris shows the extensive work of iris hybridizers.

A planting of Siberian iris will form a dense mass after only a few years.

The blooms of Siberian iris are small and delicate.

Is there any special way to divide iris?

Dividing rhizomatous iris requires a slightly different procedure from most other plants. After the flowers fade and the foliage stops growing, carefully pry the whole clump out of the ground and remove the soil. Cut the healthy leaves back to 4 to 6 inches in length and remove dead or diseased leaves and stalks. With a knife, cut off the fleshy outer rhizomes so that you have V-shaped pieces, each with two fans of leaves. Dust the cuts with an all-purpose fungicide, such as Terraclor® to prevent disease and rot. Replant immediately. (*See Figures 10-12.*)

Can I grow dwarf iris in my garden?

Many dwarf iris like the dwarf crested iris (*Iris cristata*) are favorites for cultivation in home gardens. Like most dwarf types, crested iris is tolerant of most garden situations. It grows 4 to 6 inches tall and is known for its striking yellow-crested, lavender blue flowers that appear in the spring and early summer. Dwarf iris does best in well-drained humus-rich soil and partial shade.

It can be propagated by divisions of the rhizomes after flowering, or from seed; but if

Fig. 10 *Shake off loose soil from old iris clumps and hose off remaining soil from roots and rhizomes.*

Fig. 11 *Cut off the leafless parts of rhizomes so that you have V-shaped pieces, each with two fans of leaves.*

Fig. 12 *Cut back leaf fans to 6 or 7 inches, and write the selection name or color on the leaf with a felt-tip pen.*

started from seed, crested iris may take up to 3 years to bloom. The plant spreads by rhizomes which must be mulched in the winter to protect them from frost damage. Some dwarf types like crested iris and dwarf iris (*Iris verna*) are native to the South.

Does Dutch iris bloom every year?

The bulbs of Dutch iris (*Iris* hybrida) may be left undisturbed in the ground for three to five years, but you may prefer to replace them every two years to be sure of getting the best blooms. Remove the spent flowers when the blooming season ends, and allow the foliage to die back gradually. Fertilize in the fall, when plants emerge, with ½ cup 5-10-10 per 10 square feet of bed. Dutch iris will propagate themselves and do not need to be dug up and divided until the number and quality of flowers decline.

What is the key to growing lilies successfully in the South?

Perfect drainage is the key to success with lilies (*Lilium sp.*). This is even more important than the kind of lily you plant. Although the hybrids vary slightly in their cultural requirements (and hybrids are generally more dependable than the true species of lilies), perfect drainage is a must with all types.

Planting on a slope is the best way to provide the necessary drainage; if this is not possible, or if you live in an area of heavy clay or hardpan soil, planting the bulbs in elevated beds may be the only way to have successful lilies.

Soil preparation is also important. In addition to perfect drainage, lilies need evenly moist soil. The ideal growing medium for lilies is equal parts organic matter, sharp sand (or sand mixed with fine gravel), and garden soil. A small amount of cow manure or leaf mold may be added to the mixture, provided you do so sparingly. While too-rich soil gives spectacular results the first few years, your lilies may suddenly disappear—consumed by the bacterial activity associated with a very rich organic soil.

Plant in spring. The first step in preparing the planting bed is removing existing soil to a depth of about 20 inches. Spread at least 12 inches of the prepared growing medium over the entire planting bed; water thoroughly. Then set the bulbs in place, allowing 10 to 12 inches between small bulbs and 12 to 18 inches for larger ones. Completely cover the bulbs with a layer of sand, or sand and gravel; add a 4-inch layer of the growing medium. Finally, mulch the planting bed with compost, leaf mold, pine bark mulch, or straw; water once again. Lilies grown in elevated beds should also be planted according to this layering method. (*See Figure 13.*)

If winters are unusually cold in your area, add several extra inches of mulch. Be sure to remove all extra mulch in the spring before growth begins. Foliage should appear by early May; if you have planted good-size bulbs, there should be flowers the same season.

Ideal planting depth may vary from one lily to another and according to the size of the bulb, but it is always safer to plant a lily too shallow than too deep. The 4-inch covering of soil over the tip is suitable for most lilies. However, the Madonna lily is an exception and must have no more than 2 inches of soil covering the bulb.

Although lilies can be grown in full sun, the intense summer sun may cause the flowers to fade prematurely, so they are best grown in partial shade. Protection from midday sun is essential to prolonging flower life. Some lilies prefer acid soil; others like alkaline soil. But all lilies will grow in basically neutral soil (pH 6.5 to 7.0) except the showy lily (*L. speciosum*) and its hybrids, the Trumpet hybrids, and the spectacular Aurelian hybrids. These must be grown in acid soil for success.

There are no easy rules to help you choose which lilies to plant in your garden. Since

Dutch iris will propagate themselves. You need only dig and divide them when flowering begins to decline.

The key to growing lilies like this exquisite Oriental hybrid is proper soil drainage.

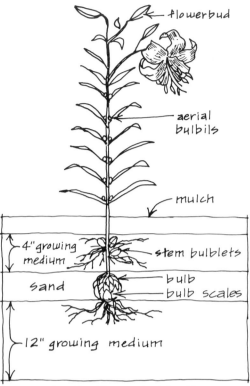

Fig. 13 *Planting bed for lilies.*

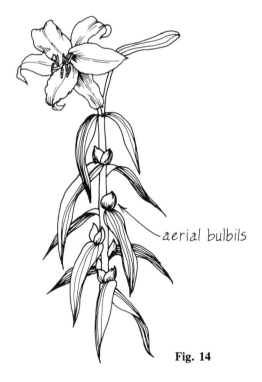

Fig. 14

new hybrids are always being developed, check with a reputable nurseryman or with growers registered with the North American Lily Society or the Royal Horticultural Society for the most recent recommended selections. However, there are some established, popular types that you can try. Regal lily (*L. regale*) is a fragrant, creamy white lily that grows to a height of 5 feet or more. It bears as many as 20 blossoms on each stem. The showy lily is one of the most elegant of all the species lilies. Its hybrids, such as the selection Rubrum, are even more spectacular. The tiger lily (*L. tigrinum*) is one of the easiest to grow of all lilies for the amateur. It is prized for its rich-orange, spotted blossoms. For spring blooms, try the Mid-Century hybrids of the Asiatic group; Aurelian hybrids bloom in midseason, followed by the exquisite, late-blooming Oriental hybrids.

How can I propagate my lilies? When is the best time to do this?

Lilies may be propagated from seeds. However, hybrid lilies grown from seeds will not be true reproductions of the parent plant unless you pollinate the plants yourself. Collect seeds in the fall, and immediately plant in well-drained containers filled with the same type soil mix used for growing lilies in the garden. Space the seeds about an inch apart on the surface of the soil, and cover with a thin layer of sand and peat or sphagnum moss. Water well, and place in a heated greenhouse or on a bright windowsill. Germination should occur in about two weeks. Grow the seedlings in the container until summer or early fall; then plant them directly in the garden, using the layer method described for initial planting of bulbs. Do not be disappointed if they do not bloom for several years.

You can also propagate lilies from the aerial bulbils, the seedlike bulbs that form between the leaf and stem of certain lilies. Treat them like seeds. (*See Figure 14.*)

The other methods of propagation (natural divisions and bulb scale separation) involve digging up the parent plant in late summer and are best done only after lilies are well established and foliage has matured. Bulb scale separation is easier than growing lilies from seeds. Simply remove the outer two layers of scales from the parent bulb, discarding any damaged or shriveled scales; replant the parent bulb. Then insert each scale in a prepared planting medium, covering its length with soil. Water lightly and frequently, and place in a warm location. Within a year, small bulblets should develop; treat them like young lilies grown from seeds.

Natural divisions are the easiest of the propagation techniques because any new bulbs produced by the parent and the bulblets on the stem have already formed beneath the soil. Gently separate them from the parent plant and replant by the layer method described for initial planting of bulbs.

What are the proper conditions for growing lily of the valley?

Lily of the valley (*Convallaria majalis*) thrives in partial shade and moist acid soil (pH 4.5 to 6.0). It will not do well in the warmer parts of the Middle and Lower South, however. The underground root stalks (pips) should be planted in the fall or early spring, 3 to 4 inches apart and 1 inch deep. Mulch lightly in the fall to encourage good growth and fertilize with 5-10-10 in early spring. A compost mulch is also conducive to good growth.

Can you tell me something about magic lily?

The magic of magic lily (*Lycoris squamigera*) is in its growth cycle. When first planted, magic lily rapidly sends up the strap-leaved foliage that is characteristic of its family, *Amaryllidaceae*. The foliage matures, then it dies back to the ground in midsummer.

Suddenly in July or early August, the plant produces a large, tall scape (a modified stem that bears only flowers) that opens into a display of as many as 12 trumpet-shaped flowers. Coming at a time of comparatively little color in the shady garden and appearing on stems that are not noticeable until the flowers open, the display is quite unexpected.

The fragrant flowers persist for as long as two weeks. Besides being hardy in the garden, they make excellent cut flowers, retaining their shape and color for as long as a week when placed in water.

Note: It often takes several years after planting for magic lilies to bloom.

The dainty white, bell-shaped flowers and sweet fragrance of lily of the valley make it a favorite for gardens in the Upper South and for those in the cooler parts of the Middle South.

Plant lily of the valley in fall or early spring.

Magic lily bursts into bloom in midsummer, bearing up to 12 trumpet-shaped, pale-pink flowers on each tall, straight stem.

Spider lily's red flowers on tall, straight stems provide an unusual flower form and bright color in a shady fall garden.

Siberian squill, known for its intense purplish blue flowers, naturalizes well in short grass or under forsythia and azalea.

Next year I will be moving to North Carolina and want to take some of my spider lily bulbs. When should they be moved?

The best time for transplanting spider lily (*Lycoris radiata*) bulbs is immediately after the foliage dies. Dig up the bulbs; let clinging soil dry, then gently remove it from the bulbs. Pack the bulbs in sphagnum moss and store according to the general instructions for bulbs on page 47. Plant the bulbs in their new site as soon as feasible.

Can Siberian squill naturalize easily?

Siberian squill naturalizes easily in the Upper and Middle South. Siberian squill prefers a sunny spot but will tolerate any kind of light. Bulbs should be set with the base 4 inches deep in the ground and may be left undisturbed for years. It is excellent for use in short grass or under azaleas, forsythia, thunberg spiraea, and pink or white flowering quince. The Siberian squill is best known for its brilliant Prussian-blue flowers, but white and purplish pink types are also available. The selection Spring Beauty is hardier and bears flowers that are twice the size of the type's blooms. Because it is sterile, its blue flowers last for several weeks.

How often should one divide snowdrops?

Snowdrops may be divided every four or five years. Dig the bulbs in early spring, soon after flowering is finished. Divide and replant them immediately so the roots will not dry out. Set the base of the bulbs 4 inches deep in the soil.

Does summer snowflake bloom in the spring?

Yes, summer snowflake (*Leucojum aestivum*) will bloom in late spring and early summer. Each 12-inch stem may bear four to eight white, bell-shaped blossoms tipped with green. The foliage dies when the flowering ends.

The members of my garden club would like information on growing tuberoses—time to plant, depth to plant, and any other information we should have.

Tuberoses (*Polianthes tuberosa*) should be planted in spring. Set the bulbs about 3 inches deep in friable, well-drained, loamy soil where they will receive full sun.

Fertilize with superphosphate or other low-nitrogen fertilizer, such as 5-10-10, after foliage develops. Water every 7 to 10 rainless days.

Tuberoses bloom spasmodically in late summer to early fall. After the foliage dies and before the first frost, dig the bulbs and prepare them for winter storage as you would most bulbs in the Upper South (*see* question on storing on page 47). In other regions of the South they can be left in the ground from 3 to 5 years before digging and separating. Propagation is by offsets, small bulblets that form on the parent plant.

The first season I planted tuberose bulbs they bloomed well. The second year I got a few blooms, and the third year I got no blooms at all. The plants grow well, and I have tried everything I know to do. What could be wrong?

One reason tuberoses fail to bloom is because the foliage is removed before it has fully matured and turned brown. The foliage manufactures food all during the growing season. After the plants have finished blooming, the food is stored in the bulbs and used to produce blooms the following season. If the foliage is removed too early, the plants have insufficient food to produce blooms.

Photo by Malak, Ottawa

Divide snowdrops in spring, after they finish flowering.

Summer snowflake is hardy and should be left in the ground undisturbed for several years.

Tuberose produces waxy white, fragrant flowers on 3½-foot stems.

Bulbs　　**61**

Plant tulips in groups of a dozen or more of the same color for the best effect. In this planting, the pansies will continue to provide spring color after the tulip show.

The tulip bulbs I planted three years ago bloomed the first year. But since then, they have produced nothing but healthy foliage. Should I dig up the bulbs and store them in a refrigerator?

Tulip bulbs should be expected to produce flowers only the first year they are planted. Any additional seasonal blooms are really a bonus.

I plan to use groupings of tulips in my garden next spring. Can you give me some pointers on how to achieve the best effects?

The classic use of tulips in the landscape is as the color infilling for the formal beds in a parterre garden. The display is breathtakingly successful because a low plant, such as Truedwarf boxwood, is used to edge the formal beds; this hides the tulip foliage and you see only the flowers.

While this effect is unsurpassed, it takes a lot of bulbs to achieve it. For example, a 2- × 3-foot bed with tulips planted every 3 inches on center would require about 100 bulbs. But carefully grouped, tulips are equally successful on a smaller scale. The following are some points to remember.

Tulips of different heights and colors are combined with creeping phlox, which complements the tulip colors and ties the bed together visually.

—In the South, most tulips rarely produce satisfactory successive seasons of bloom. For this reason, they are usually planted as annuals. When the flowers have shattered, lift the bulbs from the bed and replace them with other bedding plants.

—Plant tulips in groups of 12 or more. Group tulips of the same type and color, and avoid using more than three colors in one garden.

—Plant tulips close together. If the flowers are to be viewed from a short distance, plant the bulbs 3 to 4 inches apart. Spacing can be as wide as 6 inches if the flowers will be enjoyed from a distance.

—Tulips are short-lived color displays (lasting only about two weeks), so plant them in beds that will receive other plants for later seasonal color.

—Plant low-growing annuals like sweet alyssum, candytuft, or pansies in the tulip bed and let the tulips come up through the other flowers.

—Plant early-, midseason-, and late-flowering tulips in the same bed for a continued show. (*See* chart for tulip selections recommended for the South.)

—As an alternative to planting tulips in beds, plant them in pots and set them into the ground in the landscape; it will take at least 6 bulbs for a 12-inch pot. When the tulips have finished blooming, replace them with pots of summer color.

—Pick locations with a neutral or complementary background for tulips. While a green background generally works best, tulips could be used to complement or contrast with the color of flowering shrubs.

Variegated lilyturf provides a foreground for these tall-stemmed tulips, while azaleas complement their color.

TULIPS RECOMMENDED FOR THE SOUTH

EARLY FLOWERING	MIDSEASON FLOWERING	LATE FLOWERING
Single Early Tulips	**Darwin Hybrids**	**Parrot Tulips**
Keizerskroon	Holland's Glory	Black Parrot
Fosteriana Tulips	Oxford	Fantasy
Orange Emperor	Yellow Dover	White Parrot
White Emperor	General Eisenhower	Blue Parrot
Kaufmanniana Tulips	Gudoshnik	Orange Favorite
Shakespeare	President Kennedy	**Double Late Tulips**
	Triumph Tulips	Symphonia
	Elmus	**Darwin Tulips**
	Garden Party	Insurpassable
	Greigii Tulips	Pink Supreme
	Red Riding Hood	Queen of Bartigon
	Royal Splendour	Sweet Harmony
	Oriental Splendour	Clara Butt
		Cottage Tulips
		Balalaika
		Bond Street
		Maureen
		Halcro
		Burgundy Lace
		Mrs. John T. Scheepers
		Smiling Queen
		Artist
		Lily-Flowering Tulips
		Alladin
		Mariette
		Red Shine
		Queen of Sheba
		White Triumphator

An alternative to planting tulips in the ground is planting them in pots that may be set in the ground or placed on your terrace or patio.

The flowers of baby cyclamens last for several weeks, borne singly on tiny scapes rarely more than 5½ inches high. Once the flowers fade, the scapes become tightly coiled.

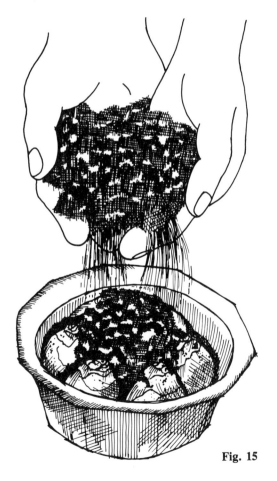

Fig. 15

I have a shaded border that needs a little extra touch of color in spring and fall. Can you suggest a flower that could be a permanent addition?

Hardy cyclamens would be ideal. The flowers are carried singly on bare stems rarely more than 5½ inches high. The tiny blossoms are quite persistent, sometimes lasting several weeks. Once the flowers fade, the stems roll into a coil and the foliage takes over as a landscape feature worthy of close inspection.

The rosy-pink blossoms of baby cyclamens (*Cyclamen hederifolium*) unfold from late July to October. Two selections, Album (white) and Roseum (clear pink), are also available. Flowers generally appear before the foliage, but it is not uncommon for them to occur simultaneously. The leaves of baby cyclamens are ivy shaped and richly marbled with silver, gray, and white. The foliage persists until summer.

C. coum begin their flower display in very early spring, with colors varying from white to pink or carmine. Two selections have also been developed: Album (white) and Roseum (brilliant rosy pink). The dark-green rounded foliage of these hardy cyclamens appears well before the flowers, usually in early fall, and lasts until summer.

Given proper growing conditions—moist, well-drained soil; plenty of organic matter; and protection from the sun—the tiny cyclamens prosper with minimum care. In fact, the less they are disturbed, the better they perform.

Their cultural requirements make the hardy cyclamens ideal plants for naturalizing or as permanent additions for a woodland garden or a border in the shade. Because of their size, they are best appreciated close at hand. And since the foliage dies back in early summer, be sure to locate hardy cyclamens where they will not be inadvertently disturbed while dormant.

General Recommendations—Indoor Use

What is the easiest way to force bulbs for early bloom indoors?

The simplest and most successful way to force bulbs for early bloom is the soil-grown technique, which is based on nature's principles—only the process may be accelerated slightly.

First, a cooling period is necessary. If the bulbs have not been precooled, you will need to refrigerate them prior to potting. Just put the bulbs in an open basket, and place it in the vegetable crisper or on the lowest shelf of your refrigerator for four to six weeks. They will then be ready to pot.

Ordinary potting soil will do, but a mixture of equal parts sterile potting soil, peat moss, and perlite or vermiculite is a better medium. Almost any type container may be used for forcing bulbs as long as it has drainage holes. Plastic pots are suitable, but old-fashioned terra-cotta pots are still preferred by most experienced gardeners. Place an inch of gravel or potsherds in the bottom of the pots to facilitate drainage.

Next, fill the pots with enough soil to bring the upper tip of each bulb to within 1 inch of the rim; then cover the bulbs with more soil. (*See Figure 15.*) Leave the tips of tulips, daffodils, and hyacinths exposed; completely cover other bulbs. Do not pack the soil, as the roots will not develop properly. Since most bulbs perform better when slightly potbound, place several bulbs in each container. An 8-inch pot will hold four or five medium-size bulbs, such as daffodils, and at least five tulip bulbs. This will also create a more impressive flower display.

Keep the pots in a cold, dark location for 13 weeks or until roots are visible from the drainage holes at the bottom of the containers. Then place the pots of bulbs in a cool, bright location, such as a north-facing window, until the foliage develops. This will take at least two weeks for crocus and daffodils and about a month for other bulbs.

Newly developed leaves will be light green, but the color will darken as the foliage matures; when this occurs, the pots are ready to be placed in a sunny window. After a few days of bright sunshine, the flowers should begin to open.

Once flowering begins, prolong the life of the blossoms by keeping the pots away from bright sun or very warm locations. It may also be necessary to water the plants occasionally since the low humidity indoors will cause them to dry out quickly.

I would like to force some bulbs for early blooming indoors. Which selections would you suggest?

Not every springtime bulb is suitable for forcing. Crocus, daffodils, hyacinths, and paper white daffodils (narcissus) are among the best; but you can also grow tulips, anemones, and amaryllis. More exotic bulbs like lily of the Nile (*Agapanthus africanus*), clivia (*Clivia* hybrida), and certain other lilies can also be grown for indoor bloom. But since their cultural requirements are rather complicated, they are not suggested for beginners.

Even recommended bulbs like hyacinths will vary to some degree in suitability. Early-blooming types tend to be more desirable than those that flower later in the season; double-flowered selections make a better show than single-flowered types; and those especially developed for outdoor fragrance will have an even more pronounced scent inside the house. The fragrance of hyacinths tantalizes with a promise of spring. Try the selection Amethystinus for early blooming indoors.

Amaryllis bulbs are not really forced because they are not induced to bloom earlier than normal even when grown indoors. However, selections recommended for growing in pots indoors include King of the Striped (white with red stripes), Pink Beauty (pure pink), Prince of Orange (reddish orange), Queen of the Whites, Queen's Page (salmon pink), and Red Master (dark red).

Recommended selections of crocus for indoor early bloom include Joan of Arc, Queen of the Blues, Striped Beauty, Remembrance, *Crocus chrysanthus* selections, *C. tomasinianus,* and *C. vernus.*

Daffodil selections recommended for early bloom include Paperwhite Grandiflora, Fortune, King Alfred, Yellow Cheerfulness, Thalia, Unsurpassable, Mount Hood, and Peeping Tom. Paperwhite Grandiflora, Thalia, and Mount Hood are white; the other selections named are yellow.

A number of tulip selections are excellent for forcing into bloom. Try General Eisenhower (red), Mrs. John T. Scheepers (light yellow), Insurpassable (lilac), Queen of Bartigon (pink), Orange Favorite (orange), Queen of Sheba (brownish red), White Triumphator (white), Gudoshnik (yellow flushed and veined with red), and Garden Party (white with rose edges).

When I plant bulbs to force for early bloom, do I need to fertilize them?

Since the bulbs themselves contain a sufficient supply of nutrients for this year's flowers, feeding really is not necessary. However, a teaspoonful of time-release 5-10-5 plant food added to each quart of soil will help the bulbs to rebuild their strength once the flowers have faded.

Daffodils are favorite bulbs for forcing into bloom indoors.

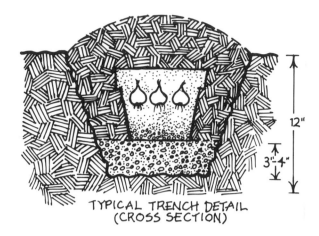

TYPICAL TRENCH DETAIL
(CROSS SECTION)

Fig. 16

I have heard that bulbs planted in pots for indoor blooming should be "planted" outside first. Would you explain this?

Potted bulbs need to rest in a cool, dark location for several months before being forced into early bloom. Although a basement is usually a good spot, the best place is the ground—just "plant" the pots outdoors in a cool, shady spot.

Choose a well-drained outdoor location, since standing water or saturated soil will cause the bulbs to rot. Dig a trench 12 inches deep, and place 3 to 4 inches of coarse gravel in the bottom. Place the pots on the gravel, and backfill the trench with soil.

If the soil is heavy clay, mix in a generous portion of shredded bark or compost with the backfill; that way, the pots will be easier to retrieve. Mound soil over the trench to insulate the bulbs against temperature fluctuations and keep them from freezing. (*See Figure 16.*) After the pots have been left undisturbed for at least 2 months outdoors (nighttime temperatures must be consistently below 45 degrees), remove them from the trench and force as previously directed.

In early October, I took my amaryllis out of their pots, removed the soil, and stored them in the basement. When and how should they be repotted?

Amaryllis need a rest period of about two months. December is a good time to pot and water them for renewed growth as indoor plants. Use a container at least 2 inches wider than the diameter of each bulb to allow 1 inch of soil around the bulbs.

Amaryllis bulbs require rich, well-drained soil. To each 6-inch potful of medium, add about 1 tablespoon of superphosphate. Before planting the bulbs, remove any dead or broken roots. Leave ⅓ to ½ of each bulb above soil level, but make sure the soil is filled in around the fleshy roots. Water well after potting, but apply little additional water until the bulbs begin to grow. The soil should always be slightly damp. (*See Figures 17–20.*)

Fig. 17 *If your bulb is 4 inches in diameter, set it in a 6-inch wide pot.*

Fig. 18 *Fill in soil around the fleshy roots.*

Fig. 19 *Leave one-third of the bulb above the soil line, or water may get into the tip of the bulb and cause rotting.*

Fig. 20 *Six or seven weeks after potting, spectacular blooms will appear. Amaryllis will bloom year after year if given proper care.*

As soon as leaves appear, move the plants to a bright location. Water them frequently, and apply a liquid houseplant fertilizer (18-18-18) at the recommended strength about every three weeks.

How should gloxinias be planted and cared for?

Plant gloxinia tubers (*Sinningia speciosa*) in February or March in pots just large enough to hold them. The soil should be light and high in organic matter. Gloxinias fare best at temperatures as near 70 degrees as possible. Keep the soil barely moist, and increase the water supply as growth develops.

Repot plants into larger containers when the first pots are filled with roots. Feed mature plants with a complete houseplant fertilizer every two weeks. Shade plants from the sun, and withhold water gradually after flowering.

What is the best way to make pineapple lilies bloom indoors?

To enjoy the blooms of pineapple lilies (*Eucomis sp.*) indoors, follow the procedure outlined for forcing bulbs for early bloom. But instead of storing the potted bulbs in a cool, dark location, place them in indirect sunlight for 10 days to 2 weeks to stimulate root development. Keep the soil moist but not wet throughout their growth period.

When the shoots are about 4 to 6 inches tall, move the plants to the coolest sunny window available and leave them there until the flowers begin to bloom. To preserve the blooms, move the plants back into indirect light.

As the leaves wither and turn brown, gradually reduce the frequency of watering. When the leaves are completely brown, store the potted bulbs in a dry, well-ventilated place at 60 to 70 degrees until the normal fall planting season. Then plant the bulbs in the garden. After two or three seasons outside, the bulbs will have recovered their vigor sufficiently to come indoors again.

Pineapple lily blooms will last longer if the plant is placed in indirect light.

Place gloxinias where they will receive bright, indirect light.

Growing on a spike and topped by leafy green tufts, the flower of pineapple lily looks like a miniature pineapple.

Vegetables, Herbs, & Small Fruits

Vine Ripened Tomatoes

Leaf Lettuce

Rosemary

Strawberries

Muscadines

Summer Squash

Few grocers' produce can compete with the fruits and vegetables that you grow in your own garden. After you have nurtured them through the season, you cannot help but believe that each head of lettuce and every juicy berry tastes a little better than any you have ever bought!

But all pride aside, homegrown edibles really do taste better, because they are fresher. Most of us know the difference in flavor between commercially-grown and garden-fresh tomatoes. The contrast is just as pronounced for other vegetables.

Raising your own vegetables, fruits, and herbs also allows you to enjoy crops that are too expensive or that you cannot find in the store. Cauliflower and broccoli can be high priced in the market, but they are economical to grow. You rarely find kale, edible podded peas, kohlrabi, or fresh horseradish in a grocery store, but they can easily be grown at home. And imagine seasoning with fresh basil or thyme, or having all the fresh raspberries or pomegranates that you can use or give away.

Giving away what you have grown can be the best part of gardening. Whether you offer the fresh produce, or give jams, pies, or canned goods, you have truly given

70

something of yourself when the gift comes from your garden.

But a garden is more than a source of food. Because of the mild climate of the South, gardeners are active year-round, getting a bonus of exercise and recreation along with nutritious vegetables and fruits. Winter garden activities entail more than just preparing the soil, pruning, and planning for the next season. Middle South gardens bear fresh greens all winter, but the Lower South has an even longer season. By making successive plantings, these gardeners can harvest peas, lettuce, radishes, carrots, and all of the cole crops through the winter and into the spring.

Fruits, vegetables, and herbs can also double as components in the landscape. For example, blueberries, figs, and pomegranates can be used as shrubs. Blueberries are medium-textured shrubs with fine fall color; figs have a prominent texture in a large, rounded form; and pomegranates have some of the most brilliant flowers in the garden. If you need a vine on an arbor to provide shade, choose a muscadine selection. Or if you need a small tree in an area where the dropping fruit will not be a problem, plant a persimmon or loquat.

Blueberries

American Persimmons

Herb Pots

Fall Vegetable Garden at Old Salem, North Carolina

Herb Garden at Colonial Williamsburg, Virginia

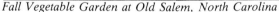

Hot Peppers

Surprisingly, vegetables can be ornamental, too. Trellised squash and cucumber vines provide fresh yellow flowers every morning. Broccoli, kale, brussels sprouts, or any of the cabbage family form delightful blue green rosettes of foliage. Then there are the herbs. Try a hedge of rosemary for an evergreen border; you will enjoy its scent each time you pass by. Use creeping thyme to trail over a wall, to fill between the cracks in stone or brick, or as a ground cover; it is probably the most versatile herb in the landscape.

But for these areas to be a part of your landscape, they must be neat. Edge the garden with landscape timbers, 1 x 6 lumber, stone, or brick. In winter, overseed with clover or green manure. Permanent paths of brick, bark, or sawdust give the vegetable garden a sense of stability while the contents of the beds continually change.

The following pages offer answers to many of your gardening questions. But you will find many more answers by simply observing your own garden. We will help you get started, and the plants will teach you the rest.

Fall Spinach

Fresh Vegetables

Lima Beans

Turk's Turban

Vegetables

What do I need to consider in choosing a site for my vegetable garden?

The most important consideration in site selection is exposure to sunlight. In order to develop properly, vegetables must receive 6 to 10 hours of sunlight every day. Tomatoes, squash, eggplant, and most other vegetables require full sun for maximum production. Other considerations are soil type and organic content, good drainage, accessibility to water, and good air movement.

Can you give me some suggestions for mapping out my vegetable garden?

Plot the garden space on graph paper, mapping out each row and vegetable location. Draw the plan to scale; otherwise, you may have more on paper than you can get into the ground.

To determine the best location for a specific crop, observe the movement of sunlight across the garden. Plant the tallest vegetables, such as staked tomatoes or trellised beans, on an end where they will not shade other vegetables. Allow plenty of room for

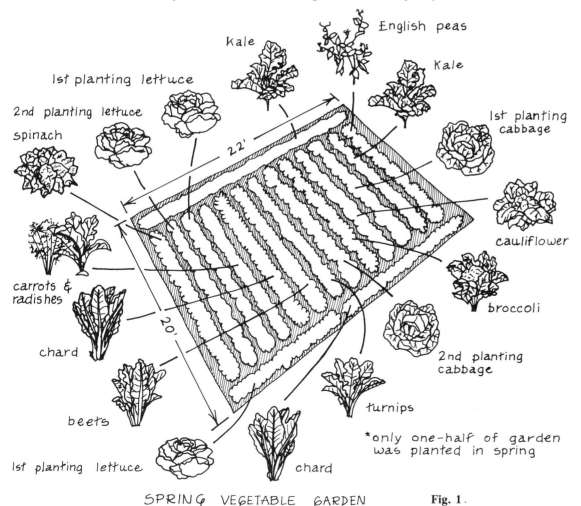

English peas

kale

Kale

1st planting lettuce

1st planting cabbage

2nd planting lettuce
spinach

22'

cauliflower

carrots &
radishes

20'

chard

broccoli

2nd planting
cabbage

beets

turnips

1st planting lettuce

chard

*only one-half of garden
was planted in spring

SPRING VEGETABLE GARDEN

Fig. 1.

spreading vegetables like squash, melons, and cucumbers. To make the most efficient use of the garden space, plant fast-maturing crops, such as radishes and leaf lettuce, alongside rows of crops that take longer to mature.

To carry your garden through spring, summer, and fall, plan to make successive plantings of seasonal crops. You will need to know about how many days it takes a crop to mature (most seed catalogs will tell you this) and how long it will continue to produce (for this information, check with your county agricultural Extension agent). Then draw the garden plan for each season (*see Figures 1–3*) and estimate the time of planting and harvest for each vegetable. For a fall garden, perhaps you can simply repeat a successful spring planting with changes only in planting dates.

Is there an easy way to line off straight rows in my garden?

To make straight rows in your vegetable garden, begin by measuring the distance that the first row is to be from the end of the garden. Drive a stake into the ground at both ends of the planned row; tie a string between the stakes, stretching the length of the row.

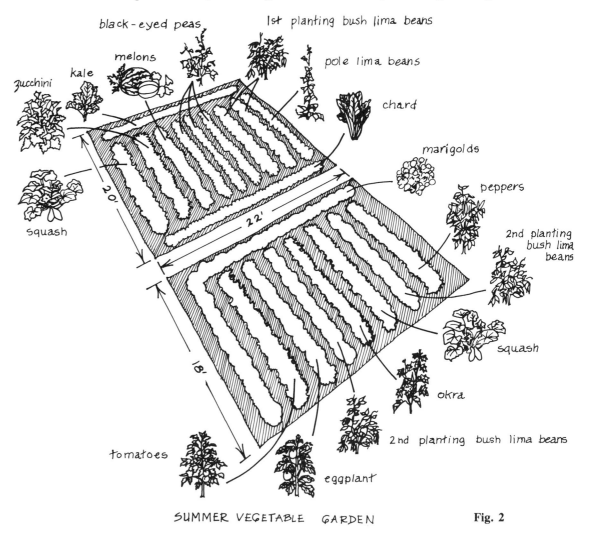

SUMMER VEGETABLE GARDEN   Fig. 2

Use the string as a guide when planting. (*See Figure 4.*) Then remove the string after planting, and repeat the marking process for the rest of the rows. Once each row is planted, label it as to the crop and date planted.

Can you give me some advice on what to plant in my vegetable garden?

The first thing to consider is your family's vegetable preferences. Next, decide which crops are the most economical to grow. Consider yield, supermarket price, and your garden size. For example, lettuce, cauliflower, and broccoli are relatively expensive at the market but very economical to grow at home in the spring and fall. On the other hand, corn is less economical. It requires a lot of garden space, produces only one to three good ears per plant, and is relatively inexpensive to buy. But freshly harvested corn has a superior flavor, and you may want to plant a few rows for that reason alone.

In addition to deciding what to plant, you need to decide how much to plant. Consider family size and whether or not you want to can, freeze, dry, or otherwise preserve the harvest. For example, to grow snap bush beans for fresh use, plant about 8

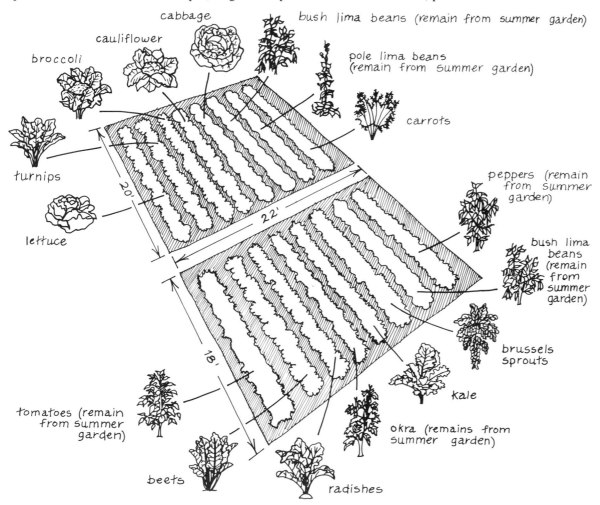

cabbage

bush lima beans (remain from summer garden)

cauliflower

pole lima beans (remain from summer garden)

broccoli

carrots

turnips

20'

22'

peppers (remain from summer garden)

lettuce

bush lima beans (remain from summer garden)

18'

brussels sprouts

tomatoes (remain from summer garden)

kale

okra (remains from summer garden)

beets

radishes

Fig. 3

FALL VEGETABLE GARDEN

Fig. 4

Vegetables, Herbs, & Small Fruits   75

feet of row per person in your family. To store or can the beans, plant 8 to 10 feet of row per person. Plant three to five tomato plants per person for fresh use, five to ten if you plan to preserve them. A 10- to 15-foot row of corn will feed one person; but if you want to can or freeze some of the crop, plant 30 to 50 feet.

What should I do to prepare the soil for my vegetable garden?

The best soil for successful gardening contains balanced amounts of sand (for good drainage), clay (for nutrient-holding capacity), and decomposed organic matter (for moisture retention). When the soil is workable in the spring, break it up 8 to 12 inches deep, using a spade or tiller. If you have heavy clay soil, improve soil texture by working in a 6- to 12-inch layer of finely ground pine bark or organic matter (manure, leaf mold, compost, or peat). Then work the soil until it is friable (easily crumbled). If you have sandy soil, add organic matter.

Soil pH is a major key to having healthy plants. The pH reading denotes how acid or alkaline the soil is, based on a scale from 0 to 14 (with 0 being the most acid and 14 the most alkaline). If the pH of your soil is not in the range of 5.5 to 6.5, the growth of many vegetables may be limited.

A common soil problem in the South is an overly acidic condition (pH below 5.5). To correct an acidic condition, incorporate lime into the soil to raise the pH to a less acidic level. Various liming products are available, with some working more rapidly than others. The safest liming products (less likely to burn plants) may take five months or more to raise the pH to the desired level. Your soil type will also influence whether lime takes two weeks or several months to change the pH. Thus, the importance of having a soil test made early cannot be overstressed; otherwise, there will not be time to correct a pH problem before a spring planting. Once the pH is corrected, regular liming thereafter will keep the soil at the desired level. However, never add more than 25 pounds of agricultural lime per 1000 square feet without having a soil test made. If the soil is too alkaline (pH above 6.5), sulfur will decrease the pH.

To help you determine the pH of your soil and how much lime or sulfur to apply, every state has a soil-testing laboratory. Your county Extension agent can tell you how to take samples and where to send them. Your soil should be tested every three years.

When should I begin preparing the soil for my vegetable garden?

Fall is the best time to prepare soil for a spring garden. The soil is warm and workable then. Fall preparation also allows plenty of time for the lime or sulfur and organic matter you have added to do their work.

When is the best time to plant vegetables?

The first planting date for the spring garden depends on the average date of the last frost in your area; the weather bureau can give you that information. (*See Figure 5.*) The very hardy crops, such as spinach and broccoli, can be planted several weeks before the frost-free date. Plant less hardy crops like carrots and beets about two weeks before that date; but wait until after the last frost to plant such tender crops as tomatoes and beans.

If you gamble with the frost date and set out tender plants early, be prepared to cover them with a cardboard box or sheet plastic should frost be predicted. Place the covering over plants in early evening to capture the ground's warmth. To keep the covering from damaging tender growth, do not allow it to touch the plants. Support sheet plastic with a wire frame or stakes. Remove the covering the next morning before the sun shines directly on it. Small transplants may be protected with plastic milk jugs that have had the bottoms removed; just place the jug over the plant in early evening.

Never plant when the soil is too wet. Wait a day or more after a heavy rain, especially in areas of poor drainage. To check the soil for moisture, squeeze some in your hand—if it forms a tight ball, it is too wet; if it crumbles, it is just right.

To avoid having to harvest an entire crop at once, stagger the planting times. Start seeds or transplants in several different groups about a week apart, planting a portion of the row at a time. Lettuce and other vegetables that do not keep long are good crops to consider for staggered plantings.

I would like to try starting a garden from seeds. Is there anything special I need to know about buying seeds?

The seeds you buy can mean success or failure for your garden. Here are some guidelines to help you buy wisely.

—Buy seeds from a reputable source. There are many excellent mail-order seed catalogs and local garden centers noted for quality seeds.

—Make sure you buy enough seeds, but do not overbuy. Most seed packages will tell you how much space is required to plant the entire package. Try to buy only the amount of seeds needed for this year's planting.

—Buy seeds packaged for the current gardening season. Old seeds may fail to germinate.

—Be sure to buy selections that perform well in your area. Each state Extension service in the South has a list of selections recommended for each region of its state. Also

Fig. 5 *Use this map as a general guide to determine the date of the last spring frost in your area. Actual dates may vary by as much as two weeks in some areas.*

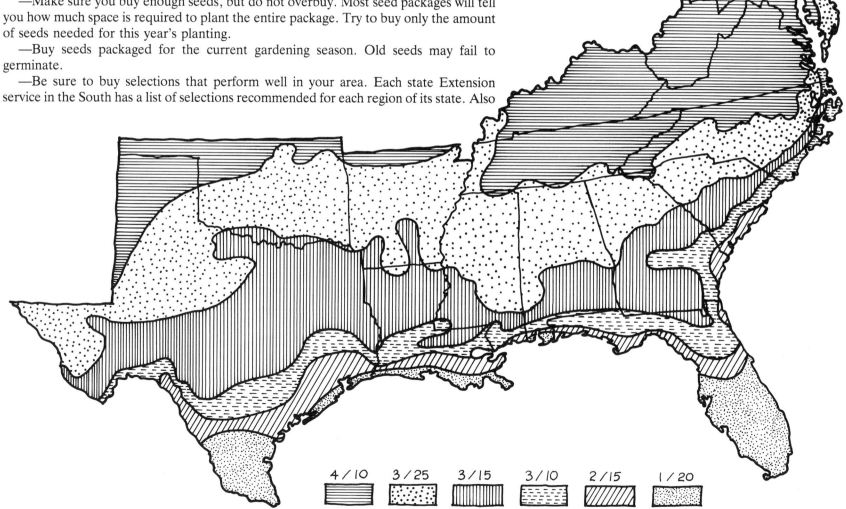

4/10   3/25   3/15   3/10   2/15   1/20

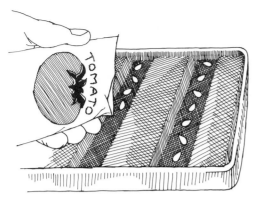

Fig. 6 *To start vegetable seedlings in a flat or tray, sow seeds in rows or scatter evenly over moistened soil and cover lightly with more soil.*

Fig. 7 *Polystyrene egg cartons make splendid seed trays for vegetables; punch holes for drainage. Plant three or four seeds in each spot, and later remove all but the strongest seedling.*

consider culinary use when making your choice. For example, some types of tomatoes are bred for canning; others are strictly for eating fresh.

—Get seeds early. Since seed catalogs often have a better selection than local sources, you may prefer to order seeds. Be sure to allow adequate delivery time so seeds will be on hand at plantingtime.

How can tomatoes, peppers, cabbages, and other vegetable garden plants grown from seeds be started in the house?

To grow seedlings of vegetable plants indoors successfully, you must either put them in a very sunny window or under fluorescent tubes where they will get light for at least eight hours each day. Place seedlings within 2 feet of the fluorescent lights.

Start vegetable seeds in containers of sterile soil or in peat pots about two months before they would normally be planted outdoors. For best results, transplant seedlings started in containers to individual peat pots as soon as a set of leaves has formed. Before setting transplants out in the garden, place them outdoors in a protected location for the last two or three weeks. If frost is predicted, take the plants indoors. (*See Figures 6–11.*)

Should I mulch my vegetables?

The wisest step in garden maintenance is mulching. It reduces moisture evaporation from the soil; aids weed control; reduces erosion; insulates the soil from excessive heat and cold; keeps ground vegetables, such as squash and melons, clean; and makes the garden look neater.

Mulch plants when they are about 4 to 8 inches high, applying at least a 2-inch layer of material. Good mulching materials include pine straw, shredded pine bark, leaves, and compost. Hay, wood chips, peanut hulls, and sawdust are also often used as mulch. If you use sawdust or wood chips, you will need to compost them first, or apply ¼ to ½ pound of ammonium nitrate per 100 square feet to aid in decomposition.

Although mulch reduces weed growth greatly, some weeds will break through. Keep them from competing with your vegetables for water and soil nutrients by handpulling weeds as they appear. You may have to use a trowel to dig up stubborn ones.

Fig. 8 *Peat pellets are excellent starters for vegetable seedlings but must be watered frequently to keep them moist.*

Fig. 9 *When seedlings are large enough to handle, transplant them from the tray or carton to another tray, spacing individual plants 2 to 3 inches apart.*

Fig. 10 *Or, to make transplanting to the garden easier, transplant seedlings to individual peat pots.*

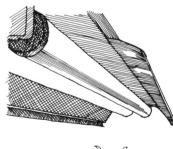

Fig. 11 *Give seedlings 12 to 16 hours of light daily, either from the sun or fluorescent lamps.*

Please give me some tips on how to stake vegetables.

The type of stake needed varies with the plants you grow. Simple stakes are best for tomatoes, eggplant, peppers, and other crops of not more than a dozen plants. The length of the stake will vary with the crop to be grown. Stakes for eggplants and peppers need be no more than 3 or 4 feet long. But tomato stakes for most selections should be at least 8 feet long and driven 12 to 18 inches into the ground. Determinate (bush type) selections only need short stakes.

To minimize damage to roots, drive the stake into the ground 4 to 6 inches away from the base of the plant. Use strips of cloth or soft twine to fasten the plant to the stake. Do not tie the cloth around the stem, then around the stake. Instead, loop the cloth strip around both stem and stake to avoid binding the stem as it continues to grow. As the plant grows, you will have to fasten it higher up on the stake.

A fence or chicken-wire trellis is best for cucumbers because they are spreading vines and require a larger area to support them. To construct the trellis, simply attach a section of chicken wire to two secure end posts. (*See Figure 12.*)

A wire-and-string trellis is best for pole beans, running lima beans, and English peas. Position two or more stakes or posts along the row (2 × 4 × 8s do well). Then run a length of clothesline wire along the top of the posts and secure it with U-nails. Run a heavy string along the bottom of the posts, about 6 inches from the ground, again fastening the string with U-nails. Tie sections of heavy twine between the wires, at 12-inch intervals, to create the vertical lines on which the beans can twine.

How can I tell when my vegetables are ready for harvesting?

For peak quality and flavor, vegetables must be picked at the right time. The following list tells you when to harvest some of the most popular vegetables.

Asparagus: Cut off the shoots at ground level when they are 5 to 6 inches long. Do not harvest asparagus the first year after planting. In beds only two years old, limit harvest to two weeks. Beds that are at least three years old may be harvested every two to three days for a period no longer than four to six weeks.

Pine straw is a good mulch for the vegetable garden. It is neat, easy to work around, and keeps vegetables clean.

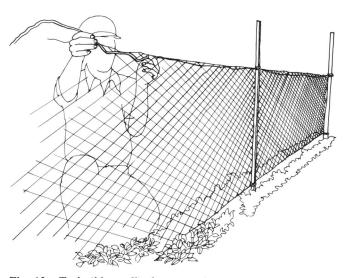

Fig. 12 *To build a trellis for cucumbers, attach a section of chicken wire to two or more posts. Run clothesline wire or heavy twine through the top loops to keep the chicken wire taut.*

A simple trellis of low end posts and horizontal twine supports is adequate for bush limas and other low-growing vines.

Tomatoes will produce better and be easier to harvest if the vines are staked.

To test corn for ripeness, insert your fingernail into a kernel. The liquid will be milky if the corn is ready for harvest.

Beans, Lima: Harvest when the beans are fully formed in the pods but before the pods become too wrinkled. Keep harvested; otherwise, production will stop.

Beans, Snap: Pick the pods beginning at the bottom of the plants before the beans begin to show inside and the pods become lumpy. Bush beans are usually harvested when 3 to 6 inches long; pole beans, when 4 to 6 inches long. Like limas, snap beans will stop producing if not kept harvested.

Beets: Start harvesting beets when they are about 1 inch in diameter. Once they reach 3 inches, harvest immediately or they will become tough.

Broccoli: Cut the stem about 6 inches below the large, central flower head while the buds are still tight (before the yellow flowers open). New shoots may develop from the base of the leaves for a later crop. Keep harvested to encourage further production.

Cabbage: Cut heads when they are firm (that is, when they do not feel spongy) and are a good size.

Carrots: Start harvesting when they are finger size, and continue until they are 1½ inches in diameter.

Cauliflower: Harvest while the head (curd) is still tight and firm, before it begins to separate. Size is not an indication of maturity. If the head is small, delaying the harvest will produce only an overmature head that will become shrunken and taste mealy. Cut the mature head with a sharp knife below the first whorl of leaves, and refrigerate it immediately to preserve freshness.

Chard, Swiss: Cut outer leaves at base when they are 4 inches or more in length. Inner leaves will continue to grow.

Corn: Test an ear as soon as the silks turn brown. About 1 to 2 inches from the bottom of the ear, insert your fingernail into a kernel. If it is ripe, the liquid will be milky; if the liquid is watery, wait a day or two before testing again. The liquid of overly ripe corn will be thick like toothpaste, and the ear will taste starchy. Harvest early in the day. Plan to use corn as soon as harvested, as it begins to lose quality immediately. To refrigerate, remove the shucks and place ears in a plastic bag.

Cucumbers: Harvest when 2 to 3 inches long for table use or wait until they reach peak maturity at 6 to 8 inches long; harvest when 2 to 4 inches long for pickling. Keep harvested to encourage further production.

Eggplant: Harvest when the fruit is about 6 inches long and very shiny. If it is a dull color, the fruit is overripe.

Kale: Harvest entire plants or just the outer leaves while young (seedling size to about 5 inches long). Older leaves are tough and stringy. Do not pinch out the growing tip.

Lettuce: Harvest anytime from seedling stage to mature size. Harvest the outer leaves of leaf lettuce, allowing inner leaves to continue growing.

Mustard: Begin harvesting when leaves are a minimum of 2 inches long. Old leaves may be tough.

Okra: Cut okra when pods are about 3 inches long; large pods are tough and stringy. Harvest daily, as old pods remaining on the plants discourage production.

Onions: Begin harvesting green onions (scallions) when they are about 6 inches tall; harvest bulbs after the leaves die.

Peas, Black-Eyed and Southern: Harvest when peas are fully formed in the pods. Pick Purple Hull selections when about half of the hull has turned purple. Peas have best flavor and are most easily shelled if picked as pods turn from green to yellow or purple (depending on the selection).

Peas, English: Pick when the peas are well formed in the pods but before the pods turn yellow. Mature peas left on the vine lose quality quickly and discourage further production.

Peppers, Hot: Harvest hot peppers at any stage of development. Generally, the pods get hotter with age.

Peppers, Sweet: Pick sweet peppers when they are 3 to 4 inches long, while bright green and crisp. Keep plants harvested to encourage production. For ripe peppers, allow the fruit to remain on the plant until they turn red.

Potatoes, Irish: Harvest when the plants begin to flower for new potatoes; harvest when the foliage starts to turn brown and die back for mature potatoes.

Potatoes, Sweet: Harvest in the fall when a large percentage of the potatoes are a desirable size. The full crop is usually ready 120 days after transplanting. Be sure to harvest before frost kills the vines.

Pumpkins: Cut pumpkins from the vine after the leaves begin to die and the pumpkins are a rich color (orange, yellow, or green, depending on the selection); leave 3-inch stems on the pumpkins.

Radishes: Harvest when the roots are about ¾ inch in diameter; the larger ones will be pithy.

Spinach: Cut entire plants when the leaves are 3 to 8 inches long; or pick only the outer leaves, allowing inner leaves to continue growing.

Squash, Summer: Harvest pattypan types when they are about 6 inches in diameter; yellow types, when 4 to 6 inches long; zucchini, when 6 to 8 inches long. Harvest promptly or the vines will stop setting flowers and fruit.

Squash, Winter: Harvest when the leaves begin to die back. Acorn squash should be dark green and 5 to 6 inches in diameter. Its rind should be too hard to puncture with your thumbnail. Butternut squash should be about 8 inches long; its rind should be tan and unstriped. Do not wash winter squash before storing; this will encourage rot. Store in a cool, dry location, placed so they do not touch each other.

Tomatoes: Pick them when brightly colored and firm, with a little green color remaining at the stem end. Ripe tomatoes do not remain in good condition if left on the vine longer than two days, so harvest frequently. (*See* page 93 for more information.)

Turnips: Begin harvesting greens when they are 2 inches long; roots, when 2 to 3 inches in diameter. If the leaves are constantly harvested, the plants will not develop good roots.

Watermelon: Cut watermelons when they sound hollow when thumped, the skins become less glossy, leaves and tendrils near the melons turn brown, and the undersides turn from white to creamy yellow. Too much rain at harvesttime will cause melons to be flavorless. If possible, wait two days after a rain to harvest.

What are some vegetables that I can grow in the fall and winter?

All the cool-season crops planted in the early spring may be grown in the fall and winter garden: English peas (Lower South), snow peas (Lower South), greens, members of the cabbage family, root crops, and onions and their relatives.

Salad greens to plant include all types of lettuce, Swiss chard, romaine, and spinach. Other greens that are easy to grow include turnip greens, mustard greens, collards, kale, and tendergreens.

In addition to cabbage, the cabbage family offers a variety of fall vegetables: broccoli, brussels sprouts, cauliflower, bok choy (Chinese cabbage), and kohlrabi. Kale, spinach,

Dig Irish potatoes when the foliage begins to die back.

Winter squash, such as butternut, is harvested after the rind has hardened.

Broccoli grows well in the cool weather of fall.

Onions are a good choice for the fall garden. Keep beds well weeded, as onions are shallow rooted.

collards, brussels sprouts, and cabbage are hardier than peas, chard, and lettuce and will remain in good condition even after a heavy frost.

Root crops for fall planting include beets, carrots, parsnips, turnips, rutabagas, and radishes. In the Lower South, September is also a good month to plant Irish potatoes, if you can find seed potatoes that will sprout.

Onions, chives, scallions (green onions), and garlic can all be set out in the fall garden.

Please give me some hints for planting vegetables for the fall.

The fall garden should be planted from mid-August through September. Very hardy crops may be planted through the first week of October. In the Lower South you may plant through the end of October.

To get the garden off to a fast start, set out vegetable transplants instead of sowing seeds. Seeds sown in October may not grow quickly enough to withstand an early frost. Buy healthy plants from a reputable source, and plant them as soon as you bring them home. Prepare soil by digging it to a depth of 8 to 12 inches; then hoe or till until the soil has a fine, even texture. Remove rocks and sticks, and work in compost, leaf mold, or other organic matter.

When setting out plants, loosen any roots that have become wrapped around the soil ball so that they can spread into the soil as quickly as possible. In the prepared soil, dig small holes with a trowel and position the plant so that the top of the root ball is even with the surrounding soil or about ⅛ inch below the soil. Firm the soil gently around each plant. After all the plants are in the ground, water the garden thoroughly.

About two weeks after planting, fertilize the garden with 5-10-10 or similar fertilizer at the rate of 1 cup per 10 feet of planted row, fertilizing both sides of the row. Water thoroughly to wash the fertilizer into the soil and remove any that you may have accidentally spilled on the plants. Repeat the application monthly, reducing the application by about half during the coldest months when the growth rate slows. Processed cow manure is a good fertilizer for the cool-season garden since it releases nutrients gradually, allowing plants to take up nutrients as they are needed.

Are there any vegetables that do not have to be harvested before frost?

Broccoli, brussels sprouts, all of the cabbages and cauliflower tolerate light frost but are damaged by severe freezes. Collards and kale can tolerate temperatures of 15 to 20 degrees. Many other fall-maturing vegetables do not have to be harvested until after frost. Oyster plant, for instance, has a better flavor if harvested after a heavy frost.

Tubers of Jerusalem artichoke may be dug anytime after the first frost. Allow them to dry for a few hours after digging, then wash and store in damp sand in a root cellar or in plastic bags in the refrigerator.

Carrots, parsnips, turnips, and other root crops planted in August and September can be kept in the garden over the winter if they are protected with a mulch of hay or straw, and dug as needed until spring. To ensure continuous production, apply ½ cup of 5-10-10 per 10 feet of row every four to six weeks. Harvest the root crops often to thin the rows and allow more room for developing roots to grow.

Horseradish should not be dug until after a hard freeze. It can be dug as needed until early spring, but the roots should be peeled and grated for use soon after digging.

Rutabagas can be harvested after a heavy frost, kept in moist sand in a cool place, and used during the winter. Or they can be dipped into melted paraffin and stored in a refrigerator or other cool place.

Our family enjoys Jerusalem artichokes in salads, but we have difficulty finding them. Do they grow in the Upper South? If so, when should they be planted and harvested; also, how do you store them?

Jerusalem artichokes should grow well in the Upper South. Most mail-order sources of plants can supply you with tubers. Plant in the spring after the last freeze; choose a location away from other vegetables, as Jerusalem artichokes multiply quickly and tend to take over an area.

Dig the tubers in the fall after the plants flower and the tops die back. Clean and store as you would potatoes. Brush off soil and store in a cool, dark, humid location that is well ventilated.

I have a nice bed of asparagus. Please tell me how to care for it this winter to ensure maximum yield next spring. Also, how and when should I fertilize?

As soon as the stalks die, cut them to ground level and dispose of them. Then apply a liberal amount of compost or manure mixed with 5 to 10 pounds of 5-10-10 or a comparable analysis fertilizer per 100 feet of row. Mulch to protect roots from frost damage and to control weeds.

Soon after the plants put out new growth in the spring, side-dress both sides of the row with 5-10-10 at the rate of 3 to 4 pounds per 100 feet of row. In late spring, side-dress with 1 pound of fertilizer high in nitrogen, such as 12-6-6, per 100 feet of row.

Because asparagus does best in a neutral or slightly alkaline soil, some gardeners must add lime at four- to five-year intervals. For an exact dosage of lime, a soil test would be necessary.

When should I transplant my asparagus, and how should the replanting be done?

Divide and transplant your asparagus early in the spring just before new growth begins. Dig trenches 18 to 24 inches wide and 10 to 12 inches deep, spacing them 4 to 6 feet apart; when digging, put topsoil on one side of the trench and subsoil on the other.

Spread 2 inches of compost or other organic material over the bottom of the trench. On top of the compost, sprinkle ½ pound of complete fertilizer, such as 5-10-10, for each 10 feet of row; cover with a 2-inch layer of the topsoil that was removed. (*See Figure 13.*)

Mix compost, fertilizer, and topsoil thoroughly; spread evenly in the trench and water well. Set the crowns 12 to 24 inches apart, spreading the roots in their natural position

Kale not only tolerates cold weather—its flavor actually improves after frost.

Cauliflower will not be damaged by light frost but should be harvested before a hard freeze.

Tubers of Jerusalem artichoke may be harvested in the fall after the first frost.

In late spring, side-dress asparagus plants with a high-nitrogen fertilizer.

and clipping off any that are broken or injured. (*See Figure 14.*) Cover the crowns with 3 inches of topsoil; then water again. As the plants grow, finish filling in the trench with the remaining soil mixed with organic matter, being careful not to cover the growing tips. (*See Figure 15.*) Water deeply when soil begins to dry out.

What kind of care do beans require?

As soon as the plants are 4 to 6 inches high, mulch according to general instructions (*see* page 78). Black sheet plastic is very effective against weeds, but be sure to punch holes in the plastic to allow rainwater and water from irrigation to enter the soil. During dry weather, water beans every three to five rainless days.

When you apply the mulch, also begin fertilizing bean plants monthly. Use 10-10-10 or a similar vegetable garden fertilizer at the rate of 1 pound per 100 feet of row. Do not exceed label recommendations. In sandy or otherwise rapidly draining soils, feed plants every two weeks and apply half the recommended dosage each time. For prolonged production, keep beans watered, weeded, harvested, and free of pests.

What is the difference between butter beans and lima beans?

There is no difference. Lima beans are often called butter beans in the South, and sometimes the small lima beans are referred to as butter beans. But the two names refer to the same vegetable.

I planted some lima beans this spring, but they never came up. Can you tell me how to grow them successfully?

Lima beans are very tender and should not be planted until weather and ground are warm—between March 20 and June 1 in the Middle South, two weeks later in the Upper South, and two weeks earlier in the Lower South. Like other beans, limas require a soil pH of 6.0 to 7.5. To reduce the possibility of disease, avoid planting beans in the same location year after year. Sow seeds of bush types 2 to 4 inches apart in rows 3 feet apart. Sow pole types 6 to 9 inches apart in rows 4 feet apart. Keep beans harvested to prolong production.

Fig. 13 *Fill the trench with compost, fertilizer, and topsoil and mix thoroughly.*

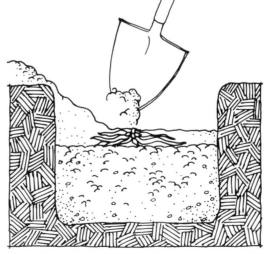

Fig. 14 *Set crowns in the trench and cover with 3 inches of topsoil.*

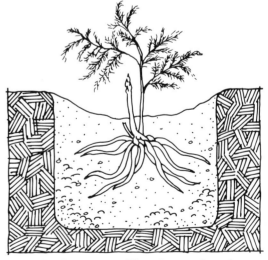

Fig. 15 *Continue to fill in the trench as the plants grow, but do not cover the growing tips.*

Broccoli is one of my favorite vegetables, and I would like to try to grow some this fall. Are there any special requirements?

Broccoli is easy to grow and is a good choice for the fall garden. If you plant seedlings in late August or early September, you should begin harvesting in 70 to 80 days.

A dozen plants, set 18 inches apart, should be adequate for a family of four. To avoid cabbage diseases, do not plant broccoli where other crops in the cabbage family were grown during the past three years. Water plants when the soil is dry; feed with an all-purpose fertilizer such as 5-10-10 when the plants are 6 to 8 inches tall, again when they are 12 to 15 inches tall, and again when the buds start to form. Scatter a wide band of fertilizer along both sides of the row at the rate of 5 ounces per 10 feet of row.

Set out broccoli transplants in late August or early September to enjoy fresh broccoli in November.

The cabbage I planted in late March was doing fine until the end of June. Then each plant sent up a long flower spike and fizzled. Please tell me why this happened.

Your cabbage plants bolted. Bolting means that a plant has stopped vegetative growth to begin reproductive growth. The flower spike will set seeds and provide another generation of its species. Cabbage bolts because, as seedlings, the plants were exposed to constant cold temperatures.

To prevent bolting, protect seedlings from severe cold and wait to transplant them until temperatures are consistently above 45 degrees. If you overwinter seedlings, you will probably get early bolting, except in the Lower South. You can also help your cabbage crop reach maturity before hot weather arrives by following a good fertilizing and watering schedule. Side-dress rows of cabbage with 5-10-10 or a similar complete fertilizer at the rate of ½ cup per 10 feet of row. Make applications every two weeks, distributing fertilizer along both sides of the row.

Water plants every four to six rainless days. If you apply a 2- to 3-inch layer of organic mulch, such as pine straw, you will conserve soil moisture and discourage weeds that would otherwise rob plants of the fertilizer you have applied.

To harvest a good cabbage crop, do not plant seedlings until temperatures are above 45 degrees, and feed and water seedlings regularly.

What does "blanching" cauliflower mean?

Blanching simply means protecting the cauliflower head (curd) from the sun. It keeps the head from turning yellow and developing an off-flavor. Blanching should begin as soon as the curd (flower) is large enough to push apart the innermost leaves. Gather the large outer leaves over the curd, and secure with soft twine. Do not tie too tightly, or you will not be able to check the maturity of the curd without untying the string. Also, tying tightly will trap moisture and promote rotting.

There are some selections available that are called "self-blanching" in garden catalogs. These have been developed so that the outer leaves of the plant naturally curl around the head to protect it from the sun. Unfortunately, the self-blanching types are usually not the fast-maturing ones suited to the South's warm spring temperatures. So in most areas, particularly the Middle and Lower South, it is best to stick with the regular cauliflower selections like Snow Crown and Super Snowball.

I have been advised to plant sweet corn in blocks of three or more rows this summer rather than in a single long row. Please give me your opinion and some information on spacing the plants.

The chances for perfect pollination are improved by block planting. The best spacing

To blanch cauliflower, tie the outer leaves over the curd.

Planting corn in blocks of several rows improves the chances of perfect pollination.

Harvest cucumbers as soon as they begin to ripen, or the vines may stop producing.

Female blooms on cucumber plants have a miniature cucumber at the base.

between plants and between rows depends partly on the hybrid you choose. Early-producing hybrids, which are generally short plants, can stand 6 to 8 inches apart in rows about 2 feet apart. Plant midseason hybrids 7 to 10 inches apart in rows that are 2½ feet apart. Later-producing hybrids, which are larger, more robust plants, should stand 9 to 12 inches apart in rows 3 feet apart. If the soil is poor, space plants farther apart than you would in fertile soil.

Modern sweet corn hybrids are bred to mature all at once. An entire block will be ready to eat within three to four days of the time the first ear is ripe. To prolong your supply of fresh corn, plant small blocks to mature two weeks apart. In each block include three or four times as many plants as you have members in your family.

Can you give me some suggestions for growing cucumbers?

Plant cucumbers in hills if you wish to grow them as creeping vines. If you prefer to grow them on a trellis or fence, sow the seeds in a raised furrow along the supporting structure. As for other garden crops, work compost, peat moss, or cow manure into the soil to improve soil structure, drainage, and moisture retention.

Once cucumber plants are about 6 inches high, mulch them with pine straw, wood chips, ground bark, or similar material. Mulching and adequate watering are important for cucumbers since a large content of the fruit is water. Without an even water supply, cucumbers may be bitter and unappetizing. Plants wilt easily on hot days, but this may not indicate a need for watering unless the plants stay wilted after the sun goes down.

Proper fertilization is also important for a satisfactory crop. Apply composted manure according to label recommendations, or use a commercial fertilizer at the rate of 1 teaspoon of 5-10-10 per plant. Make the applications every two to three weeks.

To keep your vines producing fruit continuously, harvest cucumbers as soon as they begin to ripen. If cucumbers become overripe on the vine, the seeds may mature, causing plants to stop producing.

Last year I tried to grow cucumbers in my backyard garden. The soil is good garden loam; I watered and fertilized, but the vines produced very few cucumbers. What was wrong?

One of the main reasons cucumbers and other cucurbits (members of the gourd family) fail to produce properly is the scarcity of honeybees to take care of pollination. This is especially true for backyard garden plots in the larger cities, where bees lack natural nesting places. Grow plenty of brightly colored flowers nearby to attract bees to your garden. Or handpollinate the plants with a watercolor brush. Female blooms have a miniature cucumber at the base, while male blooms do not. Also, make sure your plants receive plenty of sun. Cucumbers will not set fruit in the shade.

Last year my eggplants had many blooms but not much fruit. I did not notice any signs of pests or disease. What do you think caused our scant harvest?

Your eggplants probably did not get enough sun. They need full sun all day to produce their best. Too much nitrogen, especially before fruit begins to develop, also prevents the plants from setting fruit. Side-dress the plants with ½ cup 5-10-10 per 10 feet of row every three to four weeks after they become established.

Are there any edible gourds?

Most gourds are grown strictly for ornamental use. Turk's turban, however, may be grown and eaten like a winter squash.

Can kale be grown as a fall crop?

Kale is best grown as a fall or early-spring crop. Its flavor is sweetest after frost. Plants started in September will produce through fall and into early winter, tolerating temperatures of about 15 degrees and sometimes much lower.

Start seeds in transplant containers or a flat according to directions on the seed package, sowing them about ¼ inch deep. Keep the planting medium moist. Transplant seedlings when they are about 3 inches tall, spacing plants 8 to 12 inches apart. Seeds may also be sown directly in the ground; thin seedlings to correct spacing when 2 to 3 inches tall.

Kale grows best in a rich organic soil, but it will tolerate very sandy and heavy clay soils. For best results in poor soil, incorporate leaf mold, peat moss, or other organic matter and ⅓ pound of 10-10-10 per 10 feet of row. Kale grows best at a soil pH of around 6.5, so lime may be needed in acid soils.

From the Upper Piedmont to coastal areas, kale may be overwintered. Fertilize plants in late February or early March with 10-10-10 at the rate of 2 pounds per 25 feet of row. The leaves will remain edible until May, when the plants go to seed.

How many kinds of lettuce are there? Can you tell me something about them? I do not know which kind to plant.

There are three basic lettuce types: heading, leaf, and semiheading. Head lettuce forms a tight head. (Iceberg lettuce is a heading type.) Because head lettuce takes longer to mature (about 90 days) and is not as heat tolerant as leaf and semiheading types, it is not as widely grown in Southern home gardens.

Leaf lettuce selections produce thick bunches of loose, crisp, tender leaves. Leaf lettuce reaches full size in about 45 days.

Thicker-leaved, semiheading types such as Bibb, Boston, and Buttercrunch are dark green and more chewy (like raw spinach) than some of the leaf types. The semiheading types take longer to mature, usually about 65 to 80 days.

Cos or romaine lettuce, which also forms a loose head, is often harvested a few leaves at a time. Remove the largest outside leaves, and new leaves will grow from the center of the plant to replace them. This lettuce usually takes about 80 to 85 days to mature.

It is not necessary to wait for the lettuce to mature, however, because lettuce can be eaten at any stage of growth. You can harvest young plants as you need them.

When can I plant lettuce?

In the South, lettuce can be planted in early spring or in the fall. A fall crop remains in good shape until the first hard freeze.

To grow a fall lettuce crop, sow seeds (either indoors or out) in mid- to late August or early September. A light covering of pine straw will help keep the soil cool and moist, conditions which lettuce seeds require for germination. They will not come up if the soil is too hot (above 80 degrees). If temperatures are too warm for planting outdoors, start the seeds indoors in flats or in containers filled with sterile soil. When the weather cools, transplant the lettuce outdoors in sun or partial shade.

Eggplants need full sun and a low-nitrogen fertilizer to produce well.

Harvest kale by removing the lower leaves or cutting the entire plant.

Bibb, a semiheading type of lettuce, is chewy like raw spinach.

Salad Bowl leaf lettuce produces thick bunches of bright-green tender leaves.

Okra may be tough if harvested when it is larger than 3 inches.

Dig and divide multiplier onions every June.

In spring, sow seeds outdoors when soil temperature is between 60 and 70 degrees, or start seeds indoors and transplant after the danger of a hard freeze has passed.

Can you give me some tips for growing lettuce?

Lettuce needs a rich soil high in organic matter, although leaf lettuce does tolerate poorer soil. Soil pH should be about 6.5. Before planting, work in 1 pound of 10-10-10 fertilizer per 100 square feet of row.

Plant more than one seed in each space, keeping the planting spaces the recommended distance apart, (4 inches for leaf lettuce and 8 inches for semiheading types). Sow seeds ¼ inch deep. After the seedlings reach a height of about 2 inches, select the healthiest and most vigorous one in each space; pull up all the surrounding seedlings, being careful not to disturb the roots of the one remaining seedling.

As the plant grows, side-dress with 1 pound 10-10-10 fertilizer per 100 square feet of row every two weeks during the growing season. Apply fertilizer about 6 inches from the plant; avoid spilling fertilizer on lettuce foliage, as it will burn wet leaves.

We have planted okra for four years, but the only time we have had a good crop was the first year. When the plants are about 3 inches tall, they turn yellow and die. Please tell us what to do.

You may be planting your okra too early in the season. Okra should be planted in hot weather, when soil temperatures reach 65 degrees for five consecutive days. When planted in cool, damp soil, the seedlings often "damp off" from fungus diseases (Rhyzoctonia and Pythium). Okra is also susceptible to nematodes (*see* Chapter 5, "Pests & Diseases"). To prevent infestation, rotate the garden as much as possible. If you suspect nematodes are present, follow your okra crop with a solid planting of marigolds, then plant okra again the next year.

A few days before planting okra, incorporate manure, compost, or other decayed organic matter into the soil. Soak the seeds overnight. Plant seeds 10 to 12 inches apart, allowing 3 to 4 feet between rows. When seedlings are 3 to 4 inches tall, thin to 24 inches between plants. Water okra at least twice a week in dry weather. Fertilize monthly after the first pods begin to form, applying 1 cup of 5-10-10 per 10 feet of row.

I have seen multiplier onions listed in seed catalogs. Can you tell me something about them—when and how to plant?

Multiplier onions develop five or six new bulbs from a single transplant. New plantings can be set out much like ordinary onion transplants. Simply lay the plant along your index finger, and push your finger with the onion on it approximately two inches into the soil. Developing plants require an even supply of moisture throughout the growing season. Apply a side-dressing of a 5-10-10 fertilizer at the rate of three-eighths pound per 25-foot row as the bulbs begin to develop.

Previously established clumps of multiplier onions need to be dug and divided each June; otherwise, these plantings will gradually lose vigor, diminishing in size after several seasons. Carefully dig each clump, separating it gently into individual transplants. Store in a dry, well-ventilated area until late August, replanting them at that time for another season's growth. As they mature over the fall and winter, multiplier onions may be dug and eaten much like bunching onions or shallots.

I would like some information on storing onions through the winter.

First, discard all onions that show any sign of disease. Then cure the remainder by placing them in an airy location until the outer scales are dry enough to rustle. Place onions in mesh bags, crates, pallet boxes, or bulk bins, and store in a location where the temperature is about 35 degrees and relative humidity is between 65 percent and 70 percent. Premature sprouting indicates too high a storage temperature, poorly cured bulbs, or immature bulbs. Root growth indicates that the relative humidity is too high. When removing onions from storage, allow them to warm gradually, as moisture from condensation encourages decay.

When is the best time to plant my English peas?

Timing seems to be the greatest problem with growing English peas successfully in the South. If you plant them too early, the seeds will probably rot before they can germinate; if you plant too late, the vines will be parched by the summer sun and the peas will be hard and bitter.

For most of the South, February is the best month for planting English peas. In the Upper South, begin planting toward the end of the month; in the Middle and Lower South, plant as early as possible. February is too late to plant English peas in southern Florida; in this area, plantings are best made between October and December.

Can you give me some tips for growing English peas?

For best production, water plants every three to five days during dry weather. An erratic supply of moisture usually results in a poor crop. In clay soil, plant in raised beds to ensure proper drainage. Mix peat moss or compost into sandy soil to increase water retention.

Unless a soil test recommends otherwise, do not fertilize the soil when you are preparing the bed. Instead, wait until the plants are growing well and indicate a need for fertilizer by their yellowed leaves. Too rich a soil tends to result in excessive vine growth and diminished pod and fruit development.

To keep the plants as manageable as possible, grow them on a fence or trellis. You can build a single trellis by driving 2 × 4 × 6 stakes into the ground at 4-foot intervals; drive the stakes about 2 feet deep so the trellis will be about 4 feet high. Then staple or tack chicken wire to the stakes. To make the pods easier to pick, allow the fence or trellis to lean slightly. Plant along both sides of the trellis, spacing seeds about 4 inches apart. During harvest season, English and snow peas should receive a light application of low-nitrogen fertilizer. One-half cup of 5-10-10 per 10 feet of row is sufficient.

Can you give me some tips on choosing and growing peppers?

Most garden catalogs do a good job of describing pepper selections, but the following general groupings will help you sift through the many selections listed.

The bell group consists of the well-known sweet green or yellow, four-sided blocky types, often used raw (when it is highest in vitamin C) or in cooking. Some selections in this group have been bred for thick walls so they will hold up better when cooked whole for stuffing. There are also some hot bell pepper selections. Pimiento, a sweet conical pepper, is included in this group.

Cayenne peppers are the chile group of slim, pointed, mild or hot peppers varying from 2 to 12 inches long. Cayenne peppers are usually used for hot sauces and hot

Multiplier onions may be dug and eaten much like bunching onions or shallots.

Over most of the South, English peas should be planted in February for harvest before the hot summer sun can parch the vines.

Small red chile peppers are often used to flavor and make foods hot.

Cherry peppers are small globular peppers that are available in hot and sweet selections.

Yellow banana peppers are available in hot and sweet selections.

Cut seed or grocery-store potatoes into small chunks, each with a growth bud or "eye."

vinegars and are sometimes eaten fresh; the jalapeño belongs to this group. Some selections are used in the green stage for stuffing. The dry, mature, red peppers are used for making red chopped chili pepper, chili powder, and paprika.

Cherry peppers, which are often pickled, are globe shaped and may be sweet or hot.

The tabasco group includes some very hot selections such as Tabasco, Red Chili, and cayenne selections. The tabasco pepper is actually a different species; but all the small, pointed, red, hot types are grouped here for simplicity.

Peppers in the tomato group are flattened, four-sided peppers that look like tomatoes when mature. These are used for canning, pickling, and fresh pepper rings.

Yellow pickling peppers are elongated yellow peppers of which there are sweet and hot selections. Banana peppers and small, jalapeño types of hot yellows are often used for pickling.

Pepper transplants purchased from nurseries should be set out after the weather warms. Purchase only young, healthy transplants. Transplants already in bloom or bearing peppers will be stunted and will not produce as many peppers. If you start plants from seeds, remember that peppers are very sensitive to cold, and seeds need temperatures between 70 and 80 degrees for best germination. You may want to start seeds early in a cold frame, greenhouse, or indoors.

A week or two before planting, incorporate into the soil 3 pounds of 10-10-10 per 100 feet of row. After the plants set fruit, topdress with 1 cup of 10-10-10 per 100 feet of row twice during the growing season.

Please tell me how to grow Irish potatoes.

Buy certified "seed potatoes" at the garden center. Or cut your own seed pieces from healthy grocery-store potatoes. When cutting your own, select large potatoes with many eyes, since it is from the eyes that plants develop. Cut potatoes into 2-inch cubes, being sure that each contains at least one eye. Cut no more than 16 pieces from each pound of seed. Dust the pieces with a fungicide, such as captan, maneb, or zineb, and allow the pieces to dry for three days to help prevent rotting after the seed pieces are planted.

Prepare furrows by hilling soil up along the row about 12 inches high; then make a furrow along the top. Space rows about 3½ feet apart. Plant seed pieces 12 to 15 inches apart in the furrow. Fall potatoes do not need as much room as spring-planted ones since they will not have as much time to mature. Cover the furrow so that seed pieces are 4 to 6 inches deep in clay soil, about 6 inches deep in sandy soil. Firm the soil, and water thoroughly.

Fertilize potatoes after the tops are 4 to 6 inches high. Use 5-10-10 or a similar low-nitrogen complete fertilizer, and apply at the rate of ½ cup per 10 feet of row. Apply fertilizer along both sides of the furrow. Mulch plants, and water during dry spells when plants remain wilted after sundown.

Should spinach be started from seeds or transplants?

Spinach may be started successfully from transplants set 3 to 6 inches apart in rows 1½ feet apart. However, sowing seeds directly in the row is easier. Spinach will go to seed in warm weather, so for a spring crop, plant seeds about four weeks before the last frost date. For a fall crop, sow seeds when average daytime temperatures are below 75 degrees (usually September or October). Plant spinach in neutral or slightly alkaline soil (pH 6.0 to 7.5). Sow seeds ½ inch deep in rows 12 to 18 inches apart, or scatter the seeds evenly over a row 15 to 20 inches wide and cover with ¼ to ½ inch of soil. Thin seedlings to 3 inches apart; thin again when the plants touch each other, and feed with 10-10-10 fertilizer at the rate of 1½ to 2 pounds per 100 feet of row.

What is the difference between summer and winter squash?

Both summer and winter squash grow in the summer. The differences between them relate to harvest and storage. Summer squash is eaten when immature; but winter squash, the flesh of which is always orange, must be mature to be eaten. Winter squash also requires a longer period to reach maturity.

Another difference is the storage quality of the two types. Summer squash maintains freshness for only a few days after harvest, while winter squash may be stored in a cool, dry place for several weeks or months.

We would like to try growing squash. Can you give us any tips?

Squash is irreplaceable on Southern tables in the summer, and with proper care of vines, squash can be harvested well into the fall. For successful squash crops, follow these guidelines.

—Plant both summer and winter squash after danger of frost is past. Keep in mind that space demands of vining types (most winter squash) are greater than those of the bush-type selections; the vining types tend to sprawl over too large a space for use in small gardens. But even the bush-type squash require plenty of room to grow. If you have a small garden, you might try one of the dwarf types of summer and winter squash now available.

—If your soil is sandy and drains rapidly, sow squash seeds on the flat ground. In most Southern soil, however, the hill method is best. Rake or spade soil and composted manure into a large mound, about 24 inches in diameter and at least 12 inches high. Firm the soil with your hand; then sow six to nine seeds around the crown of each hill, covering the seeds with about 1 inch of soil. Space hills of bush selections 3 feet apart; space vining types 6 feet apart. After the plants have been up about one week, remove all but the three healthiest seedlings from each hill.

—Mulch the area around the hills before the vines begin to spread; you may damage the vines by lifting them up to mulch under them later, and a damaged vine is an open invitation to squash vine borers. During dry spells, squash need to be watered to keep production going. Avoid getting water on leaves, as this encourages powdery mildew.

—Ample fertilizer during the long growing season is also crucial to the productivity of squash. Fertilize plants monthly with 5-10-10 or a similar complete fertilizer at the rate of ¼ cup of fertilizer per hill.

Can you give me some advice on choosing tomato selections?

The first thing to consider when choosing tomato selections is how the tomatoes will be used. There is a selection for every culinary purpose: eating fresh, making tomato paste, and canning.

The second important consideration is resistance to disease. In catalogs and on seed packets and plant tags, you often find the letters V, F, or N after the selection name. These indicate that the selection is resistant to verticillium wilt (V), fusarium wilt (F), and root-knot nematodes (N). These are the major disease problems of tomatoes; other disease resistance or tolerance may also be listed in the description of the selection. Find out about the tomato problems in your area, and choose selections that are resistant or tolerant.

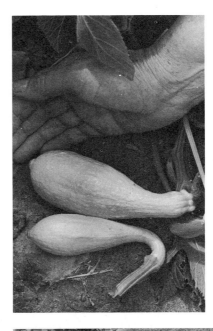

Summer squash must be used soon after harvest. Two popular types in the South are yellow straightneck (top) and yellow crookneck.

Bush-type summer squash like this pattypan selection require ample space to grow, but vining types of winter squash will need even more garden space.

Try to choose a disease-resistant tomato selection that is well adapted to the climate of the South.

Fig. 16 *Place a few tomato seeds on each moist pellet, then push the seeds into the pellet with a tapered instrument.*

Fig. 17 *Tomato seeds should germinate in one to two weeks.*

A third factor is the selection's adaptability to growing in the South. Consult your county Extension agent to make sure the selections you choose will be successful in your area. For fresh tomatoes throughout the growing season, plant early-, midseason-, and late-maturing selections.

Are there any advantages to growing tomatoes from seeds? What is the best way to grow them from seeds?

There are certain advantages to growing tomatoes from seeds. If you plan to grow a lot of tomatoes, starting from seeds can save money and shopping trips. And many of the headaches of raising tomatoes from seeds can be eliminated by planting the seeds in pressed peat pellets rather than in conventional flats.

Because peat is capable of holding more than 10 times its weight in water, seeds sown in peat pellets require less frequent watering than seeds sown in flats with garden loam or packaged potting soil. Another advantage is that the pellets are sterilized; if seeds are sown in unsterilized soil, diseases, fungi, and pests may attack the seedlings.

Pressed peat pellets are available at most retail garden supply stores. Buy pellets with a thin layer of polyethylene mesh around the pellet to hold the peat material together.

Start plants indoors in late February or early March. To plant, set the dry pellets in a small tray or shallow bowl and add water until the pellets are saturated. The pellets expand as they absorb water. After they have expanded to about 2 to 3 inches tall, place a few seeds on top of each and push into the peat about ¼ inch; use a pencil or other tapered instrument to do this. (*See Figure 16.*) Keep the pellets moist at all times, and locate them in a sunny window or greenhouse. Germination should take place in one or two weeks. (*See Figure 17.*) You can transplant the new plants outdoors, spacing them at least 4 feet apart, after the danger of frost has passed.

Please give me some tips for raising tomatoes.

The keys to growing tomatoes successfully are planting, staking, pruning, and fertilizing. Here are some guidelines to ensure success.

—Prepare the tomato bed before you buy the plants. Locate the bed in full sun. Without four to six hours of sunlight daily, fruit production may be disappointing. Dig the soil at least 10 to 12 inches deep and wide for each planting hole; space the holes at least 2 feet apart. Prepare the soil as for most vegetables (*see* page 76).

—Set plants out after the last frost. The best time to transplant tomatoes is after a rain. In the absence of rain, set out seedlings on a cloudy day or in the afternoon. Remove the leaves from the lower half of the stem. With a trowel, dig a hole in the prepared soil so that the plant will sit deep in the ground, nearly up to the lowest leaves left on the plant. Firm the soil around the plant so that it is securely anchored. Water immediately. If you purchased plants in peat pots, do not remove the pots at planting-time. Roots can grow through the sides, and the peat material will soon decompose.

—Protect plants against cutworms by placing collars around the stems. Any stiff paper or cardboard material, such as a milk carton, can be used. After plants have reached the bearing stage, cutworms no longer pose a threat.

—Apply a starter solution (mild fertilizer and water mixture) to the soil at planting-time, if desired. You can make a starter solution with any common houseplant fertilizer that is sold in liquid concentrate form. Follow label directions for mixing; then pour about 1 cup in each hole after planting.

—Erect the trellis or place stakes before planting so as not to disturb plants later (*see* page 79 on staking).

—Protect newly planted tomatoes from hot sun for the first three or four days. Keep the transplants well watered.

—Mulch the plants when they reach a height of 2 feet. Spread mulch 2 to 4 inches deep around each plant, extending out at least a foot or two from the stem. As suckers begin to develop in the junctions of the main stems, remove them so that only two main stems are allowed to develop on each plant. Removing suckers directs more of the plant's energy to fruit production. In addition, the suckers can be rooted and then planted. Unless you grow a late-season selection, top the tomato plants by removing the growing tip in late June or early July. Topping prevents excessive foliage growth and promotes larger fruit.

—Do not fertilize the plants again (if a starter solution was applied at plantingtime) until the first cluster of fruit is about half grown. Too much nitrogen fertilizer can cause rapid, leggy vine growth and poor fruit set. Use a relatively low-nitrogen, complete fertilizer, such as 5-10-10; apply about 1 tablespoon to each plant every two weeks, and water into the soil.

—Water tomatoes every five to seven days if rainfall is sparse. Apply enough water to soak the soil at least 12 inches deep.

—Inspect plants regularly to be certain that pests are not destroying either the plants or the fruit (*see* Chapter 5, "Pests & Diseases"). Pest and disease control are crucial for healthy tomatoes.

—Rotate tomato plantings each year, if possible, to reduce the risk of nematode infestation. Use the same location only once every three years.

When should I harvest tomatoes? Can you give me some tips on storage?

Most tomatoes are at their best flavor five or six days after the fruit first begins to show color. At peak ripeness, the tomato is brightly colored and firm, with a small amount of green remaining at the stem end. Ripe tomatoes will usually remain on the vine in good condition for about two days; then they begin to deteriorate.

If the fruit is overcolored, very soft, or the skin is crinkly, the tomato is overripe. These tomatoes can be used to make soups, juice, or catsup, provided the flavor has not

Remove leaves from the lower half of the stem.

Set the plants deep in the planting hole (almost up to the bottom leaves) so that roots may grow along the stem.

As the plant grows, loosely tie it to the stake with a strip of cloth.

Suckers are the shoots that grow in the junctions between stems and branches. Keep them pinched off tomato plants to ensure continued production.

Ripe tomatoes are brightly colored, firm, and a little green at the stem end. If the skins are crinkly, the tomatoes are overripe.

Start new plants from the suckers by rooting them in a mixture of equal parts sand and peat moss. Place in a shaded area and keep moist.

One way to provide good soil drainage is to grow herbs in a raised bed bordered by cinder blocks. The blocks leach lime, which helps reduce soil acidity; and they make excellent containers for growing small herbs like chives.

Fig. 18 *Fill a container with moist soil and make furrows with your finger. Sprinkle herb seeds along the furrows and cover lightly with soil. Keep the medium moist.*

been affected. If you plan to can your tomato harvest, pick only fresh, firm fruit. Never use overripe tomatoes for canning.

Do not panic when the weatherman forecasts frost and your tomato vines are loaded with green fruit. Just go outside and pick them all; if you do not have time to handpick each tomato, pull up the entire plant and hang it in a cool, dry place. Mature green tomatoes will eventually ripen, and immature green ones can be pickled or otherwise preserved. Under proper conditions, green tomatoes will keep for several weeks. Ideal storage conditions include a temperature of 55 degrees and a cool, dry place away from bright light.

If you wish to extend your tomato supply as long as possible, a little prestorage care will help. After harvesting, dip green tomatoes in a weak solution of household bleach (4 teaspoons bleach per gallon of warm water); this will kill bacteria or decay fungi on the skin. Dry thoroughly; then store.

Herbs

Are herbs difficult to grow?

Herbs can be easy to grow and use. The keys to success are proper sunlight and soil composition.

The amount and type of sunlight needed will depend on where you live. In the Lower South and Texas, filtered sunlight is best; the direct rays of the sun in these areas will quickly burn plants, so either provide a screen, such as a lattice, or plant herbs in a naturally shaded bed. In the Middle and Upper South, the direct rays of the sun are not as damaging, so the plants will tolerate full sun in those areas.

Most herbs require a well-drained, alkaline soil (pH 7). Improve water retention in sandy soils by incorporating peat moss or ground bark. If you are preparing a bed in heavy clay soil, till the soil thoroughly to a depth of 12 inches. Then work agricultural lime and peat moss or finely ground bark into the soil until it is loose and friable. A soil test will indicate how much lime to add. The lime is especially important in all areas of the South except those that already have alkaline soil, such as Texas and South Florida. In these locations, the topsoil is already sufficiently alkaline.

Adding compost or manure to the soil in early spring should supply enough nutrients to ensure good growth. Avoid using nitrogen, as vigorous growth dilutes the herbs' essential oils. However, should the plants not produce the expected growth, apply a small amount of bone meal. Each year, work in a little lime around each plant to help maintain the pH of the soil at a slightly alkaline level (pH 7).

Many herbs will also thrive in an acid soil (pH 5.5 to 6.5), including anise (*Pimpinella anisum*), basil (*Ocimum basilicum*), dill (*Anethum graveolens*), garlic (*Allium sativum*), mint (*Mentha sp.*), parsley (*Petroselinum crispum*), sage (*Salvia officinalis*), thyme (*Thymus vulgaris*), lemon balm (*Melissa officinalis*), caraway (*Carum carvi*), chives (*Allium schoenoprasum*), coriander (*Coriandrum sativum*), marjoram (*Origanum majorana*), and rosemary (*Rosmarinus officinalis*).

We want to grow some culinary herbs indoors. Can you recommend some which will grow well in containers?

Most of the popular culinary herbs may be grown indoors. However, herbs requiring full sun may need supplementary lighting from fluorescent lights. In choosing the ones you want to grow, you will need to consider each herb's light and space requirements as well as its culinary uses.

Basil, marjoram, and oregano (*Origanum vulgare*) require rich, well-drained soil and plenty of sunlight. Common, or Italian, basil is the best choice for indoor growing. Keep plants well watered and pinch out the tops to encourage bushy growth. Basil grows to about 2 feet in height. Marjoram is smaller, growing to about 10 inches; it needs good ventilation, so be sure not to crowd seeds or seedlings in the pot. Oregano is related to marjoram and has similar cultural requirements.

Chives and parsley are favorites for indoor herb gardens. (*See* specific questions on these herbs for growing information.)

Rosemary, sage, and thyme require well-drained soil and full sunlight. Rosemary grows from 10 inches to 3 feet. This pungent herb should be placed in a cool location, misted weekly, and watered frequently—the roots must not be allowed to dry out. Sage will grow to 2 feet in height and may need trimming after flowering. Both rosemary and sage are subject to attack by spider mites, but washing the leaves frequently should keep the pests under control. Thyme may be creeping or upright but will not grow taller than 10 inches.

Spearmint (*Mentha spicata*) and tarragon (*Artemisia dracunculus*) are good, easy-care herbs to grow indoors. Spearmint is not particular about soil or sunlight and will reach its height of 12 inches in either indirect light or full sun. Tarragon prefers poor, slightly dry soil and full sun. It grows 12 to 18 inches tall and requires little care other than regular misting.

If you have limited space to grow culinary herbs indoors, plant several different herbs in a wide, deep clay pot. Just be sure their light, soil, and watering requirements are similar.

Which herbs are considered annuals and which are perennials?

Among annual herbs are anise, borage (*Borago officinalis*), coriander, dill, fennel (*Foeniculum vulgare*), and summer savory (*Satureja hortensis*). Although caraway and parsley are technically biennials, they are usually grown as annuals.

Perennial herbs include horehound (*Marrubium sp.*), horseradish (*Armoracia lapathifolia*), lemon balm, mint, sage, tarragon, lavender (*Lavandula sp.*), winter savory (*S. montana*), and rosemary. All will perform well in relatively poor, alkaline soil.

Do you recommend starting herbs from seeds?

Although herbs are generally started from nursery-grown transplants, you can grow your own transplants from seeds. Herbs easily grown from seeds include basil, chives, sweet marjoram, parsley, sage, and summer savory.

Sow seeds in a moist medium of topsoil, sand, and peat moss in small, manageable containers like milk cartons, foam cups, or clay pots. Place them in bright indirect light; move to a sunny window as germination begins. When seedlings are 2 to 3 inches tall, transplant into pots for growing on a terrace or balcony or into peat pots for planting in the garden after the last frost. (*See* Figure 18.)

Can herbs be propagated by cuttings?

Garden herbs, like other herbaceous plants, are easy to propagate from cuttings of new growth. Most common culinary herbs can be propagated by this method at any time

An herb rack that hangs in your kitchen window is a good way to increase the space you have to grow herbs indoors.

To propagate herbs, take cuttings from new growth anytime during the growing season.

Strip leaves from the bottom half of each cutting, and insert the cuttings upright in flats filled with rooting medium.

Keep cuttings watered so that the medium does not dry out.

Harvest herbs before the plants bloom and hang them in bunches in a dry, dimly-lit, well-ventilated place to dry.

To encourage basil to develop bushy growth, cut off the flowers and tops of plants.

during the growing season. You can use newly rooted cuttings to increase outdoor plantings or to grow in pots.

Make cuttings about 4 inches long from new growth on plants growing in pots or in the garden. Fill peat pots or nursery trays with a mixture of equal parts of perlite and peat moss, and moisten before inserting the cuttings. Strip the leaves from the bottom half of each cutting and insert the cut end of the stem in the rooting medium. Firm the medium around each stem.

Locate the pots or flats in a shady place outdoors where they will not be disturbed. Keep the rooting medium moist; during hot, dry weather this may mean daily watering. Once the medium dries out, it is difficult to moisten again. Root formation should take place within two to four weeks. Gently lift the cuttings in nursery flats to see if any have rooted. Roots of cuttings in peat pots will begin to protrude through the sides of the pot. When roots are visible, cuttings are ready to plant in the garden or in pots.

How can I preserve the herbs I grow in my garden? How long will they keep?

You can preserve herbs by drying or by freezing. Dried leaves and bulbs will keep at room temperature for a year and seeds for three years or more. Frozen herbs will be flavorful for a year, but the leaves will wilt when defrosted.

Generally, herbs grown for their foliage should be harvested before the plants bloom. Cut the stems above the last two sets of leaves at the base of the stem, so the plant will continue growing. Herbs to harvest before flowering include basil, chives, dill, mint, oregano, parsley, rosemary, and sage.

To dry herbs, wash the leaves, tie the stems in small bunches and hang the plants upside down in a dry, ventilated, shady location for two weeks. When the leaves are dry and crisp, strip them from the stems and spread them on a cookie sheet. Place them in an oven set to its lowest temperature and dry the herbs until the leaves crumble to the touch. (However, do not crumble all of the leaves before storing.) If you have a microwave oven, you can dry herbs by simply placing them on a paper towel in the oven for two or three minutes. Whether you use a microwave or a conventional oven, store the dried herbs in airtight containers.

To freeze herbs, simply wash, dry, and place them whole or chopped in plastic bags. Freezer storage preserves the delicate flavor of herbs such as borage, chives, and parsley better than drying.

How does the use of fresh herbs compare to that of the dried herb?

Generally, when you use fresh herbs to flavor foods, use twice as much as the dried amount called for in the recipe. The flavor of herbs like oregano intensifies when the plant is dried.

I grow basil from seeds and it flowers at an early age. Should the flowers be pinched out? Also, are there any special harvesting precautions?

Keep the flowers removed and the tops of the plants pinched back to encourage bushy growth. Use the top growth you have pinched off as a fresh seasoning for poultry, meat, fish, vegetables, salads, cheese dishes, and tomato dishes. To harvest basil for drying, cut the stem just above the second pair of leaves when flower buds begin forming again. A second cut may be made in the fall, before the first frost.

I would like to grow a small bed of caraway. Please give me some information about the culture and harvesting of this herb.

Biennials grown for their seeds, like caraway, need a cool rest period between growing seasons and so will not do well in the Lower South. In the Middle and Upper South, sow caraway seeds outdoors in late April or May.

Soil that is not too rich produces the best harvest of seeds. Prepare the bed carefully, remove all dirt clods and rocks, level, and soak with water. When the soil is dry enough to be workable, make furrows 8 to 10 inches apart and about the depth of a pencil point; then sprinkle the seeds evenly in the furrow. Cover lightly with soil, firm it, and keep it moist until seeds have sprouted.

When seedlings are 2 to 3 inches high, thin to 8 to 10 inches apart. After young plants are established, water sparingly; too much moisture tends to soften stems and cause blossoms to fall before setting seeds.

Plants develop during the first year but do not produce seed until the second year, when seeds ripen in late summer or early fall; then the plants die. In harvesting caraway, cut the entire plant, and place it in a paper bag with the seed head down. As the seeds dry, they will drop into the bag.

Please tell me how to grow chives in pots on my kitchen windowsill.

The general culture of chives is the same as that of onions. To grow them in containers, prepare a soil mixture of topsoil, sand, and peat moss. Space groups of bulbs 2 to 3 inches apart, with the bulbs ½ inch beneath the soil.

Indoors, chives grow best in full sun. Check plants daily for watering and feed about once a month with a general-purpose houseplant fertilizer mixed according to package directions. Bulbs should be divided occasionally so that they do not become too crowded. In the winter, set pots outdoors and allow the plants to freeze. This allows the bulbs to go dormant and produce stronger foliage the following year.

What is the best way to harvest chives?

Cut the foliage just above the white base of the leaf to harvest chives. The more you cut chives, the more they will grow. If the cluster becomes too large for the pot, divide it into several sections and plant in separate pots.

When and how do you propagate chives?

Growing chives from seeds is slow. Propagate chives in early spring by dividing a clump of bulbs into several smaller sections of four or five bulbs each. (*See Figure 19.*) To grow outdoors, plant divisions in partial shade and rich, moist soil, spaced about 10 inches apart. Flowers will appear in early summer; keep them removed to encourage continued leaf growth.

How can I grow coriander?

Coriander requires a light, well-drained soil and full sun. Seedlings do not transplant well, so start plants from seed sown in early spring. Thin the seedlings to 9 or 10 inches apart. Leaves are ready for harvest in early summer and may be used fresh in curries and other hot, spicy foods. Seed heads should be cut when seeds begin to turn light brown; hang seed heads over a cloth in a well-ventilated area to allow seeds to ripen and fall.

Chives require full sun and may need daily watering when grown indoors on a windowsill.

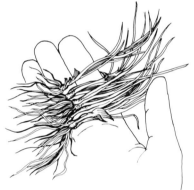

Fig. 19 *A clump of chives divides easily into smaller sections of bulbs.*

To harvest chives, cut the foliage just above the white base of the leaf.

Vegetable Selections for the South

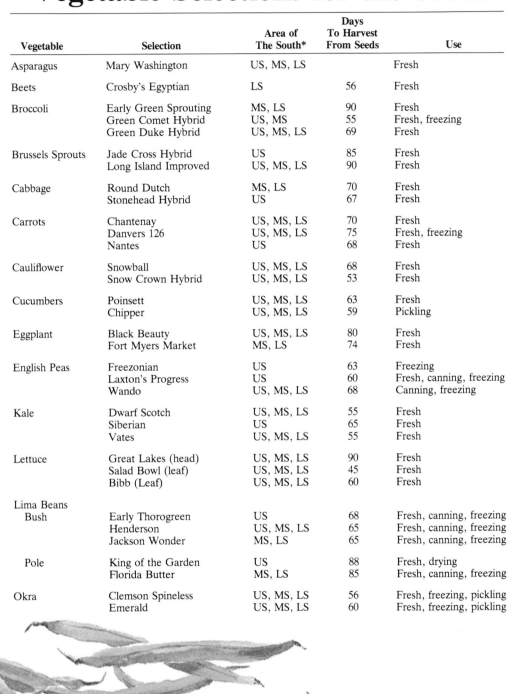

Vegetable	Selection	Area of The South*	Days To Harvest From Seeds	Use
Asparagus	Mary Washington	US, MS, LS		Fresh
Beets	Crosby's Egyptian	LS	56	Fresh
Broccoli	Early Green Sprouting	MS, LS	90	Fresh
	Green Comet Hybrid	US, MS	55	Fresh, freezing
	Green Duke Hybrid	US, MS, LS	69	Fresh
Brussels Sprouts	Jade Cross Hybrid	US	85	Fresh
	Long Island Improved	US, MS, LS	90	Fresh
Cabbage	Round Dutch	MS, LS	70	Fresh
	Stonehead Hybrid	US	67	Fresh
Carrots	Chantenay	US, MS, LS	70	Fresh
	Danvers 126	US, MS, LS	75	Fresh, freezing
	Nantes	US	68	Fresh
Cauliflower	Snowball	US, MS, LS	68	Fresh
	Snow Crown Hybrid	US, MS, LS	53	Fresh
Cucumbers	Poinsett	US, MS, LS	63	Fresh
	Chipper	US, MS, LS	59	Pickling
Eggplant	Black Beauty	US, MS, LS	80	Fresh
	Fort Myers Market	MS, LS	74	Fresh
English Peas	Freezonian	US	63	Freezing
	Laxton's Progress	US	60	Fresh, canning, freezing
	Wando	US, MS, LS	68	Canning, freezing
Kale	Dwarf Scotch	US, MS, LS	55	Fresh
	Siberian	US	65	Fresh
	Vates	US, MS, LS	55	Fresh
Lettuce	Great Lakes (head)	US, MS, LS	90	Fresh
	Salad Bowl (leaf)	US, MS, LS	45	Fresh
	Bibb (Leaf)	US, MS, LS	60	Fresh
Lima Beans				
Bush	Early Thorogreen	US	68	Fresh, canning, freezing
	Henderson	US, MS, LS	65	Fresh, canning, freezing
	Jackson Wonder	MS, LS	65	Fresh, canning, freezing
Pole	King of the Garden	US	88	Fresh, drying
	Florida Butter	MS, LS	85	Fresh, canning, freezing
Okra	Clemson Spineless	US, MS, LS	56	Fresh, freezing, pickling
	Emerald	US, MS, LS	60	Fresh, freezing, pickling

Vegetable	Selection	Area of The South*	Days To Harvest From Seeds	Use
Peppers				
Hot	Cayenne	MS, LS	72	Canning, drying
	Hungarian Wax	US	65	Fresh
Sweet	California Wonder	US	62	Fresh
	Keystone Resistant Giant	LS	80	Fresh
	Yolo Wonder	US, MS, LS	78	Fresh
Potatoes, Irish	Kennebec	US, MS, LS	100	Fresh
	Pontiac	US, MS, LS	100	Fresh
Potatoes, Sweet	Centennial	US, MS, LS	110	Fresh
	Jewel	US, MS, LS	125	Fresh
Radishes	Cherry Belle	US	22	Fresh
	Scarlet Globe	US, MS, LS	24	Fresh
	White Icicle	LS	28	Fresh
Snapbeans, Bush	Provider	US, MS, LS	50	Fresh, canning, freezing
	Tendercrop	US, MS	53	Fresh, canning, freezing
	Tenderette	US	55	Fresh, canning, freezing
	Topcrop	US, MS, LS	49	Fresh, canning
Snapbeans, Pole	Dade	MS, LS	55	Fresh
	Kentucky Wonder	US, MS, LS	65	Fresh, drying, freezing
Snap Peas	Sugar Snap	US, MS, LS	70	Fresh
Southern Peas	Mississippi Silver	MS	70	Fresh, canning, freezing
	Pink Eye Purple Hull	LS	70	Fresh, canning, freezing
	Queen Anne	US	68	Fresh, canning, freezing
Spinach	Bloomsdale Long-standing	US, MS, LS	48	Fresh
Squash				
Summer	Aristocrat Hybrid (zucchini hybrid)	US, MS LS	48	Fresh
	Early Prolific (straightneck hybrid)	MS, LS	50	Fresh
	Yellow Crookneck	MS, LS	53	Fresh
Winter	Butternut	US, MS, LS	85	Fresh
	Table Queen (acorn hybrid)	US, MS, LS	90	Fresh
	Royal Acorn	MS, LS	82	Fresh
Sweet Corn	Silver Queen	US, MS, LS	92	Fresh
	Seneca Chief	US, MS, LS	82	Fresh
Swiss Chard	Lucullus	US	55	Fresh
Tomatoes	Auburn 76	US, MS, LS	70	Fresh, canning, juice, paste
	Better Boy	US, MS, LS	70	Fresh, canning
	Floramerica	US, MS	75	Fresh
	Manalucie	MS, LS	85	Fresh, canning
	Marion	MS, LS	70	Fresh, canning
	Tropic	US, MS	80	Fresh
	Beefsteak	US, MS, LS	96	Fresh, canning
Turnips	Just Right Hybrid (greens)	US, MS, LS	60	Fresh
	Purple-Top White Globe (roots)	US, MS, LS	55	Fresh

*(US) Upper South, (MS) Middle South, (LS) Lower South

Vegetables, Herbs, & Small Fruits   99

Lemon balm is best grown from divisions or cuttings, as seeds germinate slowly.

My dill transplants never grow prolifically. What is the problem?

Dill seedlings do not transplant well. Their root systems are small and delicate, and the herb may flower prematurely if disturbed. Try growing dill from seed sown outdoors in spring. Plant it in a sunny, protected spot in slightly acid soil (pH 5.5 to 6.5) to which compost or manure has been added. Keep the plants well watered and free from weeds for an abundant supply of leaves, seeds, and flower heads to use for pickling and flavoring.

What is lemon balm?

Lemon balm is a bushy perennial whose crinkled leaves produce a sweet lemon scent that makes it a fragrant plant to grow indoors or out. The leaves can be used fresh in stuffings, salads, sauces, fruit salads, drinks, and wine. Dried leaves make a delicious tea and are a good addition to potpourri.

Spearmint or garden mint is easy to grow and spreads rapidly.

Lemon balm grows easily from cuttings or divisions in most types of soil. It may also be grown from seeds, but germination is slow. Plant lemon balm in full sun or light shade in the spring. Outdoors, the herb grows to 3 feet in height, but indoors it will reach about 1 foot and benefits from being frequently cut back.

Are marjoram and sweet marjoram the same plant?

No. Two kinds of marjoram are usually grown in herb gardens—sweet or knotted marjoram and pot or French marjoram (*Origanum onites*). Both are perennials; but sweet marjoram, which produces an essential oil, is more widely used for culinary purposes. Since it is not cold hardy, sweet marjoram is grown as an annual in the Upper South, but may be grown as a perennial in the Middle and Lower South. It grows about 2 feet tall and is started from seeds sown indoors and transplanted after danger of frost is past. Its delicate, sweet flavor accents salads, egg and meat dishes, vegetables, and stuffings. Pot marjoram grows in a spreading clump about 2 feet tall. Start it from seeds, root divisions, or cuttings planted after frost. Its flavor is more like oregano and is best suited to soups and stews, sausages, and stuffings.

I have heard that there are many types of mint. Can you tell me which are the culinary types and how to use them?

Spearmint or garden mint is the most popular culinary species. Use it to make mint jellies and sauces and to add a special fresh flavor to vegetables, freshwater fish, rice pilaf, and pea soup, as well as iced tea and, of course, mint juleps. Bowles mint (*Mentha villosa*) and apple mint (*M. suaveolens*) are also good for general seasoning purposes. Several kinds of mint make refreshing teas, including spearmint, apple mint, orange mint, and peppermint.

To use fresh mint, harvest leaves at any time. To dry leaves, cut stems above the first two sets of leaves as flowers begin to open.

How can I raise mint in my apartment?

Mint is one of the easiest herbs to grow indoors; it thrives in full sun or indirect light. However, indoor environments may be too dry. Try increasing humidity for your potted mint by growing it in a completely enclosed container to keep the humidity high. Perhaps you could place the potted mint in a plastic bag, opening it occasionally for ventilation.

Please give me some tips for growing parsley.

Parsley can be grown in the vegetable or flower garden, in pots on a terrace, or in a container set in a sunny window, where it will grow year-round.

Parsley seeds can take several weeks to germinate unless you soak them in water for 24 hours prior to planting. Sow seeds outdoors in March on the surface of moist, rich soil in partial shade. Thin the seedlings to one plant per 6 to 8 inches in the row or one plant per 6-inch pot.

Be especially careful not to allow container-grown parsley to dry out. If allowed to dry, the foliage will yellow around the leaf edges.

Although parsley is a biennial herb (it dies the second season), it is best grown as an annual to ensure a continuous supply of foliage. If you sow seeds each year, the young plants will have reached an adequate size before the older ones die.

Harvest parsley anytime to use fresh or to dry.

Parsley prefers full sun but also tolerates shade. Its ruffled, evergreen foliage makes an attractive border for vegetable or flower gardens.

The creeping, bushy growth of common thyme makes it a good plant to cascade over a garden wall.

There are several kinds of parsley you can plant. The flat-leaved selections are used primarily for flavoring. The curly-leaved selections, such as Extra Curled Dwarf and Evergreen, are excellent for garnishes as well as for cooking. A less-common form known as Hamburg parsley is grown for its edible root.

Will sage overwinter well? What kind of care does it need?

Sage is hardy outdoors and should overwinter with no problem if the plant is healthy. It requires a sunny location and slightly alkaline, well-drained soil. Sage should be watered sparingly. Plant seedlings in the spring, spacing the plants 12 inches apart in rows 2 feet apart. Fertilize the plants lightly and harvest only a few leaves or branches the first year. The following spring, cut the plants back to encourage new growth to develop. Sage will begin flowering in the summer of the second year. To harvest, cut the shoots before they bloom, or strip the leaves in late summer.

Can you recommend some different kinds of thyme that I could grow for culinary purposes? What are their cultural requirements?

The following thymes are good for seasoning soups, poultry, salads, and vegetables.

Common thyme, a bushy plant that grows to about 12 inches, bears oval gray green leaves and is propagated from cuttings.

Caraway thyme (*Thymus herba-barona*) is a creeping plant with dark-green leaves and lavender flowers. Propagate it from divisions.

French thyme (*T. vulgaris*) is also bushy, but somewhat smaller than common thyme. This type has a strong flavor and is propagated from cuttings.

Lemon thyme (*T.* x *citriodorous*) is a good ornamental planting and makes an excellent tea. Propagate it from cuttings or division.

Orange balsam thyme (*T.* x *citriodorus*), makes a good border plant, growing to about 6 inches in height and bearing pale pink flowers. Its citrus-thyme flavor is a delightful accent for fruit salads.

Oregano thyme (*T. vulgaris*), an evergreen that grows about 10 inches tall. Propagate it from cuttings.

All of these thymes are hardy, easy-to-grow perennials. They require full sun and light, sandy, neutral soil that drains well. Caraway thyme should be planted shallow; set the other thymes deep in the soil. Thyme needs little water or care (besides weeding) to spread rapidly. Lemon thyme is less hardy than the others and may require winter protection in the Upper South. To harvest thyme, cut the stems 2 inches above the ground as the flower buds begin to open. Hang in a warm, shady place to dry, and store the dried leaves in an airtight container.

Small Fruits

We have just moved to Florida. What are some of the tropical fruits we can grow in our backyard? How can we tell when they are ripe?

Gardeners in North Florida (north of Orlando and Ocala) can grow the same kinds of fruits as gardeners in most of the Lower South. But, except for the Mexican types of avocado, they generally cannot grow the tropical fruits that gardeners in Central and South Florida can grow. And in Central and South Florida, gardeners must take proper precautions when winter temperatures occasionally plunge to freezing or below.

The most common of these tropical fruits for the home garden include avocados, bananas, grapefruit, mangoes, oranges, papayas, tangelos, and tangerines. There are hundreds of selections of some of these fruits, so check with your agricultural Extension agent for selections adapted to your area.

Citrus fruits may be ready for harvest in late fall, winter, or spring, depending on the selection you plant. If you know your specific selection, your nurseryman or Extension service can tell you when to harvest it.

Avocado selections may be grown in most of Florida except in wet areas, where root rot will kill them. In southern Florida, the bright green, smooth-skinned Guatemalan × West Indian hybrids are most common in home gardens. Mexican types are cold hardy and will grow in North and Central Florida. These turn from reddish to ebony as they mature. Avocados ripen from late June through March of the following year, depending on the selection. When the fruit is mature, it will fall off the tree and can then be ripened at room temperature. Falling to the ground may bruise the fruit, however, so you may prefer to test an avocado for maturity by picking one when its ridges have filled out. If, after a day or two indoors, the stem end has not shriveled or turned brown or black, you can safely pick other avocados of that size and allow them to ripen. To determine whether an avocado is ripe enough to eat, gently squeeze it in the palm of your hand; if it yields slightly to the pressure, it is ready to be eaten.

Banana selections most commonly planted in home gardens for table use include Cavendish, Lady Fingers, and Apple. With average weather, bananas will ripen roughly 120 days after blossom. Harvest them before they are actually ripe, however, or the bananas will split open. Cut the stem (made up of many bunches of bananas) about two weeks before the selection is expected to be ripe; hang the stem in an open shaded place, protected from heat or cold, to let the bananas ripen. Individual bananas are ready to pick when the cross-section is rounded instead of angular. If you prefer not to cut the whole stem off, you may pick the hands (bunches) of bananas just before they ripen, starting with the oldest fruits at the top of the stem and working down to the youngest at the bottom of the stem.

Mangoes can be tested for maturity by snapping a fruit from the stem and inspecting the sap that flows from the stem end. If the sap oozes slowly and is clear, fruit of that size on the tree is ready to be picked to ripen at room temperature. If the sap flows freely and is milky looking, the fruit is still immature. When you snap a fruit from its stem, always be sure to point the stem end away from you to avoid being hit by the stream of sap that an immature fruit will squirt. Another way to check for maturity is to carefully slice through the fruit lengthwise and slightly off-center, so that the knife slides past the seed. If the interior is turning yellow, the fruit is ready for harvest. Mature mangoes feel soft and are fully colored.

Papaya is ready to pick when the blossom end begins to turn from green to orange or yellow. Then allow it to ripen at room temperature. Papaya may also be picked when still green and steamed like summer squash.

What is the best way to propagate bramble fruits?

Bramble fruits, including blackberries, raspberries, and dewberries, are among the easiest fruits for the home gardener to propagate. Although plants are easy to dig up and transplant, they can also be grown from tip cuttings of the current year's canes. Softwood cuttings, made from the fresh, new summer growth, are the easiest cuttings to root.

The tangelo, a cross between a tangerine and a grapefruit, is very sweet and juicy and peels easily.

Valencia is a popular, late-maturing orange selection that extends the citrus season into June or July.

Fig. 20 *Make cuttings of the current season's (fruitless) canes. The canes that bear berries will die soon after fruiting.*

Fig. 21 *Remove leaves from the bottom half of each cutting, and insert the cuttings upright in moistened rooting medium.*

Fig. 22 *Regular feeding and watering will help ensure a good crop of blackberries.*

Make cuttings only from healthy, prolific plants. (*See Figure 20.*) If you are trying to propagate a plant found growing in the wild, make cuttings from plants which produce large berries. However, most wild plants tend to be sparse and produce small berries and are not worth propagating. Do not make cuttings from canes on which berries are borne, because canes of bramble fruits die after fruiting.

Wear gloves when working around bramble fruits. The canes of most selections are thorny. When picking berries or making cuttings from plants in the wild, wear protective clothing and bring a small bucket and some wet paper towels to wrap the cut ends of your cuttings.

Make cuttings 4 to 6 inches long. Strip the leaves from the bottom half of each cutting, and insert the cuttings upright in a moistened rooting medium of equal parts perlite and peat moss. (*See Figure 21.*) Place flats of cuttings in a light but shaded place, and keep the medium moist at all times. Root formation should take place in a few weeks. Pot rooted cuttings in containers 6 inches in diameter at the top until plantingtime in the fall.

Bramble fruits may also be propagated by suckering, root cuttings, and tip layering. Red raspberries and bush-type blackberries send up suckers that you can dig and replant in early spring. Choose healthy canes about 3 feet long and prune them back by about ⅓ after transplanting. If you need to propagate these types of bramble fruits rapidly, you can make cuttings of the roots in late winter. Select roots about ⅛ inch in diameter. Cut them into 3-inch lengths and plant horizontally, covering them with 3 to 4 inches of sand or light soil. Transplant them in the fall or the following spring.

Trailing blackberries and black and purple raspberries spread by tip layering. To encourage tips to root, in late summer allow them to rest on the soil undisturbed. Tips will become fleshy and put out roots. You can dig the tip layer the following spring and transplant it, covering the bud with about 2 inches of soil. Cut off the old cane to avoid transmitting anthracnose to the new plant.

When is the best time to transplant bramble fruits?

In most of the South, March is the best month for moving blackberries. Raspberries, which grow in the Upper South, may be transplanted in March also. When digging up the plants, try to retain as much soil as possible around the roots to promote rapid reestablishment in their new location.

If you plant nursery-grown plants, set them out in the fall. They can become established over the winter and survive better in the warm weather of the following spring and summer.

Both blackberries and raspberries prefer well-drained soil but can adapt well to a wide range of soils. During dry spells, water every three to five rainless days, and feed monthly until harvest with 5-10-10 or a similar complete fertilizer. Apply ½ cup of fertilizer per square yard of planted area. (*See Figure 22.*)

What are the differences between growing blackberries and raspberries?

The differences between growing blackberries and raspberries depend on the types you choose to grow. Blackberries are generally divided into bush types and trailing types. Raspberries are divided according to color and growth habit.

Bush blackberries and red and yellow raspberries have erect, thorny canes that do not require support but may be trellised to make care and harvesting easier. Blackberries and some types of red and yellow raspberries produce one crop each summer on canes that grew the previous year; the berry-producing canes die after fruiting. These types multiply by sending out suckers from the roots of the main plant. The new plants that start from suckers will quickly widen crop rows and make care and harvesting more difficult. Pull suckers as they appear and transplant them in the established rows.

Trailing blackberries and black and purple raspberries, on the other hand, are vinelike and should be grown on trellises. Like their upright cousins, these types produce one crop annually on canes that grew the year before. But propagation is by tip rooting rather than suckering. This makes them easy to maintain in narrow rows; simply prune the tips to keep them from taking root in the soil.

The everbearing red and yellow raspberries form still another group. These produce one crop in the fall and another the following summer on canes that die after the second fruiting. Everbearing raspberries also spread by suckering, and culture is essentially the same as for bush blackberries and the other red and yellow raspberries. However, you have the option of growing two crops each year or of cutting back all canes after the fall crop to produce one vigorous crop the following fall.

Blackberries may be harvested every three or four days during a three- to four-week period. The harvest period for raspberries lasts one to two weeks, and berries should be picked every two or three days.

Beyond these differences in growth habit and harvest time, blackberries and raspberries are very similar in culture. Both require soil rich in organic matter and a fertilizer with high nitrogen content. They do best in full sun, but blackberries will tolerate partial shade. Bramble fruits are susceptible to fungus diseases if they become too crowded. To promote good air circulation, set plants two feet apart in rows spaced 5 feet apart, prune out old canes after harvest, and remove weak or diseased canes. Heading, or cutting back the top 2 or 3 inches of canes, will promote lateral branching and increase the next year's fruit production. A layer of mulch will reduce the risk of injury to the shallow roots.

Raspberries grow well in the Upper South.

Which do you recommend—transplanting wild blackberries and raspberries from the woods, or buying plants from the nursery? What are the selections that grow best in the South?

The problem with transplanting wild plants is that fruit size and quality are unpredictable. With developed strains of blackberries and raspberries, you are more likely to get good berry production.

Among the best blackberry selections for the Upper South are Comanche, Raven, and Thornfree; for the Middle and Upper South, Darrow and Ebony King; for the Lower South (but not southern Florida), Georgia Thornless, Brazos, and Oklawaha. Raspberry selections recommended for the Upper South include Cumberland, Latham, Newburgh, September, Dorman Red, and Heritage. For selection recommendations geared specifically to your locale, contact your county agricultural Extension agent.

For the past two years, my entire patch of Darrow blackberries have borne hard, seedy little knots instead of big, juicy berries. Can you help?

Dry weather during the growing period the previous summer may have contributed to the poor harvest. Blackberries require irrigation during drought. Soaker hoses or trickle irrigation work well in the home garden. Also apply a thick mulch of hay, wood chips, or leaves to help keep the soil evenly moist. Mulch also prevents the growth of weeds, which compete with blackberries for moisture. After harvest, cut old canes to the ground.

Some selections of blackberries spread by tip-rooting; to maintain narrow rows, simply prune back the tips.

Rabbit-eye blueberries are native to the South. Early-, mid-, and late-season selections are available.

Fig. 23 *To ensure pollination (and subsequent fruiting), plant two or more blueberry selections.*

Fig. 24 *Blueberries require moist, slightly acid soil that is rich in organic matter. Work plenty of compost or other partially decomposed organic matter into each planting hole.*

Please recommend some selections of blueberries that will grow well in the South.

Rabbit-eye blueberries are native to the woodlands of Georgia, North Florida, and South Alabama. Standard selections which produce large, sweet berries and grow well over most of the South include Woodard, Tifblue, Delite, Climax, and Briteblue. Woodard and Climax mature early in the season. A planting of Tifblue, Briteblue, and Delite bushes will provide berries all season, since these selections mature in early, mid-, and late season respectively. In addition to these selections, gardeners in North Florida can plant Aliceblue and Beckyblue, both early maturing. Three highbush types have been especially bred for the Central Florida climate: Avonblue, Sharpeblue, and Flordablue (all early maturing).

Three rabbit-eye blueberry selections have recently been released from North Carolina. These are Centurion (late), Powderblue (midseason), and Premier (early). Their adaptability has not been tested in all states, however, and they may not do well in the Lower South.

For proper pollination (and subsequent fruiting), you must plant two or more blueberry selections. (*See Figure 23.*) For example, if you have space for six plants, plant two each of Tifblue, Woodard, and Delite or three each of two of the selections.

In Florida, because of the climate, all blueberries do not bloom at the same time. For successful pollination, Florida gardeners must choose selections that bloom simultaneously, such as the following combinations: Sharpeblue and Flordablue; Bluegem, Woodard, and Delite; Tifblue, Briteblue, and Climax; Aliceblue and Beckyblue. Avonblue is self-fruiting and does not require a pollinator.

How do I plant blueberries in my home garden?

Like azaleas, blueberries have a shallow, fibrous root system that requires light, acid (pH 4.2 to 5.5), well-drained soil. The only way to plant blueberries is in soil amended with plenty of peat moss. Dig a hole 2 to 3 feet wide and 1 foot deep (2 feet deep in heavy clay), and mix the backfill with an equal volume of peat moss. Be generous with the peat moss. It will help ensure proper soil pH and good drainage, both of which are crucial to successful blueberry culture. (*See Figure 24.*)

When planting blueberries, be sure to loosen roots that have become matted around the root ball of the container-grown plant. Space plants about 6 feet apart, setting them in the planting holes so the top of the root ball is slightly above soil level (like you would plant azaleas); then backfill the hole with the peat moss-soil mixture, mounding it up around the roots. Mulch the planting with pine straw to protect the shallow roots; and keep well watered until established. Also, water well during dry periods.

After blueberry plants are established (about two years), you may fertilize in spring with ½ cup of 10-10-10 per plant; if plants are old enough to bear fruit, feed again four to six weeks later. Blueberries are not heavy feeders, but if additional fertilizer is needed to keep plants healthy, apply again in early summer. Water the fertilizer in well to avoid burning the shallow roots.

When should blueberries be planted? Will they grow in the shade?

Although early-spring planting is acceptable, fall planting gives blueberries much longer to become established before they leaf out in the spring. For best fruiting, plant blueberries in full sun; if planted in the shade, they will produce only about half a crop.

How can I tell when blueberries are ready to be picked?

Most blueberries turn blue long before they are ready for picking, so color is no indication of ripeness. Cup your hand under a cluster of berries, and rub your thumb across the fruit. Those that fall from the cluster readily are ripe. Berries that must be pulled off are not ripe.

My blueberries seem to produce smaller fruit each year. What can I do?

To improve fruiting of blueberries, remove dead or diseased wood in March. Prune weak growth from older wood, and cut back healthy new shoots to a vigorous branch; remove suckers at ground level. On plants that tend to overbear, remove one-third of the flower buds from the ends of the branches; this will result in larger, higher quality berries and healthier plants. Also, keep plants well watered during dry weather in spring and summer so that fruit will reach full size.

In which regions of the South will figs grow best? Can you recommend some selections?

Figs will grow throughout the South but require winter protection in the Upper South.

Figs will thrive and bear fruit abundantly in the Middle and Lower South. They will also grow in the Upper South but must have winter protection, such as newspaper wrapped around the trunk.

Recommended selections for the South are Celeste and Brown Turkey. Both are self-fruiting and do not require cross-pollination with another tree. In the Middle and Lower South, the selections will produce two crops each year; in the very mild areas of the Gulf Coast and southern Florida, gardeners can harvest three crops annually.

Gardeners in the Lower South may also try Hunt, Magnolia, and Florentine. However, Hunt yields less than Celeste; the fruit of Magnolia may crack or sour if left to ripen to full maturity. And Florentine's fruit may crack and sour in areas of high rainfall. One way to obtain a satisfactory fig tree is to plant a sucker from a fruit-bearing tree of proven quality. The sucker should produce the same quality as the parent.

When is the proper time to plant fig trees?

Late winter and early spring are recommended times to plant fig trees. Be careful not to let the roots dry out at plantingtime. (*See* page 193 in the chapter "Trees & Shrubs" for information on planting bare-rooted trees.)

When is the best time to harvest figs?

The flavor of fresh figs is best when the fruit has just ripened; but if you plan to preserve them, harvest several days before they are fully ripe. Otherwise, they may lose their firmness and shape during the preserving process. When picking figs, leave the stem attached to the fruit.

Please tell me how to propagate fig trees.

Figs are easily propagated by rooting 3- to 4-inch hardwood cuttings during the dormant season. Make cuttings so that each has three or four joints or nodes; the basal cut should be at the base of the bottom node.

Root cuttings in water or soil. For soil rooting, use containers that are 6 to 8 inches in

Fig. 25 *Fig trees are fast-growing, low-maintenance plants that can be propagated as soon as the leaves have fallen off.*

Fig. 26 *Cut suckers (new stems arising from the base of the plant) at their point of origin, then cut the individual suckers into 6- or 8-inch sections just above a node.*

diameter and at least 6 inches deep. Fill them with a moist planting medium of equal parts garden loam or potting soil, builder's sand, and perlite. Insert the cuttings into the mixture, leaving only the top node above the surface; the base of the cutting should extend no more than two-thirds the distance to the bottom of the container. Water carefully, and keep the soil slightly moist but not wet. (*See Figures 25–27.*)

I have an old, overgrown fig bush that has almost stopped bearing fruit. How can I make it productive again?

Pruning is the key to a productive fig bush. In the case of an older plant that has been neglected, select three to eight vigorous, widely spaced stems to serve as leaders. Remove all other stems, and prune the leaders back about halfway. Thereafter, cut back the bush each spring just before the growth begins. At that time, remove one-third to one-half the length of the previous season's growth.

My figs have been damaged by cold weather. What can I do?

Figs may be damaged by cold weather, even in the warmest parts of the South. In the Upper South, they may be repeatedly killed back. The root portions of the trees are durable, however, so figs usually recover from severe winters.

You can help restore cold-damaged figs to good health by pruning the injured parts. It

Cut damaged branches back to shoots from which new leaves are growing.

Fig. 27 *Root the cuttings in solid medium or plain water. Roots and new leaves will begin to appear in two to four weeks.*

Wait until figs leaf out to prune cold-damaged wood.

is best to wait until after the trees have leafed out so that you can easily distinguish the healthy wood from the damaged. You will not hurt the plants' recovery by waiting until leaves have appeared; but do not delay pruning too long, or you will invite the entry of disease organisms. On mature plants, use a pruning saw and a strong pair of loppers to cut all damaged branches back to living shoots. Do not apply pruning compound to cuts. If plants have been severely damaged, it may be necessary to cut them back nearly to the ground. Fertilize with 5-10-10 or other complete fertilizer, and mulch. Regular watering and monthly fertilization will help damaged trees resume normal growth.

What types of grapes will do best in my area?

The three species of grapes that grow in this country (American bunch, muscadine, and European) can be cultivated in the South. Bunch grapes are best suited to the Upper and Middle South. Among the best selections for Southern gardens are Portland, Seneca, Delaware, Concord, Catawba, Fredonia, and Niagara.

Muscadines are native to the Middle and Lower South.

Muscadines are at home in the Middle and Lower South. Today's muscadine selections have evolved from the native grape and have superior characteristics—improved fruit quality, increased cold hardiness, and specific disease resistance. Recommended selections for the Upper and Middle South include Hunt, Carlos, Albemarle, Noble, and Magnolia. In the Lower South, however, grape growing may be limited by Pierce's disease (a degeneration of the vine). To avoid the disease, select resistant selections like Chief, Cowart, Creek, Magoon, Noble, Southland, Tarheel, Dixie, and Welder. Especially recommended for Florida are Blue Lake, Lake Emerald, and Stover.

French grapes and French-American hybrids will grow in the Upper and Middle South (*see* next question).

For all three species, check with your nurseryman and county Extension agent to find out which selections are best suited to your specific area.

Will grapes for fine wines grow in the South? If so, are there any special precautions?

The French grapes and French-American hybrids, noted for the excellent quality of wine they produce, have been successfully established throughout much of the Middle and Upper South—in North and West Texas, Kentucky, the hills of Virginia, and areas in between. Only the humid coastal climate of the Lower South has proved unsatisfactory for their culture.

Some of the French types which have been grown include Pinot Noir, Riesling, Sauvignon Blanc, and Petite Sirah; among the French-American hybrids are Seyval Blanc, Villard Blanc, Aurora, and Léon Millot. In Florida, try SV-12309 (Roucaneuf), which is resistant to Pierce's disease.

When considering growing the French grapes or the French-American hybrids, here are some things you need to know.

—French grapes are highly susceptible to fruit and leaf diseases, so they grow best in warm, dry conditions. In highly humid areas, serious damage will result from outbreaks of Pierce's disease. Since French grapes lack a well-defined chilling requirement, they may be damaged by extreme fluctuations in winter temperatures.

—The French-American hybrids were developed in an attempt to combat the cultural problems of the French grapes. They combine the flavor and quality of the French types with the disease resistance and hardiness of American selections. Thus, the hybrids have

Prune muscadines in the winter, after the leaves have fallen from the vines.

Cut back last summer's growth to within a few inches of its point of origin. This forces growth of lateral shoots that will bear next season's crop.

This portion of the vine shows three seasons of growth, properly pruned.

a slightly wider growing range than the French types and are also more tolerant of environmental conditions.

To be successful with both French grapes and French-American hybrids, it is important to select the proper site. Gently sloping sites are recommended; avoid low-lying sites because they become frost pockets in winter. Steeply sloping hills should also be avoided since they erode easily.

The best grapes are produced in deep, sandy soils to which organic matter has been added. Adequate sunlight and good drainage are also essential. Lack of sunlight not only retards fruit ripening but also encourages spread of disease.

You may plant in spring or fall, but spring is generally recommended. Before planting, cut back each vine to a single cane with two buds. Do not fertilize at plantingtime. When new growth appears, apply ¼ pound ammonium nitrate per vine; broadcast it in a 3-foot-wide band around the vine, beginning 1 foot from the trunk.

Begin pruning and trellising grapevines the second year. This should be done in late fall or winter when the vines are fully dormant. Consult your county Extension agent for pruning and trellising instructions.

Do not allow grapevines to bear any fruit the first two years; keep all young fruit clusters removed. And keep the crop light the third season. The fourth season should produce a good crop, with the vines in full production after the fifth year.

Are muscadines much trouble to grow? What sort of care is involved?

Muscadine grapes can survive with little or no attention, provided they are given the correct growing conditions: full sun, well-drained soil, and adequate fertilization. Muscadines do not grow well in clay or hardpan soils or where the water table is low. Nor do they tolerate poor drainage. Sandy sites should be improved with organic matter for best growth.

Purchase container-grown or bare-root plants from a reliable source, and set them out during the dormant season (October to February). Muscadines should be trained to grow on a strong support, such as a fence, arbor, or trellis.

Fertilize new plants in the early spring with a complete fertilizer, such as 10-10-10, at the rate of ½ pound per plant. In late spring or midsummer, additional nitrogen may be needed; apply at the rate of ⅛ pound ammonium nitrate per plant. As the plants become established during the second and third years, double the first year's dosage. Fertilize established vines (more than 3 years old) with 3 to 5 pounds of 10-10-10 or similar complete fertilizer in early spring. Apply additional nitrogen in June, using ½ pound ammonium nitrate per vine.

In some soils, grapes may develop a magnesium deficiency; this results in yellowing between the leaf veins of older leaves. To correct the deficiency, broadcast Epsom salts evenly over a 3- to 6-foot area around the vines at the rate of about 3 ounces for 1- to 2-year-old vines and 6 ounces for older vines.

When is the best time to prune muscadines?

Established muscadines must be pruned every winter to attain maximum production, and the best time to do this is soon after they drop their leaves. Muscadines fruit on new wood produced in the spring, so pruning is necessary to create spurs from which new shoots can arise.

Prune last year's growth to within 4 inches of the point of origin. Remove canes that have outlived their productivity. If vines have been neglected for several years, you may have to prune them severely and sacrifice a year's production in order to restore the plants to their correct growth habit. Cut overgrown vines back to their trunks; then cut the trunks to stumps about 12 inches high.

However, if you do not wish to take such radical action, you may be able to restore old vines by cutting back all 1-year-old canes to 6-inch stubs and removing all other shoots. Or, to avoid losing an entire year of fruit production, you can try cutting back all new growth to 6-inch stubs on half of the plant this winter. Then next winter, cut back the new growth in the same manner on the remaining half.

What is the best way to train new muscadine vines?

Training vines is easy and will be worth the effort. At plantingtime, drive a 4- or 5-foot stake into the ground beside the plants. When growth begins in spring, select the strongest shoot to become the main stem, and tie it to the stake. During the first summer, encourage development of the main stem by keeping all side shoots removed. When the end of the stem reaches the top of the stake, pinch it out to encourage side shoots to develop during the second summer.

Before the second summer, drive 4 × 4 × 5 posts 18 inches into the ground, spacing them 15 feet apart. Stretch a No. 9 gauge wire along the top; for a four-arm system, fasten a second wire about 2 feet from the ground. As the side shoots develop during the second summer, select two near the bottom wire and two near the top wire to become the lateral arms and tie them to the wires. Continue to remove all other side shoots arising from the main stem. Thereafter, prune every year during the dormant season. (*See Figure 28.*)

When should muscadines be harvested?

Muscadines are ready for harvest when the fruit has fully developed its characteristic color. After ripening, the fruit of some selections will remain on the vine in good condition for about two weeks. Other selections should be harvested soon after ripening or the grapes will shrivel or shatter (fall from the vine). Local growers can probably provide information on the keeping quality of area selections.

If you have more muscadines than you can eat, store the extras. Grapes for storage should be clipped from the vines in full clusters, placed in a sealed container, and stored at 35 to 40 degrees (a refrigerator is a good place). Grapes removed from cold storage deteriorate rapidly and should be used immediately.

Is there a simple way to grow grapes without an arbor?

Some kind of support for grapevines will make them easier to care for. One of the simplest ways to grow grapes is by planting them along a fence. Because the plants are at shoulder level or lower, depending on the height of the fence, pruning and harvesting are easier. Also, protecting the fruit from birds is simplified because protective netting can be applied more easily to a fence-supported planting than to an arbor or an espalier.

When growing grapes on a fence, space plants 8 to 10 feet apart along both sides of the fence, staggering the plants as you go. Most grape selections are vigorous growers, so do not overplant. For 30 feet of fence, four plants are adequate.

Where will loquat grow?

The loquat is a bushy, sub-tropical evergreen shrub grown as an ornamental in most of the South and for its fruit in the Lower South and lower parts of the Middle South (as

When a main lateral arm has outlived its productivity, select the strongest shoot to take its place. Allow it to attain its full length in the summer; then next winter, remove the old arm and train the new one to grow on the trellis.

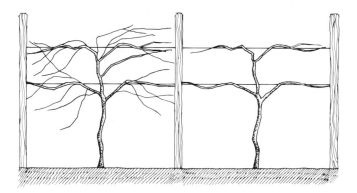

Fig. 28 *Muscadines trained to a four-arm system should be pruned every year during the dormant season.*

Loquat is grown as an ornamental shrub over most of the South. Gardeners in the Lower South may also enjoy its fruit.

Plant persimmon trees in a permanent location where dropping fruit will not present a problem.

far north as Austin, Texas and Montgomery, Alabama). Loquat is sensitive to cold weather and is not likely to bear fruit much further north of this region.

Can you give me some tips for planting a persimmon tree?

Plant persimmons away from walks, terraces, and other areas where the dropping fruit will create an untidy appearance. Since they are deep rooted and do not transplant easily, select a permanent location initially. Young trees (1 to 3 years old) are more easily established than larger trees, but it may be two to six years before they begin to bear fruit.

For best growth and fruiting, persimmons need rich, well-drained soil, full sun, and plenty of space. However, they will grow in sandy and clay soils if well drained. Persimmons need a consistent moisture supply, so be sure to water plants regularly during periods of drought. Generally, persimmons are free of pests.

American persimmons produce male and female flowers on separate trees, so you must plant both to ensure cross-pollination and fruit production. Unlike the native type, some Oriental persimmons, such as Tanenashi, do not require a pollinator. They produce a much larger, seedless fruit, which is not bitter like American types. So when buying an Oriental persimmon, check with your source to find out if you need to plant a pollinator.

Can anything be done with ripe persimmons that have not been exposed to frost to make them palatable?

Place ripe persimmons in a plastic bag with one or more apples (depending on the quantity), tie the open end of the bag, and store in a cool place for four or five days. Persimmons should then be as soft as a ripe peach and not quite as sour.

In the spring my eight-year-old Oriental persimmon has many blooms and young fruit but soon afterward begins to drop the fruit. By fall all the fruit is gone. What can be the trouble?

Insufficient moisture and uneven moisture seem to be the main reasons fruit drops

Persimmons that ripen on the tree may be made more palatable by placing them in a plastic bag with an apple.

A persimmon is best eaten when it is as soft as a ripe peach.

Tanenashi is a good selection of Oriental persimmon for the South but must have an even supply of moisture to bear fruit.

from Oriental persimmon trees. Try mulching the tree heavily with compost, peat moss, pine straw, or other organic matter and watering it regularly during the growing season.

Pineapple guavas are considered tropical fruits. Can they be grown for fruit production in the South? If so, what are the secrets to growing these plants?

Pineapple guavas will grow in the Lower South. For successful fruit production, plant in full sun in well-drained, sandy loam to which compost or peat moss has been added. Most pineapple guavas must cross-pollinate to produce, so plant several selections near each other. Two new selections, Coolidge and Pineapple Gem, are self-fruiting.

The 2- to 3-inch-long green fruit has a red blush and white flesh. It ripens in late summer or early fall, depending on the location. In southern Florida, the fruit will drop before it ripens, so it should be picked when mature and allowed to ripen indoors.

What are the ideal growing conditions for pomegranate?

Pomegranate, a deciduous ornamental shrub, is best adapted to dry regions, but it will grow throughout the South. Both the ornamental and the fruiting types of this deciduous shrub tolerate a variety of soils, provided drainage is good. Pomegranate is somewhat drought resistant, but it will have better appearance and produce better if not subjected to long periods without water. It is hardy in the mild winters of the Middle and Lower South but requires winter protection in the Upper South. Pomegranate needs little fertilizing. If foliage yellows, apply nitrogen-rich fertilizer; if the plant becomes chlorotic, apply a complete fertilizer with added micronutrients (magnesium, manganese, copper, and boron).

Two selections of fruiting pomegranate are generally available, Wonderful and Ruby. Wonderful is considered the better selection to plant, since its fruit is large and of good quality with small soft seeds. Ruby produces smaller fruit with larger, harder seeds and a more acidic flesh.

Pineapple guava is ready for harvest in October in warmer regions of the South.

Pomegranate is a somewhat drought-resistant ornamental shrub that will grow throughout the South.

Vegetables, Herbs, & Small Fruits   113

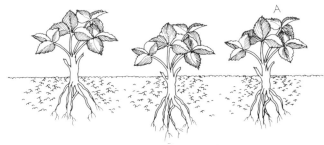

"A" is set up proper depth

Fig. 29

Fig. 30 *A young matted row system. Eventually the rows will become a solid planting.*

Strawberry selections are adapted to specific climates, so check with your county Extension agent for those that are best for your area.

Friends from Indiana offered to send us some of their strawberry plants. Do you think we could grow them successfully here in the South?

Probably not. Although strawberries grow in most areas of the United States, selections are adapted to specific climates. Check with your agricultural Extension agent for selections that are best for your area.

Generally, you can grow Apollo and Atlas in the Middle South. Selections adapted to both the Upper and Middle South include Earlibelle, Pocahantas, Surecrop, Redchief, and Tennessee Beauty. In the Lower South, try Dabreak, Headliner, Tangi, Konvoy, Massey, Missionary, or Florida 90.

Another reason for purchasing your own plants is that gift plants may come with an unwanted bonus of nematodes or foliar diseases. Purchase disease-free plants from a reputable nursery.

How should strawberries be planted?

Plant strawberries in the fall in full sun and fertile, well-drained soil high in organic matter. Locate the bed on a slope, if possible, to promote good drainage. Dig the soil 8 to 10 inches deep, working in compost or peat moss to improve soil structure.

When you set the plants out, be sure to position the plants so that the top of the root ball is level with the surrounding soil. Plants set too low are susceptible to crown rot; those set too high may dry out and die. (*See Figure 29.*)

The most common method for planting is the matted row system. Space plants 18 to 24 inches apart on beds that are 2 feet wide. Allow 3½ to 4 feet between the rows. As runners develop, train them back into the row. Do not allow the runners to spread into the paths between the rows. (*See Figure 30.*) In poorly drained soil, you may prefer to mound the soil 12 to 15 inches high in a raised furrow. Firm the soil and set the plants about 8 inches apart in the row.

Another method of planting is the hill system. With this method, you avoid having to replant every year, because you treat the plants like the perennials they are. Set plants 12 inches apart each way and keep all runners removed. After planting, apply a 1- to 2-inch layer of mulch of pine straw, sawdust, or similar weed-free organic mulch. Either wait to mulch until plants reach a height of about 4 inches, or mulch the entire bed after preparing the soil; part the mulch around planting holes to set plants, then tuck the mulch back against stems. Or, you can use black plastic sheeting as mulch.

Water plants thoroughly every three or four rainless days regardless of planting method. Size and quality of the fruit depend heavily on a constant supply of water.

Do strawberries need any special care while they are ripening on the plants?

Strawberries require the most care during the preharvest period in April and May. An even supply of moisture is crucial for proper development of the fruit. If rainfall has been sparse in your area, water the plants regularly, every three to seven rainless days, depending on how quickly your soil dries out.

Pest control is also critical at this time (*see* Chapter 5, "Pests & Diseases"). Frequency of picking will affect the degree to which your crop is troubled by pests. Roly-polies do most of their damage on ripe fruit, so if the fruit is picked as soon as it is ripe, damage will be minimized.

I planted a small bed of strawberries early this spring. What should I do to keep the bed producing year after year?

With proper care, a strawberry bed may be perpetuated for three or four years. Since you planted in spring, remove flower clusters as they appear during the first year. This is important to the plant's growth and productivity.

In late June, topdress the bed with cattle or poultry manure, or apply 8-8-8 fertilizer at the rate of ½ cup per square yard of bed. In warmer areas of the South, make a second application of fertilizer in early September.

As winter approaches, mulch plants heavily for protection against frost and soil temperature fluctuations. Loosely pile hay, pine straw, sawdust, wood shavings, or similar mulch material on plants to a depth of 2 to 3 inches.

Plants will begin to bear regularly in their second spring. Pick the berries as they ripen, and keep new runners removed. After harvest, prepare the beds for the next year; if you planted in the hill system, simply fertilize the plants and continue removing runners as they appear. If you planted in the matted row system, narrow the rows to about 1 foot by chopping out plants. Clean out all weeds, and fertilize the beds as before. New runners will soon widen the bed again; train them to grow into the bed as you did the first year. Continue to water as dry weather demands. As before, fertilize in September in mild regions; throughout the South, mulch for winter protection.

While fruit is still immature, mulch plants with pine straw to keep the berries off the ground.

Houseplants

Cattleya Orchids

Houseplants can enliven any interior, bringing the special freshness and vitality of the garden indoors. Growing houseplants successfully need not be difficult, if you select plants adapted to the available light and know their cultural requirements.

Most plants will flourish in bright indirect light, but many will also adapt to medium light. Low light, however, is often a problem for indoor gardeners. Many popular houseplants will languish in poorly lit interiors without the help of plant lights. For these situations, try peace plant, cast-iron plant, snake plant, and Chinese evergreen. There are even some orchids that will grow in the weak light of a northern exposure. Use our chart of light requirements of common houseplants to help you choose plants adapted to your available light.

If you want to increase your available light with plant lights, try to provide a mixture of fluorescent (rich in blue light) and incandescent (rich in red). Generally, too much blue light induces low, stocky growth; too much red causes plants to become tall and spindly. To obtain the proper balance, use two fluorescent watts for every incandescent lamp watt. Most incandescent lamps have built-in reflectors. To prevent heat damage, position reflector lamps at least 3 feet from plants. Fluorescent tubes should be 6 to 14 inches above plants.

Providing adequate light is just the first step in growing houseplants. Proper watering

Bromeliad *Piggyback Plant*

Christmas Cactus

Jubilee English Ivy

is also important. Overwatering and underwatering are equally disastrous for most plants, although a few, such as Chinese evergreen, may tolerate either extreme. Sansevieria, certain orchids, and some other plants require rest periods when they receive little or no water. Cast-iron plant, spider plant, some ferns, dracaena, and other plants require evenly moist (but not wet) soil. As a general rule, however, water houseplants when the top ½ inch of soil is slightly dry. Then water thoroughly, until excess water runs out of the drainage hole. Do not allow pots to stand in water.

Houseplants require higher humidity than is found in most homes. To increase humidity, mist plants (except those with hairy leaves). Or set pots in a tray filled with pebbles; half-cover the pebbles with water so that the bottoms of the pots do not come in contact with the water.

Regular feeding is also important for healthy houseplants. A liquid fertilizer containing minor elements is generally recommended for houseplants. But if you move your plants outdoors for the summer, use a slow-release fertilizer applied at the beginning of the summer. The granules break down too slowly indoors to benefit plants much but will work well in warm summer temperatures. Do not apply fertilizer to dry soil, as it may burn plant roots. Periodically flush the soil with water to remove salt residues that may accumulate from plant food. Since fertilization rates vary for houseplants, check our

Gloxinias

Corn Plant

Iron Cross Begonias

Chinese Evergreen

Sansevieria

119

recommendations for specific plants.

If your houseplants begin to decline in spite of proper care, they may need repotting. Potbound plants wilt quickly between waterings, exhibit growth that is generally slow and stunted, or have roots that begin to protrude through the drainage hole or on the surface of the soil.

To determine if your plant is potbound, remove it from its container and inspect its roots. To remove a small plant, moisten the soil slightly to make it stay together; then tip the pot upside down to slide the plant out. To remove a large plant, lay the container on its side, and gently tap the container off the root ball with a block of wood and a hammer. Do not pull the plant out by the stem. If the roots are matted on the surface of the soil ball, repotting is in order. Some flowering plants, such as African violets, geraniums, peace plants, and begonias, grow best when they are slightly potbound, but these are the exception.

Be sure to use sterile soil and to sterilize containers before repotting. Dip containers in a solution of 1 part liquid household bleach to 9 parts water. Rinse well to remove bleach, and let the containers dry before putting soil in them.

Kalanchoe

Poinsettia

Pink Starlite Bromeliads

Breakfast Room Window of Houseplants

Bromeliads

General Recommendations

Can you give me some suggestions for keeping my houseplants attractive and healthy?

Proper sun exposure, watering, and fertilizing are essential to your plants' good health, but the extras make the difference between a plant that is simply alive and one that is truly splendid. One such extra is regular care, including dusting, misting, and pruning.

Dust-coated leaves receive less light than clean ones; this hampers growth. To keep leaves clean, dust with a dry cloth, paper towel, or sponge. A wet cloth only rubs dust into the pores of the leaves, further reducing light absorption. As you dust, inspect your plants for pests. Dusting may spread spider mites from one plant to another; if you detect mites, take the plant outdoors and hose off the pests.

Mist plants (except those with hairy leaves) every few days to supply humidity lost due to air conditioning or forced-air heating. A better way to supply humidity is to place plants on a tray or saucer filled with pebbles or gravel and water. Just be sure the water does not come in contact with the bottom of the pot.

In early spring, prune woody houseplants. Cut off yellowed leaves and all dead, diseased, unproductive, or spindly wood. Remove at the point of origin any excess branches and twigs that detract from the plants' form. Plants that will respond favorably to spring pruning include weeping fig (*Ficus benjamina*), English ivy (*Hedera helix*), forced azaleas (*Azalea sp.*), coral ardisia (*Ardisia crenata*), dwarf gardenia (*Gardenia jasminoides* Radicans), Wheeler's dwarf pittosporum (*Pittosporum tobira* Wheeler's Dwarf), gold-dust plant (*Aucuba japonica* Variegata), natal plum (*Carissa grandiflora*), glorybower (*Clerodendrum thomsoniae*), cast-iron plant (*Aspidistra elatior*), sweet or tea olive (*Osmanthus fragrans*), and calamondin orange (x *Citrofortunella mitis*).

Herbaceous plants may become leggy during the winter. Prune elongated stems back to bushy growth or to within a few inches of the soil. Make cuts just above a bud where new leaves will sprout. Some houseplants that benefit from such pinching back include geraniums (*Pelargonium sp.*), impatiens (*Impatiens sp.*), wandering Jew (*Tradescantia fluminensis*), coleus (*Coleus sp.*), Swedish ivy (*Plectranthus australis*), and peperomia (*Peperomia sp.*).

What are some common houseplant problems?

Very few houseplants are 100 percent trouble-free. Indoor plants are susceptible to most of the problems experienced by plants growing in the open ground, as well as a few problems unique to container-grown plants.

The following are common symptoms of houseplant troubles and possible causes.

—Brown leaf tips and/or margins: Too much water, exposure to drafts from forced-air heating or air conditioning, too much fertilizer, too little water, or too little humidity; may also be caused by chlorine or fluoride in the water (see page 140, "prayer plant"); in high traffic areas, often a result of the plant being brushed by passersby.

—Yellowing and dropping leaves: Air pollution, sudden change of environment, inadequate light, chilling, overwatering, or poor drainage and aeration; may also be caused by root rot diseases (result of overwatering) or by certain pests.

—Weak growth and light-green or yellow foliage: Too much light or inadequate fertilization.

An important part of houseplant care is removing dust and insecticide residues from leaves.

English ivy benefits from spring pruning.

—Small leaves with long internodes (spaces on stem between leaves): Inadequate fertilization or light.

—Small new leaves curl under: Too much light or certain pests.

—Leaves mottled, curled, yellowed: Usually pest damage; spray for spider mites, scale, or whiteflies.

—Wilting: Overwatering, underwatering, overcrowded roots, too much sun, or excessive temperatures.

If I am using plant lights, how can I tell how much light to give my houseplants?

Light is rated in terms of footcandles (a footcandle is the amount of light cast by one candle on a surface 1 foot away). A houseplant classified as a low-light plant requires 50 to 150 footcandles of light; medium-light plants, 200 to 500 footcandles of light; bright-light plants, 500 to 1200. (The light requirements for some common plants are listed below.)

Almost all plants except delicate ones, such as ferns, will grow better with more than the recommended minimum light. If there is some question about the number of footcandles your plant lights are producing, you can check them with a footcandle meter available at electrical supply stores. Or, you can use a photographic light meter, but you will have to convert its reading into footcandle units according to the manufacturer's instructions.

Although many plants can grow under continuous light for 24 hours, certain plants must have some darkness to grow well or to trigger flower and seed production. And with some plants, the length of the dark period initiates seed germination; tuber and bulb formation; and other growth characteristics such as color, enlargement of leaves, and the elongation and branching of stems. Some, such as cacti and other succulents, coleus, and scheffleras (*Brassaia actinophylla*), need long days and short nights; other plants, the reverse; and some have no specific requirements for the length of day-night periods. However, most houseplants do well with 14 to 16 hours of light a day, with flowering plants generally requiring longer periods of light than foliage plants.

Full-spectrum lamps produce the closest simulation of sunshine.

An incandescent plant lamp can be used in any indoor receptacle.

LIGHT REQUIREMENTS FOR COMMON HOUSEPLANTS

LOW LIGHT (50 TO 150 FOOTCANDLES)	MEDIUM LIGHT (200 TO 500 FOOTCANDLES)	HIGH LIGHT (500 TO 1200 FOOTCANDLES)
Bamboo palm (*Chamaedorea erumpens*)	African violet (*Saintpaulia sp.*)	African fern pine (*Podocarpus gracilior*)
Boston fern (*Nephrolepis exaltata* Bostoniensis)	Areca palm (*Chrysalidocarpus lutescens*)	Calamondin orange
Cast-iron plant	Bird's-nest fern (*Asplenium nidus*)	Climbing fern (*Lygodium sp.*)
Chinese evergreen (*Aglaonema sp.*)	Dumb cane (*Dieffenbachia sp.*)	Coleus
Dracaena (*Dracaena sp.*)	False aralia (*Dizygotheca elegantissima*)	Copperleaf (*Acalypha wilkesiana*)
Heart-leaf philodendron (*Philodendron cordatum*)	Jade plant (*Crassula argentea*)	Croton (*Codiaeum variegatum*)
Parlor palm (*Chamaedorea elegans*)	Kangaroo vine (*Cissus antarctica*)	Ice plant (*Lampranthus emarginatus*)
Saddle-leaf philodendron (*Philodendron selloum*)	Lady palm (*Rhapis sp.*)	Japanese fatsia (*Fatsia japonica*)
Sansevieria (*Sansevieria sp.*)	Norfolk Island pine (*Araucaria heterophylla*)	Japanese pittosporum (*Pittosporum tobira*)
Peace plant (*Spathiphyllum sp.*)	Peperomia	Ming aralia (*Polyscias fruticosa*)
	Piggyback plant (*Tolmiea menziesii*)	Velvet plant (*Gynura aurantiaca*)
	Prayer plant (*Maranta leuconeura* Kerchoviana)	
	Queensland umbrella tree or schefflera	
	Rubber plant (*Ficus elastica*)	
	Spider plant (*Chlorophytum comosum*)	
	Wandering Jew	
	Wax plant (*Hoya carnosa*)	

Fig. 1 *Break the root mass at the bottom of the root ball and cut off straggling roots.*

Fig. 2 *Place the plant in the new pot at the same level that it grew previously.*

Fig. 3 *Fill the pot with fresh soil mix and firm the plant gently into place.*

What is the best way to repot houseplants?

Carefully loosen the larger roots that are matted and unwrap those that have coiled around in the pot. Try not to crumble the soil ball. Remove any roots that have rotted.

To repot, select a container at least 2 inches larger in diameter than the one in which the plant was growing. Add enough well-drained, porous potting soil so that the top of the root ball is 1 inch below the rim of the pot. Fill in around the root ball with potting soil, and firm it.

Water the soil gently to settle it; then add more soil as needed to bring the level of the soil up to the top of the root ball. Water the plant thoroughly, but withhold fertilizer for at least one month or until roots are established. (*See Figures 1–3.*)

Repotting does not always mean transferring the plant to a larger container. Mature plants that might become difficult to handle if allowed to grow any larger should have their roots pruned and be repotted in the same size container. At the same time, cut back the top growth proportionately to maintain a balance between roots and top; if roots are cut but the top growth is not, the root system may be unable to support the plant.

How can I propagate plants that grow in clumps?

Many houseplants that grow in clumps, with two or more stems arising from the roots, can be divided to form as many plants as there are stems. Other plants, such as peace

Fig. 4 *Sansevieria propagates easily from root division.*

plant, continually send up new plantlets from the base. These also can be separated from the parent plant at the roots.

To propagate a plant from root divisions, remove the plant from its pot and gently crumble off enough soil to allow you to see the crowns. Many plants divide easily, and you need only pull the stems apart with your hands. (*See Figure 4.*) Pot the divisions immediately in individual containers. Thickly matted or fleshy roots may have to be cut apart with a sharp knife. If some of your divisions have poor roots or no roots at all, insert the divisions in a rooting medium as you would leaf or stem cuttings. A mixture of either peat moss and sand or peat moss and perlite provides a good rooting medium for rootless divisions.

Plants to propagate by root division include African violet; airplane plant, also called spider plant; cast-iron plant; most indoor ferns; prayer plant; peperomia; sansevieria or snake plant (*Sansevieria trifasciata*); peace plant; Chinese evergreen; and screw pine (*Pandanus sp.*).

What is air layering?

Air layering is a way to propagate such plants as rubber plant, schefflera, croton, and Swiss cheese plant (*Monstera deliciosa*). It also induces branching on these plants. To air layer, make an upward cut one-fourth to one-half way through a healthy stem near the top of the plant. Insert a toothpick or matchstick in the cut to keep the two surfaces apart. Apply rooting hormone to the cut surfaces to help speed the rooting process.

Cover the cut with a ball of damp sphagnum moss, and secure with string. Then wrap the ball with a piece of plastic, tying each end with string to prevent moisture loss. Within four to six weeks, roots will become visible through the plastic. Remove the newly rooted plant by cutting at a point just below the ball of moss and roots. Discard the plastic film and string, but leave the moss in place to protect the tender roots when potting the young plant. Within two to three weeks, two branches will also sprout on the parent plant where its stem was severed. (*See Figures 5–10.*)

Fig. 7 *Slit the bark vertically between cuts and peel it away. Notched handles of the shears are used here to grasp the bark and force it off.*

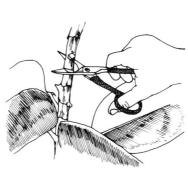

Fig. 6 *Make two cuts between the nodes, completely through the bark and all the way around the stem. Here, a pair of utility shears with cutting edges modified for this particular purpose is used.*

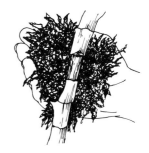

Fig. 8 *Scrape away any of the green cambium layer still attached to the wood. Place moist sphagnum moss over the wounded area.*

Fig. 5 *Select a healthy, vigorously growing branch and remove five to seven leaves at the area where root development is desired.*

Can you suggest some guidelines for grouping my houseplants attractively?

Before you get started, there is one basic consideration to keep in mind—group only those plants with similar light requirements. An understanding of form, color, texture, and balance will be helpful in creating an attractive collage.

The general form of a plant will have considerable influence on its position in the design, as will its size. A tall vertical plant is probably best used at the back of a grouping, while a short vertical plant will look better at the front. A plant with a strong horizontal form gives the design a sense of stability, while an irregular form will help fill in the voids. Remember, if the forms are too similar, the overall composition will seem artificial; if they are too diverse, it will look unresolved. (*See Figures 11–13.*)

The variety of color in the plant world is astounding. But it can be overpowering when it occurs with too much diversity. Dark-green plants will tend to recede, while light greens have just the opposite effect. So color can be used to give the collage a sense of depth and movement. Variegation and bright colors can add interest, but give them a dark background for maximum effect. Too much variegation is distracting; save it for accents and special effects.

Texture is both visual and tactile. The leaves of a rubber plant are not just big, they are big and smooth; African tree fern looks and feels soft. The feel is important, but it is the visual texture that must be considered. Bold texture against fine texture is the strongest combination. Fine textures against medium textures are still striking, but uniform textures will make the design monotonous.

Balance is probably the most important consideration of all. A well-balanced collage is the result of adjusting mass and scale, color, form, and texture until they all work as a unit. The process may take some time, but it will be worth the effort.

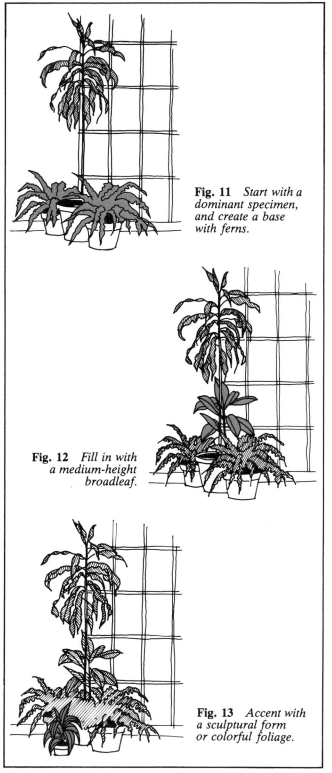

Fig. 11 *Start with a dominant specimen, and create a base with ferns.*

Fig. 12 *Fill in with a medium-height broadleaf.*

Fig. 13 *Accent with a sculptural form or colorful foliage.*

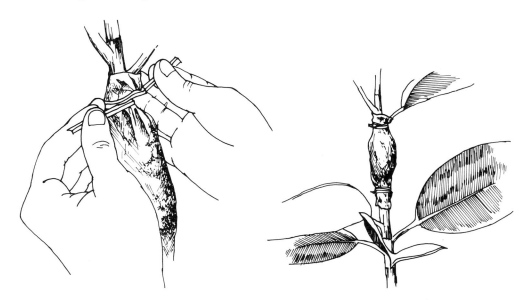

Fig. 9 *Fold a piece of polyethylene over the moss to hold it in place. Fasten the plastic securely at each end to keep the moisture from escaping.*

Fig. 10 *Cover the plastic with aluminum foil if air layering is being done outside. This will exclude sunlight, which could cause growth of algae and result in unsuccessful rooting.*

Use a soft spray of warm water to clean the foliage of an African violet. Allow the leaves to dry before placing the plant in strong light.

The sap of an aloe plant provides a soothing treatment for minor burns.

To produce its glossy, bright-red blooms, anthurium requires high humidity, bright indirect light, and warm temperatures.

Specific Plants

Once a month I wash the leaves of all my plants except African violets. What is the best way to clean their leaves?

The easiest way to keep African violets clean is to set the pot in the kitchen sink and apply a soft spray of warm water; do not use cold water. One caution—do not allow direct sunlight on wet foliage. The drops of water magnify the sun's heat, and spots may be burned on the leaves. Set the plants in the shade until the water evaporates from the leaves. Then return them to their original place.

I have heard that the sap of aloe is good for soothing sunburn, itching, and minor cuts. Is it a difficult houseplant to grow?

Aloe (*Aloe vera*) is easy to grow indoors. Give it plenty of light and a well-drained soil; apply a soluble plant fertilizer about every eight weeks, and let the soil dry out between waterings. Potted plants receiving bright sunlight will sucker from the base and soon cover the entire pot. To start new plants, remove young suckers from the base of the parent plant and repot in a clay pot that drains well.

What can I do to make my anthurium bloom? It is four years old but has never flowered.

There are many types of anthuriums (*Anthurium sp.*), and some bloom more quickly than others. In South Florida, anthurium is used in the landscape; but over most of the South, it will only grow indoors. Anthurium needs high humidity, warm temperatures for active growth, and bright indirect light. Be sure the crown is above the soil, the pot is well drained, and that the soil mixture contains plenty of organic matter. In time, it should flower.

I think my asparagus fern is potbound. What should I do?

If your asparagus fern (*Asparagus sp.*) stops growing or if the soil in the pot dries out daily, divide the plant and repot the divisions. To repot, slide the plant out of the pot (*see* directions for repotting, page 127) and cut the root ball into halves or quarters, depending on how overgrown the fern's roots are. Make clean cuts with a sharp knife to avoid damaging roots. Next, gently untangle the matted roots so that they will spread out in the new container. Place a mound of sterile, well-drained potting soil in the container and spread the root system over it. Fill in with the soil, pressing the soil and plant base lightly in place. Water so the soil will settle; then add more soil, if necessary, to fill the pot to the lower level of the lip. (*See Figures 14–17.*)

What kind of care do begonias require?

Begonias (*Begonia sp.*) can be very temperamental houseplants. They require a higher level of humidity than is usually found in homes, but they should not be misted. Water droplets may condense on leaves and stems, encouraging the development of fungus and bacterial diseases. To increase humidity for your begonias, place them on a pebble tray.

Watering is the most difficult part of caring for a begonia, as regular, predetermined watering schedules do not work. The amount of water a begonia will require depends on the temperature, humidity, and the amount of light it is receiving. If the foliage feels crisp and rigid, chances are it requires no water. But if the foliage feels the least bit soft and droopy, then it is time to water the plant.

Most begonias prefer a soil that is evenly (not excessively) saturated, with a drying-out period between waterings. The easiest way to ensure complete saturation is to place the pot in a sink or basin and fill the sink until water overflows the rim of the pot. Leave the pot submerged until air bubbles stop rising to the surface; then remove the pot from the water, and allow it to drain thoroughly. Do not water again until the foliage indicates that it is time.

A word of caution—never submerge the entire plant. Begonias are very susceptible to mildew; water on the leaves simply aggravates this situation. If you cannot flood the begonia without wetting the leaves, set the pot in a shallow pan and pour water into the top of the pot until it seeps out of the bottom. Let the plant sit in a few inches of water for 10 to 15 minutes, then allow it to drain thoroughly.

Feed begonias with a balanced fertilizer, such as 10-10-10, in a diluted solution of ¼ teaspoon per 2 gallons of water. Feed the plants every other week when they are actively growing. Many begonias become dormant in the winter and should not be fed until they begin to develop new shoots. Be careful not to overfertilize, however; this causes leaf and flower distortion as well as chemical build-up in the soil, which can damage the root system.

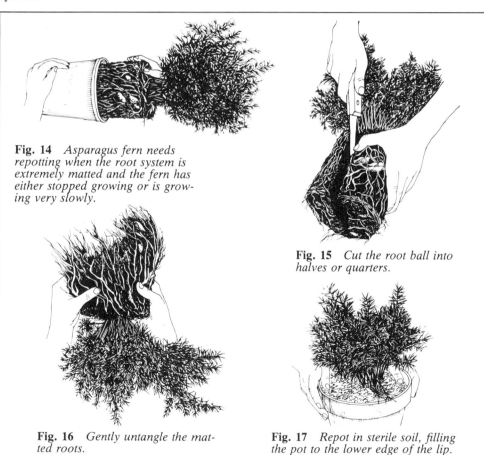

Fig. 14 *Asparagus fern needs repotting when the root system is extremely matted and the fern has either stopped growing or is growing very slowly.*

Fig. 15 *Cut the root ball into halves or quarters.*

Fig. 16 *Gently untangle the matted roots.*

Fig. 17 *Repot in sterile soil, filling the pot to the lower edge of the lip.*

Begonias prefer an evenly moist soil and a drying-out period between waterings. Flooding the pot is a good way to ensure thorough saturation, but avoid wetting the foliage.

Rieger begonias produce long, gracefully arching flower stalks with up to seven blossoms per stalk. This specimen is Begonia × hiemalis *Rieger's Improved Schwabenland Pink.*

Aechmea fulgens *Discolor* is an epiphytic bromeliad. After it flowers, rose-red berries form and sometimes last a year.

Bromeliads are available in a wide range of colors, forms, and textures. Combine different selections for an intriguing effect.

Christmas cactus requires cool night temperatures for several weeks in the fall to bloom between Thanksgiving and Christmas.

The flowers of Christmas cactus are short and delicate, with upturned petals that look like a windblown skirt. Plants may bloom in red, orange, lavender, pink, or white, depending on the selection.

My bird-of-paradise plants are healthy and grow vigorously, but they have never flowered. What can I do to make them bloom?

The bird-of-paradise (*Strelitzia reginae*) blooms best when crowded, so do not divide your plants often. Your plants may not be large enough or old enough to start blooming. Plants need at least ten healthy leaves before they begin to produce flowers, which appear most often in late summer or fall. And most plants do not flower until they are three to five years old. Bird-of-paradise also benefits greatly from frequent, heavy feedings.

Can you recommend some bromeliads that will make good houseplants? What kind of care do they need?

Nearly 20 genera and several hundred species of bromeliads are being sold as houseplants, but not all are desirable selections for indoor growing. In terms of beauty, cost, and durability, six genera provide outstanding choices: *Aechmea, Cryptanthus, Guzmania, Neoregelia, Tillandsia,* and *Vriesea.*

Aechmea bromeliads are some of the most widely grown, prized for their striking foliage, sculptural form, and showy, lasting flowers. Because of their extreme durability, they are ideal for people who have never grown bromeliads. Most are epiphytic (deriving nutrients and moisture from the air), but all make perfect container plants.

Cryptanthus bromeliads are known as earth stars because the foliage is usually arranged in flattish, symmetrical, star-shaped patterns. They are rarely more than a few inches high and less than a foot wide. Most have brightly colored foliage; however, it loses intensity when the plants are grown in low light. All are terrestrial and have inconspicuous white flowers in the center of the plants.

Guzmania bromeliads are characterized by straplike leaves and an arching form. These are generally container-grown epiphytes. *Neoregelia,* a group that includes terrestrial and epiphytic plants, requires bright light to produce colorful foliage. In low light, the foliage will be dull. The *Tillandsia* and *Vriesea* groups also include both terrestrial and epiphytic plants. The *Tillandsia* group accounts for almost half of the known bromeliads, including Spanish moss (*T. usneoides*). They are also the most varied, with forms ranging from vase shaped to grasslike. The *Vriesea* group is a delightful exception to the rule "brightly colored foliage in bright light." These plants maintain their richest colors in low light.

Your success with growing bromeliads indoors will be determined by the growing medium, water, and light. The growing medium and water needs of bromeliads are based on whether the plant is epiphytic or terrestrial. Light requirements are best determined by the plant's general appearance.

What kind of care does Christmas cactus require? What is the best way to induce flowering?

Provided Christmas cactus (*Schlumbergera bridgesii*) receives bright light (not direct sunlight), only minimum care is required to keep it attractive and healthy year-round. In fact, the plant is best left alone except for occasional watering and feeding. Water only when the soil becomes dry, and fertilize monthly, except during the winter after flowers have faded.

The best way to induce flowers is to take the plant outdoors in the fall, when night temperatures are consistently between 50 and 55 degrees for several weeks. To encourage most of the buds to open at the same time, do not water the plant while it is outdoors. When the tiny flower buds form at the tips of mature leaves, take the plant indoors and resume your regular watering schedule. To avoid bud drop, do not place the plant near doorways, heating vents, or other drafty locations.

If placed outdoors in early October, Christmas cactus should begin flowering sometime between Thanksgiving and Christmas. The exact time will depend on environmental conditions and the selection of Christmas cactus you have.

Cast-iron plant provides bold texture and sculptural form in a low-light interior.

Chinese evergreens tolerate low light and neglect, but they will really thrive with proper care.

I have read that cast-iron plant will grow indoors. Do you recommend it? What kind of care does it need?

Cast-iron plant is normally considered an outdoor plant but will survive adverse conditions indoors very well. It needs little care and tolerates low-light situations. One of the few requirements of cast-iron plant is weekly watering to keep the soil evenly moist. If the soil dries out occasionally, it will not hurt the plant; but if dry soil coincides with high temperatures (75 degrees or more), yellow foliage or browning of the leaf margins may result.

When cast-iron plant becomes rootbound, you will need to divide it, preferably in winter or early spring. Since the foliage arises from clumps of underground stems called rhizomes, be sure each division contains a portion of rhizome to provide buds for new growth. Repot the divisions in loamy soil, and withhold fertilizer the first two months. This allows time for the roots to become established before the application of nitrogen stimulates the foliage into growth. Feed established plants every two months with a soluble houseplant fertilizer during spring, summer, and fall. Reduce watering and withhold fertilizer in winter.

What kind of care do Chinese evergreens prefer?

Chinese evergreens are just as undemanding about water, soil, and temperature as they are tolerant of low- to medium-light situations. They are the perfect plant for the person who occasionally forgets to water, but they will also perform well for the overzealous waterer who keeps them saturated. To keep them in top condition, however, water Chinese evergreens on a regular basis (once a week is recommended). Waterings should be deep and thorough, followed by a drying-out period to avoid the possibility of root rot.

Chinese evergreens prefer warm days (85 degrees) and cooler nights (60 to 65 degrees), but they adjust remarkably well to the constant temperatures of air conditioning. Avoid placing them in direct drafts and overheating in winter. An occasional misting is also beneficial.

While they can be maintained for years in the same container, an annual repotting will keep your Chinese evergreens in a healthy, vigorous condition. A commercial potting soil combined with equal parts of perlite and peat is recommended.

Florist's chrysanthemums will bloom for two to three weeks indoors if given direct sunlight and cool temperatures.

Can chrysanthemums be grown as houseplants?

Marguerites (*Chrysanthemum frutescens*) and florist's chrysanthemums (*C.* x *morifolium*) may be grown indoors if you can provide cool temperatures (40 to 55 degrees at night and 68 degrees or lower during the day) and at least four hours of direct sunlight daily. Chrysanthemums should be protected from direct sun when they begin flowering. Keep the soil moist and fertilize potted chrysanthemums every two weeks.

Cyclamen's nodding blossoms will last for weeks if given proper care. Place it in a cool location and keep the soil evenly moist, but do not wet the plant's crown.

Large dracaenas are particularly handsome in groupings. This one includes (left to right) Dracaena deremensis *Janet Craig*, D. sanderiana, D. fragrans *Massangeana*, a compact form of D. deremensis *Warneckii*, and a full-size *Warneckii* selection.

Marguerites produce yellow, white, or pink daisylike flowers throughout the year. Keep the plants small (18 inches tall or less) by pinching off the tips of stems. Florist's chrysanthemums bloom for two to three weeks, producing white, yellow, bronze, maroon, pink, or lavender flowers.

When the flowers fade, you can set the plants in the garden. To have more chrysanthemums for indoor blooming, make stem cuttings from marguerites anytime; divide or make stem cuttings from florist's chrysanthemums in early spring.

The cyclamen I received as a gift stayed green and bloomed beautifully for awhile. Now the foliage has died and all that is left is the bulb. Will it sprout again?

It is highly unlikely that you will be able to bring your cyclamen (*Cyclamen persicum*) into bloom again. This plant is brought into bloom initially in a greenhouse, where lighting and temperatures are carefully controlled. These conditions cannot be duplicated in the home or outdoors in the South. Your best course with a gift cyclamen is to enjoy the flowers and foliage while they last, then dispose of the plant.

I water my corn plant, let the soil dry before watering it again, fertilize it often, clean the foliage, and give it partial sunlight. However, it does not seem to grow. What else can I do?

If your corn plant (*Dracaena fragrans* Massangeana) has been growing in the same container for four or five years, it may be potbound. Remove it from its container and inspect the roots. If they are matted on the surface of the soil ball, the plant needs repotting. If the plant is not potbound, bear in mind that corn plant is a slow grower. Continue to give the plant enough light, water, and fertilizer and it will eventually reach a desirable size. Remember, overfertilization will burn the roots.

I would like to use some dracaenas as floor plants. Can you recommend some large types?

Large dracaenas are bold enough to use as a single specimen, an important element in design. They are generally used as floor plants, either alone or in groups. The following are three types to try.

Dracaena deremensis: This species may grow up to 15 feet tall; leaves are green and about 2 inches wide and 2 feet long. The cultivar Warneckii has many white stripes on the leaves; Janet Craig has green leaves that are ribbed and thick.

D. fragrans: Often reaching a height of 15 feet, this dracaena has green leaves up to 3 feet long and 3 inches wide. The cultivar Massangeana, commonly known as corn plant, has a wide yellow band down each leaf.

D. marginata: This plant is known as Madagascar dragon tree and is the most sculptural dracaena, due to its long, slender, and often twisting bare stems. This plant will reach a height of about 12 feet; leaves are long (up to 2 feet), slender, and green with a red margin. The leaves of the cultivar Tricolor are striped in white, red, and green.

How can I cut back my leggy dracaena to make it bushier? Can I use the parts I cut off to start new plants?

One leggy plant in a pot with shorter ones can be attractive. However, getting your leggy dracaenas back in shape is easy, and you can multiply the number of plants you have in the process. Cut the stem just above the lowest leaves to encourage new growth.

If there are no leaves on the lower portion of the stem, cut the stem about 12 inches above soil level.

To start new plants, cut the bare portion of the removed stem into several 3- or 4-inch sections, and lay each leafless section horizontally into the rooting medium. Firm the sections into the medium and mist regularly. Shoots and roots will develop along the stem segment. If the leafy portion of the removed stem is very long, you may want to cut it into two or more sections. Remove leaves from the bottom of each section and insert the stem section upright in a pot of equal parts perlite and peat moss. Packaged potting soil will also suffice. (*See Figures 18–20.*)

To ensure rapid root formation, keep the rooting medium moist. Frequent misting of the upright cuttings will also aid root formation. When new leaves appear on these cuttings, repot the plants. You can keep your plants bushy by giving them bright indirect light and fertilizing twice a year with a liquid fertilizer such as 18-18-18.

How can I propagate echeveria?

Echeveria (*Echeveria sp.*) and many other succulents are extremely easy to propagate. Just pinch or cut the offsets borne in small rosettes on the stem of the mother plant. (*See Figure* 21.) Place the offsets directly in sterile, well-drained potting soil. (*See Figure* 22.) Some of the lower leaves of the offset can be trimmed, if necessary, so that it will sit well in the soil. In very little time, the plantlet will produce its own roots. To help the plantlet stay in contact with the soil, it can be held between pins or toothpicks placed on either side. Since these plants need a dry environment, allow the soil to become moderately dry between waterings.

Fig. 18 *To restore a leggy dracaena to a bushier habit, cut the stem just above the lowest leaves. Use the removed portion to start new plants.*

Fig. 19 *Cut the bare portion of the removed stem into 3- or 4-inch sections.*

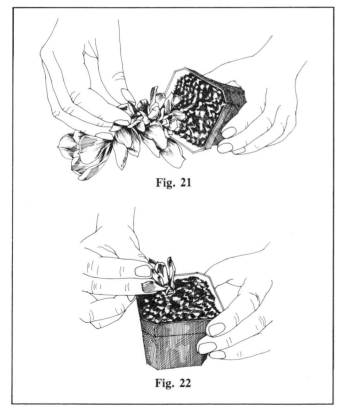

Fig. 21

Fig. 22

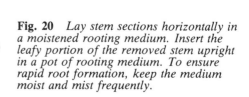

Fig. 20 *Lay stem sections horizontally in a moistened rooting medium. Insert the leafy portion of the removed stem upright in a pot of rooting medium. To ensure rapid root formation, keep the medium moist and mist frequently.*

Are there any ferns that do not require high humidity?

The popular indoor ferns, like Boston fern, require a lot of bright indirect light, high humidity, and temperatures somewhat cooler than those generally found inside a house. However, there are several rugged ferns that are well adapted to less humid situations, not unlike the inside of your house. Native to the warmer, drier regions of the tropics, the rugged ferns have leathery foliage that helps to protect them from the loss of moisture caused by drying winds. Specialized roots or rhizomes provide reserves of moisture for periods of drought. The rugged ferns may adjust to low-light situations but prefer bright indirect light. You may have to shop around to find these ferns, but they will be worth the effort.

Holly fern (*Cyrtomium falcatum* Rochfordianum) bears lustrous, dark-green, deeply serrated fronds arranged alternately along a central stem or rachis. Although the holly fern prefers the indirect light of a north-facing window, it performs exceptionally well in artificial light (especially fluorescent). Keep the soil evenly moist, but avoid overwatering. A good choice for drafty locations, holly fern may withstand both central air conditioning and forced-air heat.

Crisped hart's-tongue fern (*Phyllitis scolopendrium* Crispifolia) is a compact plant, rarely growing more than 12 inches high and 16 inches across. Despite its rather delicate appearance, crisped hart's-tongue is not a plant to overpamper. A deep, thorough soaking once a week is the best technique for watering; this can be supplemented every six months with an application of liquid plant food mixed at half the recommended strength.

Staghorn fern (*Platycerium bifurcatum*) is an epiphyte, or air-growing fern. Although it is most often grown in hanging baskets or mounted on a plaque of wood or palm bark,

The arching, almost symmetrical form of holly fern makes it a good choice for locations where it can be seen from several different angles.

The crisped hart's-tongue fern is one of the most durable of all the rugged ferns. Soft indirect light and weekly waterings are all that is necessary to keep it in top condition.

Fish-tail fern is a ruffled version of climbing bird's-nest fern. Although it looks more delicate than climbing bird's-nest, it has the same dependability and stamina in difficult locations.

Aside from its dramatic blue green color, crisped blue fern offers the distinct advantage of low-light requirements. The coarsely textured foliage also withstands the low humidity of forced-air heat and cooling.

staghorn fern can also be grown in a container. Since this plant receives most of its nutrients from the air, neither fertilizer nor a heavy potting soil is required. All the fern really needs is a mixture of equal parts long-fiber sphagnum moss and coarse peat to help retain moisture at the roots.

Maintenance of staghorn fern is quite simple. Place it in bright indirect light and water weekly or whenever the planting medium begins to dry out. To water, submerge the board or container in tepid water for about 10 minutes or until air bubbles stop forming on the surface of the water. Regular misting of the plant is also recommended.

The polypodium ferns (*Polypodium sp.*) are some of the most dependable and varied houseplants on the market. Although their foliage presents a great diversity of colors, forms, and textures, the members of this genus are easily identified by their creeping, hairy rhizomes that develop on the surface of the soil. Amazingly durable even in the most difficult conditions, the four polypodiums discussed below are almost sure to be successful.

As the common name suggests, the handsome ruffled foliage of crisped blue fern (*P. aureum* Mandaianum) has a distinctive bluish cast. The habit of growth is typically fernlike with large, deeply serrated fronds carried on a thin brown rachis. An upright spreading form makes crisped blue fern useful for almost any container and particularly attractive in hanging baskets. One of the most low-light tolerant of the polypodiums, the crisped blue fern performs exceptionally well in artificial light. But when it receives plenty of bright indirect light, the foliage of this fern will be larger, more abundant, and an even deeper shade of blue.

Climbing bird's-nest fern (*P. punctatum*) has an upright habit of growth. The long tapering fronds are thick and waxy, usually growing to a height of 12 to 20 inches. Fish-tail fern (*P. punctatum* Grandiceps) is a crested version of the climbing bird's-nest fern with rufflelike indentations at the end of every frond. Since the waxy coating on the fronds protects both of these ferns from dehydration, they can take the blast of forced-air heat or cooling with amazing stamina. Plants exposed to such conditions will, of course, require more frequent waterings; but with a little extra care, they will survive where other ferns would perish.

Lacy pine fern (*P. subauriculatum* Knightiae) is more delicate looking and slower growing than the other polypodiums, but it is every bit as tough. Although it may eventually attain a height and spread of 20 inches, the lacy pine fern can be maintained at almost any stage of growth by simply not repotting it. And the smaller scale of potbound plants will only help to emphasize the delicate appearance.

Can brake ferns be grown as houseplants?

Two selections of brake ferns or table ferns (*Pteris sp.*) well adapted to growing indoors are Cretan brake fern (*P. cretica*) and Australian brake fern (*P. tremula*). Cretan brake fern grows 6 to 12 inches tall. Three good types are *P. cretica* Albo-lineata (white striped, dark-green foliage, low growing), *P. cretica* Childsii (frilly, bright-green leaflets), and *P. cretica* Wilsonii (low growing, with fan-shaped frond tips). Australian brake fern grows rapidly. As a small plant (1 foot tall), it makes a good centerpiece; at its maximum height of 4 feet, the fern is an excellent floor plant.

The brake ferns require only the low light of a northern exposure. However, they do not tolerate the drying effects of home heating. Mist them occasionally, or place them on a pebble tray filled with water. Keep the soil barely moist. Moving the ferns outdoors during a spring or summer shower will also refresh them.

Despite its rather curious, exotic form, climbing bird's-nest fern is extremely durable. It is one of the few ferns you can forget to water for a week without seriously damaging the plant.

The drooping fronds of staghorn fern make it a fine choice for hanging baskets, especially since the plant is epiphytic (air growing) by nature.

Brake ferns will grow in the weak light of a northern exposure, but they require regular misting to counter the drying effects of indoor heating and cooling.

Rabbit's-foot ferns are characterized by surface-creeping hairy rhizomes.

Rabbit's-foot fern does not require high humidity but will benefit from weekly misting.

Staghorn ferns look best when mounted on a board so the long, handsome fronds hang downward. Here, moist sphagnum moss covers the roots of the fern.

Hammer nails into the board in a circle about twice the diameter of the fern's container. Cover the inside of the circle with a thin layer of moist sphagnum moss and place the fern on top; completely cover the roots with additional moist moss.

Attach the moss-covered base of the fern to the board with fishing line. Work the line back and forth over the moss mound, catching it on the nails to secure it. Tie it firmly on the last nail.

I have just bought a beautiful rabbit's-foot fern. How can I keep it looking as healthy as it does now?

Rabbit's-foot fern (*Polypodium aureum*) tolerates drier air than most popular ferns. It requires plenty of bright indirect light, but keep it out of direct sunlight and away from drafts. Soil should be porous and moist but never soggy. Mist the fronds once a week. Feed once a month with a liquid houseplant fertilizer such as 18-18-18 at half the recommended strength.

My staghorn fern developed large brown spots as soon as I brought it inside in the fall. Why?

Usually the problem is caused by inadequate moisture and humidity. The solution is simple—more water. If your fern is mounted on a plaque of sphagnum moss, keep the plaque moist at all times. The plant may require a little water every day, depending on the rate at which it dries out. Mist the fern every few days to be sure that at least a small amount of water will reach the leaves directly. Another way of providing moisture directly to the leaves and keeping the leaves clean at the same time is to wipe them off at least once a week with a damp sponge or cloth.

Please tell me how to attach my staghorn fern to a plaque.

One way to mount a staghorn fern on a plaque is to choose a piece of rough-cut cedar, a round of wood, or other attractive board into which you can hammer small nails (be sure the wood has not been treated with a preservative). You will also need small galvanized nails that have flat, round heads; sphagnum moss; and fishing line.

To mount the fern, first hammer the nails into the board to form a circle about twice the diameter of the pot the plant is growing in. Cover the area inside the circle with a thin layer of moist sphagnum moss; then remove the staghorn fern from the pot, and place it

upright on top of the moss. Cover the roots of the fern with additional moist sphagnum moss, being sure that the base of the plant is thoroughly covered. (To moisten dry moss, submerge it in a container of water and squeeze out excess water.)

To attach the fern to the board, wrap the moss-covered base with fishing line; work the line back and forth across the moss mound, catching it around the nails to hold it securely. When the fern is well fastened to the board, tie the line around the last nail to keep it secure.

Gloxinia produces velvety blooms in a variety of rich colors.

Our gloxinia, which we received as a gift, has stopped blooming and the leaves have withered. A friend told us that it will put out new growth. Is this true?

Yes, although the quality of new growth will probably not equal that of the original plant. When gloxinia (*Sinningia speciosa*) flowers fade and leaves wither, the plant has gone dormant. New growth should appear two to four months later. Withhold water during dormancy. Then, when sprouts develop, repot the plant in a mixture of 2 parts peat moss, 1 part packaged potting soil, and 1 part sharp sand or perlite. Keep the soil moist and fertilize monthly during the plant's growth period. Gloxinia does best in bright indirect or filtered sunlight and warm temperatures (75 degrees or higher in the daytime). When flowers begin to fade, withhold fertilizer and reduce watering gradually until the plant becomes dormant again.

I have some English ivy growing in my yard. Can I bring some of it indoors to use as a houseplant?

English ivy makes an excellent indoor plant. The variety of leaf shapes makes it as striking as the most exotic houseplant. In addition to bird's-foot, fan-shaped, curly leaf, and heart-shaped, there are variegated types and miniature forms.

Ivy is at its best when allowed to cascade over the container to create a graceful, flowing effect. Ivy grows slowly in an indoor environment, so pruning should not be necessary. If the plant becomes leggy, just pinch it back. Plant ivy in well-drained soil and place it in a sunny window or brightly lit location.

When you bring ivy indoors, it may lose some leaves while adjusting to the lower humidity of a home environment. You can increase humidity around the plant by setting the container in a pebble tray filled with water. Ivy likes the soil neither too wet nor too dry. If the soil stays too wet, the leaves will develop black spots, signaling the onset of rot. Let the soil dry, and resume watering only when the top inch of soil is dry. Feed ivy monthly (twice a month in summer) with 18-18-18 at the rate recommended on the container label. However, if ivy begins to turn solid green, decrease fertilizer until the foliage regains its original variegation.

I have two fairly large jade plants that receive regular care, but for quite some time a number of the lower leaves have been shrinking, shriveling, and dropping.

Jade plant is considered a tree. Many trees lose lower leaves; some lose lower branches. Unless a jade plant is growing in the most ideal situation, it will eventually begin to lose lower leaves. Although the plant will grow in bright indirect light, it prefers direct sun for at least four hours a day. If leaf margins are red, the plant is receiving enough light. Allow the soil to dry out between waterings and feed the plant every three or four months. Jade plants rarely need repotting, since they can thrive for years while rootbound.

Jade plant is actually a tree, and it can be expected to lose lower leaves as the trunks develop.

Kalanchoe is one of the best indoor flowering plants, blooming for as long as two months.

I received a kalanchoe for Christmas. How should I care for it?

Drought-tolerant kalanchoe (*Kalanchoe blossfeldiana*) is one of the best indoor flowering plants, producing masses of red or yellow blossoms for up to two months. Kalanchoe requires bright light. From October until May, it should be placed where it will receive at least three to four hours of direct sunlight daily. During the summer months it should be kept in bright light, but not in direct sunlight.

Nighttime temperatures can affect the growth rate of kalanchoe. The optimum nighttime temperature is about 65 degrees. Placed in a sunny window, the plants will receive adequate light during the day and the coolest temperature in the room at night. Warmer temperatures may delay or inhibit flowering.

Plant kalanchoe in well-drained soil. To avoid overwatering, water the plant thoroughly, then wait until the soil is dry at least 1 inch deep before watering again.

Are there any orchids that can be grown as houseplants?

Contrary to popular belief, orchids make excellent houseplants. They adapt well to average home temperatures (60 to 80 degrees), and can even tolerate brief periods of hot weather (90 to 100 degrees) if humidity is high. Good ventilation is the most important factor in growing orchids indoors. Place pots on shelves made of slats to allow air circulation all around the plant. Avoid overwatering; if the pot feels heavy, it probably needs no water. If the pot feels light, water the plant. A gravel-filled tray or saucer placed on a shelf below the pot will catch excess water that drains through the pot and help supply humidity. You may also increase humidity by spraying the air around the plants. Do not spray the plants themselves, however, as wet foliage is susceptible to disease. Pot orchids in osmunda fiber or fir bark. Plants in osmunda require little fertilizer; once every five weeks while they are growing is enough. Fir bark will require more fertilizer.

Orchids vary widely in their lighting requirements. There are plants for nearly every lighting situation. The following are a few of the types that are easy to grow in a south-facing window.

Cattleyas, especially *C. citrina* (bright yellow), *C.* x *dolosa* (magenta), *C. nobilior* (rose colored), and *C. schillerana* (rose brown). These epiphytic orchids flower in summer, except for *C.* x *dolosa,* which blooms in winter. The blooms may last two to four weeks. *Cattleyas* prefer a slightly dry soil between waterings. After the flowers fade, withhold water for five to seven weeks to allow the plants to rest.

Dendrobium, especially *D. chrysotoxum* and *D. aggregatum.* These orchids bear drooping spikes of flowers in spring. They require four hours of sunlight and plenty of water until foliage matures. Then, to induce blooming, withhold water for three to four weeks. Resume watering when flowers appear. After they fade, allow a waterless rest period of five to seven weeks.

Oncidium, especially *O. ampliatum, O. ornithorhynchum, O. sarcodes, O. splendidum, O. leucochilum,* and *O. wentworthianum.* Most of these evergreen epiphytic orchids produce long-lasting yellow and brown flowers. *O. ornithorhynchum* bears hundreds of tiny lilac blossoms. The plants require plenty of water and high humidity while growing, but they should be allowed to dry out for two to five weeks when growth stops and again after flowers fade. *Oncidiums* respond well to being moved outdoors in summer.

Brassia, especially *B. caudata, B. maculata,* and *B. gireoudiana.* These evergreen epiphytes produce light-green or yellow green flowers spotted with brown. During spring and summer, keep the potting medium moist and feed the plants every two weeks with 20-10-10. At the end of the summer, withhold fertilizer and allow the medium to dry slightly between waterings to encourage flower spikes to appear. In winter, water just enough to prevent the pseudobulbs (stems) from shriveling.

In an east-facing window, try the *Oncidiums* or *Brassavola cucullata* and *B. nodosa.* Both *Brassavolas* are excellent houseplants, bearing fragrant pale-green flowers. They need three to five hours of sunlight to bloom but require little water. The medium should be allowed to dry out between waterings, and after flowering they may be watered even less. Place the orchids outdoors in the summer.

For a western exposure, try *Coelogyne* orchids, especially *C. cristata, C. flaccida, C. fuscescens,* and *C. ochracea.* These evergreen epiphytic orchids require a moist medium while the plants are growing; but do not let water accumulate in the new growth, or it may rot. After the flowers fade, withhold water for five to seven weeks.

In a north-facing window, try *Stanhopea* orchids, especially *S. wardii, S. insignis, S. oculata, S. tigrina,* and *S. ecornuta.* The flower scapes grow from the base of the plant, so *Stanhopea* orchids must be grown in open baskets especially designed for this purpose, or in bottomless pots. These plants need warm temperatures (no lower than 60 degrees on a winter night), high humidity, and plenty of water. In the winter, decrease the frequency of watering, but never let the medium dry out.

How much water do palms require? How often should they be fertilized?

The amount of water a palm, or any other plant, requires varies with changes in the humidity, temperature, and the amount of light it receives. To help maintain a consistent soil moisture, add water only when the upper inch of soil has dried completely. Central heating and cooling systems reduce humidity, so mist palms frequently. Low humidity causes many palms to develop brown leaf tips. Feed palms monthly during spring and summer with an 18-18-18 fertilizer. Do not feed plants in fall and winter months.

What kind of light do palms require?

The amount of light a palm receives may well be the most important element in determining its success. A general rule for palms is the brighter, the better. Even the parlor palm and the bamboo palm, which tolerate relatively low-light situations, perform much better when they receive a higher amount of light. Just make sure that the light is filtered or indirect. Due to the magnifying effect of window glass, direct sunshine will cause the leaves of most palms to burn. A south-facing window with six to eight hours of light each day would be ideal for a palm. When the light situation is less than perfect, the other environmental factors (temperature, humidity, and soil moisture) become all the more important in maintaining a healthy plant.

Bamboo palm tolerates low-light situations, but it will grow even better in a garden room or near a tall window.

Dendrobium is one of several kinds of orchids that may be grown as a houseplant.

Mauna Loa (top) is the largest of the three popular peace plants, growing over 2 feet tall. The more abundant flowers of Clevelandii make up for its smaller size.

Spade-leaf philodendron is a medium-size plant, small enough to fit on a tabletop or large enough to anchor the corner of a room.

What is the best temperature for palms?

Most home environments are suitable. Avoid extreme fluctuations. Daytime temperatures should range from 75 to 85 degrees, with a 65- to 75-degree range at night. The lady palm is an exception. It prefers milder days (68 to 72 degrees) and cooler nights (50 to 55 degrees). Be sure to avoid drafts from heating and cooling vents.

Will peace plant grow in a room that receives very little light?

While no plant will grow in total darkness, peace plant will do exceptionally well in low-light situations; and as a bonus, it blooms intermittently throughout the year. The greenish white flowers, cloaked in a white hood, last at least a month.

Some of the more commonly available selections are Mauna Loa, Clevelandii, and Wallisii. Mauna Loa, the largest of the three, usually grows more upright than the others (2 feet or more) and has 4- to 6-inch flowers. Clevelandii and Wallisii have smaller leaves and flowers, but Clevelandii has a better flower display. Wallisii is the smallest and has less of the elegant dark-green foliage than Clevelandii.

Peace plant prefers filtered light or the indirect light of a north-facing window; at no time should peace plant receive direct sunlight. In winter, when days are shorter, move the plant into brighter light. If you garden under artificial light, 10 to 15 watts per square foot of growing space or 50 to 100 footcandles is adequate. While comfortable in a variety of temperature and humidity conditions, peace plant will not tolerate wet, soggy soil. A thorough watering each week is usually sufficient.

Propagating peace plant is easy; but if the plant is slightly rootbound, it will bloom more often and more profusely. When the plant becomes overcrowded, however, divide the roots and repot the divisions at any time of the year.

Pests and diseases are rarely a problem with peace plant. An occasional gentle shower of lukewarm water will keep the leaves glossy and wash off small infestations of pests. If the plant container has a drainage hole, flooding the root system now and then will minimize the build-up of fertilizer salts, which cause the leaf tips to brown. Too much or too little water also can cause the leaves to brown.

How can I start new plants from my peperomia? How should I care for them?

Fleshy-leaved peperomia, such as ovalleaf peperomia (*Peperomia obtusifolia*), may be propagated by either stem or leaf cuttings. Each stem cutting should include at least two leaf-joints or nodes. Place cuttings in rooting medium so that the lower node is below the soil, and keep the medium moist. Other types of peperomia, like Emerald ripple peperomia (*P. caperata*), may be propagated by leaf (petiole) cuttings placed in the soil. When roots are established, pot each new peperomia in a sterile potting soil. Place the plants where they will receive bright indirect or filtered sunlight. Water thoroughly from the bottom when the soil becomes slightly dry, but do not allow the plants to stand in water. After your new peperomias are established (in about four to six months), feed with a houseplant fertilizer every three to four months.

Please give me some tips for growing philodendrons.

Philodendrons are among the easiest indoor plants to grow. Most types will adapt to nearly any lighting situation, but it is best to avoid locations with extremely bright or extremely low light. Rooms with a southern, western, or eastern exposure are ideal.

Water frequently enough to keep the soil moist but never wet; overwatering is probably the greatest enemy of philodendrons. Soil moisture is more difficult to determine in large containers, since the soil tends to dry out more slowly than in small containers. For plants in large containers, check the soil moisture 2 to 3 inches below soil level before you water.

Plants should be potted in a well-drained yet moisture-retentive medium. Most packaged soil mixes are fine for philodendrons; but if drainage is slow, you can mix in additional sand or perlite.

The leaves of my piggyback plant are turning brown around the edges and dying. I keep the soil moist, and the plant is in a semishady location. What is wrong?

You may be wetting the leaves of your piggyback plant when you water it. This plant, like the African violet, does not like to have wet foliage. Either water the plant from the bottom (do not let it stand in water too long), or water with a container that has a slender spout; keep the soil moist but not waterlogged. Overwatering could also cause leaves to turn brown.

The problem could also be caused by a deficiency in manganese. Correct this with a fertilizer containing minor elements.

How do I propagate piggyback plants?

The piggyback plant produces tiny plantlets (called offsets) on its leaves, and reproduction of the plant consists of simply separating the offset from the mother plant and rooting it. Fill a shallow flat or 3-inch pot with sterile potting soil. Snip off a leaf on which an offset is growing; include at least 1 inch of the stem (petiole) with the leaf. (*See Figure 23.*) Insert the cutting into the medium so that the leaf rests flat against the medium; the leaf itself will root. (*See Figure 24.*)

Water carefully so as not to disturb the rooting offsets. Keeping the rooting medium moist will require almost daily watering. Take care not to overwater.

Do not place leaf cuttings where they will receive direct sunlight. Soil will dry out rapidly in strong light, and the mother leaf will curl away from the rooting medium. The leaf cutting should root in two or three weeks.

Please tell me how to care for my new Norfolk Island pine.

Locate your Norfolk Island pine where it will receive bright indirect or filtered sunlight; in the winter, place it in full sun. The plant prefers moderate temperatures but can tolerate a range from 45 degrees at night to 85 degrees in the day. Keep the soil barely moist. A newly purchased plant will have been fertilized by the commercial grower and will not need feeding for about six months. Fertilize an established plant every three or four months. When your Norfolk Island pine shows signs of being rootbound, repot it in highly organic potting soil like that used for African violets. This should only be necessary every three or four years. Norfolk Island pine is temperamental and may be a difficult houseplant to grow.

I have recently purchased a pocketbook plant. Please advise me as to the care of this plant.

Pocketbook plant (*Calceolaria crenatiflora*) is native to the cool Andes Mountains of Chile, so give it plenty of light but no direct, hot sunlight. Keep the soil barely moist. Overwatering is one of the biggest problems with growing pocketbook plant in the home. Since the leaves are hairy, avoid wetting them when watering. Feed every three or four weeks during the growing season with a general-purpose houseplant fertilizer

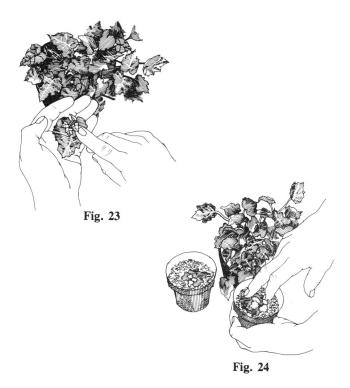

Fig. 23

Fig. 24

Pocketbook plant requires bright indirect light and cool temperatures.

(18-18-18). Growing a pocketbook plant to blooming size is very difficult. The exotic-looking plant is usually purchased from a florist at blooming time and discarded a month later, when flowering stops.

This Christmas I purchased a number of poinsettias for my home. Please tell me how to care for these plants so they will bloom again next Christmas.

Coaxing poinsettias (*Euphorbia pulcherrima*) into bloom again is very difficult, as it requires the carefully controlled lighting conditions of a greenhouse. However, if you want to try, here are some suggestions.

Once the poinsettias fade, treat them like any other houseplant. Then when warm weather arrives, take them outdoors for the summer and cut all stems back to within 3 inches of the soil. In September, bring them inside to start the blooming cycle, which is triggered by long nights and short days. From about September 15 to October 10, give the plants 14 to 16 hours of light a day; then beginning about October 10, keep the plants in total darkness for 14 to 16 hours a day until the desired intensity of bract color is reached. This schedule of light and darkness must be followed diligently. If one of the dark periods is disturbed by even a dim light for a very short time, the flowering cycle will be interrupted.

The leaves of my prayer plant have always folded up at night, but now they remain open all the time. Also, the tips of the leaves are turning brown and they seem to be dying. What is wrong?

Insufficient water and low humidity encourage brown tips on the leaves of prayer plant. To increase humidity, set the pot in a tray of pebbles, with water barely covering the pebbles. Prayer plant needs consistently moist soil during most of the year. In winter, allow soil to dry slightly between waterings. Fluoride or chlorine in the water may be adding to your plant's problem. Try collecting rainwater for the plant, or let tapwater sit in a pan at room temperature overnight to allow chlorine to evaporate. In severe cases, turn the pot on its side and allow the soil to dry out. Then resume watering. Once the plant is restored to a healthy condition, it will probably start folding its leaves at night. Repot your prayer plant in fresh soil every spring; feed once in the summer and once in early fall. Be sure the plant receives bright indirect light.

Can you give me some guidance on caring for rubber plants? The leaves on the first one I bought turned yellow, then brown, and finally fell off. I bought another one recently, and it is beginning to do the same thing.

Rubber plant is usually a reliable houseplant if it receives enough sunlight and humidity. Adjusting to indoor light after having been raised in bright light in a nursery is sometimes difficult for this plant. Place it where it will receive very bright light or filtered sunlight for several hours each day. The most practical way to increase the humidity around the plant is to place it in a pebble tray with water not quite covering the pebbles.

Excessive or improper applications of fertilizer can contribute to the problem you describe. Frequent, weak solutions of fertilizer are safer than infrequent heavy applications. Also, avoid fertilizing when the soil is dry.

What is the best way to propagate a rubber plant?

The most popular method of propagating the rubber plant is air layering (*see* page

To keep a prayer plant healthy, keep the soil consistently moist, except during the winter when the soil should dry slightly between waterings.

124). However, this yields only one plant at a time. To start several new plants at once, try rooting leaf cuttings. If you make cuttings from a leggy plant, the mother plant will benefit from being cut back. New growth will arise below where you have made cuts on the mother plant.

First, cut off a portion of stem below one or more leaves. (*See Figure 25.*) Then cut the piece of stem into sections, with a leaf attached to each. Make each cut just below a leaf. (*See Figure 26.*) Prepare a rooting medium of equal parts of perlite and peat moss; moisten it, and fill peat pots or large plastic foam cups with the medium. Insert each stem upright in a filled pot, and firm the medium around the cutting. With a pair of scissors or pruning shears, remove the upper two-thirds of the leaf. (*See Figure 27.*) Keep the medium moist while the cuttings are rooting. In a few weeks, a new shoot will arise from the base of the cutting. (*See Figure 28.*)

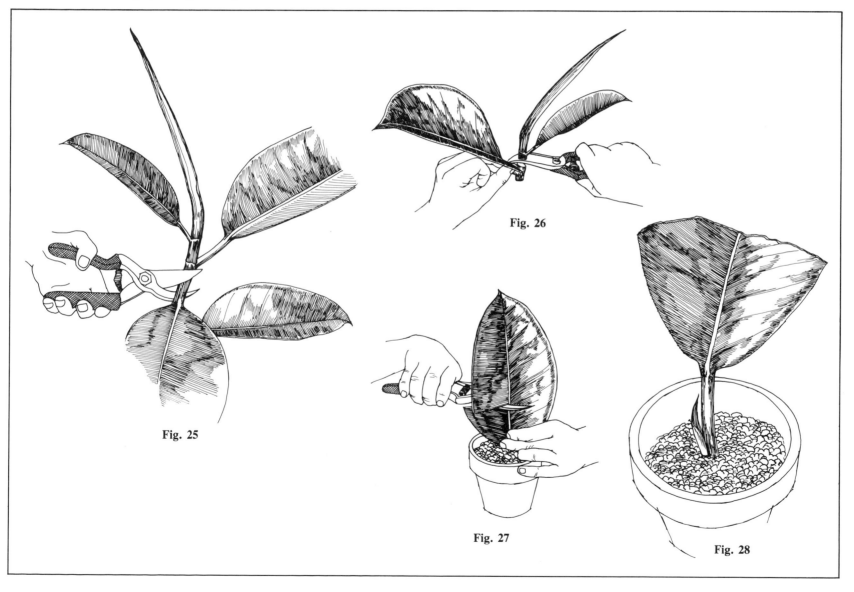

Fig. 25

Fig. 26

Fig. 27

Fig. 28

What kind of care do sansevierias require?

Sansevierias will thrive in almost any lighting situation, from full sun to the weak light of a north-facing window. During spring, summer, and fall, water your sansevierias only when the upper layer of soil (at least the top ½ inch) feels dry and crusty. Then give the plants a deep, prolonged soaking. In the winter, water sparingly—just enough to keep the foliage from shriveling. Feed established plants every three or four months, except during the winter, when you should withhold fertilizer.

Please give me information on the care and feeding of shrimp plant.

Shrimp plant (*Beloperone guttata*) performs best in a loamy soil, medium humidity, and direct sunlight. Allow the soil to become slightly dry between thorough waterings. Feed the plant every two weeks with light applications of houseplant fertilizer. Pinch off tips of stems to keep the plant 12 to 18 inches tall.

Please tell me why my spider plant is not sending out "babies."

Spider plants generally do not produce "babies" until they are in a rootbound condition. Just give your plant time, and the young spiders will eventually come. When runners bearing plantlets do appear, place each new plant in a soil-filled pot and hold it in place with a bent paper clip until roots can form. After two or three weeks, cut the plantlet from the runner. Or you can wait until the plantlet's aerial roots (small, white nubs) are about ¼ inch long. Then cut the baby plant from the runner and put it in its own container.

Wait four to six months to fertilize newly potted spider plants; thereafter, fertilize every three or four months. Give the plants bright indirect light and keep the soil moist.

What causes the tips of the leaves on my spider plant's babies to turn brown? Also, the mother plant is beginning to look faded. Does that mean that it needs repotting?

Both mother plant and babies could be suffering from any of several problems—low humidity, inadequate moisture, overfertilization, or fluoride in the water. Letting the soil dry out could also cause brown tips.

To increase humidity, set the plant in a pebble tray. Check soil often to be sure it is always moist, and feed plants every three or four months. To remove chlorine or fluoride from the water, leave tapwater in an uncovered container overnight to allow the gas to dissipate.

Is Swedish ivy easy to grow?

Yes, Swedish ivy is easy to grow and will even thrive in plain water. However, it must have very bright indirect light to grow well indoors. Keep the soil barely moist and feed the plant every two months with houseplant fertilizer diluted to half-strength. When stems become leggy, pinch them back to encourage branching, and root the cuttings to make new plants.

Swedish ivy thrives in bright indirect light.

A ti plant requires direct sunlight or at least 12 hours of artificial light.

I am considering a plant light for my ti plant, which is in a fairly dark corner. Please tell me how many hours the light should shine on the plant and from what distance.

A ti (*Cordyline terminalis*) receiving no direct sunlight needs 12 to 16 hours of artificial light a day (800 footcandles). Two 40-watt fluorescent tubes with a reflector can supply this amount only if placed about 6 inches directly above the ti plant. An incandescent 150-watt reflector spotlight will provide enough light at a distance of 3½ feet. Keep the soil moist at all times, and place the container on a pebble tray to raise the humidity.

I recently received a dwarf umbrella tree as a gift. How should I care for it?

The dwarf umbrella tree (*Brassaia actinophylla* Arboricola), often called schefflera, is a long-lived plant, even more tolerant of relatively low-light levels and cool temperatures than the standard umbrella tree. But to look its best, this miniature tree prefers plenty of bright indirect light and a warm environment (nighttime temperatures of 65 to 70 degrees and daytime levels of 70 to 75 degrees). Avoid setting your plant in direct sunlight, as it may burn or scorch the tender foliage.

Dwarf umbrella trees may drop leaves if given too much or too little water. Allow the soil to become partially dry, then water thoroughly, gently flooding the soil until water runs from the container's drainage holes. Numerous light sprinklings usually do little more than allow salt residues to build up in the soil. The residues burn the leaf tips and cause browning.

Wait about six months to fertilize new plants or those that have just been repotted. Then feed young specimens bimonthly with an 18-18-18 liquid fertilizer during the spring and summer months. Fertilize mature plants once or twice a year.

Few pests or diseases trouble dwarf umbrella trees except spider mites. Even these pests may be discouraged by spraying the plants monthly with warm, soapy water. If large numbers of mites appear, a Kelthane spray applied according to label directions usually provides complete control. (Never spray the plant indoors.)

When dwarf umbrella trees become severely rootbound, repot them in a rich, well-drained sterile potting soil.

A young specimen of dwarf umbrella tree is both compact and bushy.

My wax plant is at least three years old. It has an abundance of beautiful foliage but has never bloomed. I was told that the blooms are borne on the runners and that I should not trim them as I had been doing. Now some of the runners are 3 or 4 feet long, and I still have no blossoms. Can you tell me why?

Most gardeners grow wax plant for its rich, glossy foliage. It normally blooms in summer but has a reputation for being reluctant to bloom until completely potbound. During its growing and blooming season, give it at least five hours of sun. During winter, let it rest or grow very slowly. Withhold food and give it just enough water to prevent wilting. If possible, keep it in a rather dry place where the temperature is about 50 degrees.

Toward spring, start it into growth again by keeping the soil moist, not wet, and by feeding every two or three weeks with a regular houseplant fertilizer according to directions on the label. As summer approaches, begin feeding with a low-nitrogen fertilizer. Fertilizer high in nitrogen encourages foliage growth at the expense of flower bud development. If the plant blooms, leave the flower heads undisturbed. New flower clusters form on the stems of the old ones.

Wax plant is usually grown for its foliage but may be coaxed into bloom once it becomes potbound.

Pests & Diseases

Larvae of Pine Sawfly

Japanese Wax Scale

Insects, diseases, and weeds in the garden are problems for most people; but there are steps you can take to keep pests and diseases to a minimum. To discourage diseases from forming on ornamentals, water them in late morning after the dew has dried, or in early afternoon so that the foliage dries before the dew falls; this will help eliminate the moist conditions that many fungi need to develop. Thin and space plants properly to allow good air circulation, which helps keep foliage dry. Remove fallen leaves and diseased plant parts to eliminate a source of reinfection, and use clean mulches like pine straw to help discourage some soilborne diseases. To prevent the development of recurring diseases, spray every year before the problem starts.

Most of these practices also help prevent diseases in the vegetable garden. However, some diseases, like powdery mildew, develop in spring and fall when the humidity and temperature are favorable. In these cases, early spraying and planting resistant selections are the best solutions. To delay insect entry into the garden, clean up garden waste regularly during the year to eliminate breeding and overwintering sites. Turn the soil

Squash Vine Borer

Cross-Striped Cabbageworms

Grasshopper

Aphids

Japanese Wax Scale

146

after the last fall harvest and again in late winter; this procedure will kill overwintering insects by exposing them to freezing temperatures.

If, in spite of taking precautions to prevent pests or diseases, a problem does develop, then the next course of action is to correctly identify the cause. On ornamentals, for example, leaf yellowing or stippling, deformed leaves, and chewed foliage are typical signs of insect damage. Leaf yellowing, which may be spotty or may cover the entire leaf, can point to sap-sucking insects such as aphids, scales, lacebugs, mealybugs, mites, whiteflies, and psyllids; most of these insects are present on the undersides of leaves or on stems. Deformed leaves may also result from their feeding. Chewed foliage is the work of caterpillars, grasshoppers, and beetles.

After you identify the problem, you can select an appropriate pesticide or control; but keep in mind that a pesticide that will control one pest or disease may not affect another pest or disease. If you have doubts about the identification or solution of a problem, consult your county Extension agent or a nurseryman. And before you apply any

Mexican Bean Beetle

Sooty Mold

Pine Sawfly Larvae

Fire Blight

Leaf Miner

Cabbageworm

Bagworm

pesticides, be sure to read the label carefully and follow its directions. Water plants several hours before applying chemicals, because drought-stressed plants can be burned by pesticides. Plants may also be injured if pesticides are applied when temperatures are above 85 degrees or below 40 degrees on the day of application or up to 48 hours afterward. Try to spray in early morning, late afternoon, or on an overcast day, since plants may be burned if direct sun falls on the foliage before the pesticide evaporates. To protect yourself when using pesticides, wear rubber gloves and protective clothing, and do not stand downwind in pesticide drifts.

If you prefer to keep the use of chemical controls to a minimum, you can enlist the aid of some beneficial insects. Insectivorous insects, which eat harmful pests, include dragonflies, praying mantids, ladybugs, lacewings (and their larvae, known as aphid lions), firefly grubs, ground beetles, centipedes and larvae of syrphid flies. Parasitic insects, such as some tiny wasps and certain flies, lay eggs on the bodies of pests. When the eggs hatch, the larvae feed on the host's body until it is destroyed.

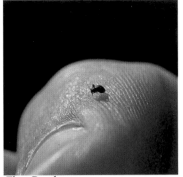

Flea Beetle

Tomato Hornworm

Black Spot

Dandelions

Tea Scale

Plantain

Trees, Shrubs, and Flowers

The leaves on my ornamentals are yellowing between the veins and growth is stunted. What is causing this?

The leaf yellowing, or chlorosis, and stunted growth you describe are probably caused by a mineral deficiency. Although most Southern soils contain adequate amounts of most or all essential nutrients, soil pH should be about 6.5 for these nutrients to be available and absorbed through the plant roots. In neutral or alkaline soils, minerals such as iron, magnesium, and manganese may be present in an insoluble form, and therefore unavailable to plants.

Correct iron chlorosis with a foliar spray of ferrous sulfate. For a long-term solution, treat the soil with ferrous sulfate and sulfur, or with chelated iron. Magnesium deficiency can be corrected by adding dolomitic limestone, Epsom salts, or fertilizers containing magnesium. Manganese deficiency can be corrected by adding manganese sulfate to the soil, or spraying foliage with a minor element spray.

I cannot seem to keep powdery mildew off of my ornamentals, especially my crepe myrtle. Any suggestions?

Under extreme conditions of high humidity and poor air circulation, powdery mildew on crepe myrtle and other ornamentals is difficult to control. It can be recognized by the white, circular spots that form on the leaves. These spots become irregularly shaped and darker in color. Leaves may curl and become distorted, but generally powdery mildew does not cause serious damage.

Most fungicides are preventives, not cures. That means that the fungicide must be on the plants before the disease organisms invade. Use cycloheximide, karathane, or benomyl for best results. Either continue to spray your plants for partial control, or replace them with plants that are less subject to disease attack. Check with your nurseryman for appropriate replacements.

Some of my landscape plants are covered with a black sootlike coating. What could it be?

It is sooty mold, a fungus that grows on the excretions (honeydew) of sucking pests like aphids, whiteflies, soft scales, and mealybugs. The fungus is not directly harmful to the plant. But the thick, black coating that it forms blocks out light so that the plant

Chlorosis, or leaf yellowing, due to mineral deficiency can usually be corrected with a minor element spray applied to the foliage.

Powdery mildew on ornamentals appears as a white, powdery fungus covering the leaves.

Most aphids are green, black, or brown. They are usually inconspicuous, feeding in junctions of leaves and stems.

Sooty mold is the black fungus that grows on the excretions of sucking insects such as whiteflies, aphids, mealybugs, and soft scales.

In an early stage of development, whiteflies attach themselves to the underside of leaves. It is then that they are most destructive, not during the flying stage.

Soft scales are usually found on stems or the underside of leaves. They are attached to the plant and not free to move.

Wax scale shows up on plant stems and branches as white, waxy balls that look like candle wax.

foliage does not receive enough sunlight to manufacture food. Consequently, the plant is weakened.

Sooty mold will eventually flake off the foliage, or you can use dormant oil to peel it off. The only way to prevent its occurrence is to prevent infestations of the sucking insects that secrete honeydew. If the insects are present, treat with Diazinon® or malathion, mixed and applied according to label directions.

How can I tell if my garden plants have wax scale?

Wax scale is one of the easiest scale insects to spot on your garden plants. This soft, white scale is found on ornamentals such as podocarpus, gardenia, camellia, and Southern magnolia. The ⅛- to ¼-inch scales resemble white candle wax. Their color ranges from pink (when young) to white or creamy white when mature.

Wax scale is most often found on limbs and stems of plants, rarely on the leaves. It can be difficult to control, and repeated applications of pesticides may be needed. On small shrubs, or for limited populations, remove the scales by hand before you spray the plant. In removing the adults, you will also be removing the many eggs they are holding underneath. Each scale may contain a hundred eggs that are unaffected by sprays, and repeated applications are necessary to kill young crawlers after they hatch. Spray infested plants with dormant oil as described for camellias.

Japanese beetles are ruining our trees and shrubs. How can we control them?

Japanese beetles feed on hundreds of shade trees, flowers, shrubs, and fruits. The foliage looks like lace after they finish eating the tissue between the veins; flowers and ripening fruit may be completely demolished.

Female beetles lay eggs under grass roots. Grubs hatch 10 to 12 days later and spend the summer feeding on the grass roots. They overwinter in the soil, then emerge the

Japanese beetles are destructive throughout the summer.

following spring as ⅜-inch-long, metallic-green and brown adult beetles that are active from spring through fall. Adults may be controlled with methoxychlor, Isotox®, malathion, carbaryl, or rotenone, applied according to label directions. Or, if you prefer not to use chemicals, try beetle traps, which attract the pests with a combination of floral lure and sex pheromones. Grubs may be controlled with bacterial milky disease spores, but this may take three years to produce results. In addition, the spores are only effective if used over a large area, such as a whole neighborhood. If you treat a small area, it will be quickly reinfested by adult beetles from nearby areas because beetles are constantly moving from place to place.

Some of my trees have tent caterpillars. Will they spread to other trees? How can I control them?

Eastern tent caterpillars will often spread from tree to tree, feeding on foliage and young twigs. The caterpillars hatch in early March and build a webby tent in a fork of the tree on which they overwintered. To control these pests, spray the tents and caterpillars with *Bacillus thuringiensis* or carbaryl according to label directions. Begin sprays when tents first appear, and completely cover the infested area. Repeat *Bacillus* sprays after two weeks; use carbaryl every seven days until the caterpillars are under control. Acephate also controls tent caterpillars on certain trees. Check the label for specific recommendations.

The leaves on my azaleas are rust-colored on the underside and bleached and splotched on the upper side. What is causing this?

The damage probably signals azalea lacebug, the major pest of azaleas. These bugs also feed on firethorn and cotoneaster, sucking sap from the underside of the leaves. The almost colorless nymphs begin appearing in early spring. By early summer, they are ⅛-inch-long adults with lacy brown and black wings. They lay eggs in the leaves along the veins, and a month later, a second population emerges.

Control lacebugs with Isotox®, malathion, methoxychlor (nymphs), acephate, or carbaryl, applied according to label directions. Be sure to cover the underside of leaves thoroughly. Two applications will probably be necessary to control both generations.

Last summer my boxwoods developed blistered, yellow leaves, which dropped off. What should I do to prevent this from recurring?

Your boxwoods were probably infested with boxwood leaf miner, the most destructive boxwood pest. Although a different insect from the holly leaf miner, the boxwood leaf miner works in basically the same way, tunneling between the upper and lower surfaces of the leaves. This causes irregular swellings or blisters in the leaf and eventual defoliation.

The boxwood leaf miner overwinters in the leaf as a partly grown larva. In early spring it completes its growth, emerging as a fly and leaving a white pupal skin attached to the underside of the leaf. Females lay eggs on the underside of new leaves within 24 hours of emergence. The eggs hatch in early summer and the larvae begin feeding on the new growth. To control boxwood leaf miners, spray in early spring as soon as you see gnatlike, orange yellow flies beginning to emerge. Or, contact your county Extension agent for the timing of sprays in your area. Use carbaryl, Diazinon®, malathion, or dimethoate (a systemic insecticide), according to label directions. You can also use dimethoate in the summer to kill young miners as they feed.

Eastern tent caterpillars are easily recognized by their tentlike webs.

During the day, tent caterpillars leave their webs to feed on flower buds, foliage, and young twigs.

Lacebugs leave a rusty residue on the underside of firethorn, azalea, and cotoneaster leaves.

Fig. 1 *Camellias infected with petal blight are marred by brown spots and soft areas on the blossoms.*

Enlarged, thickened growth on camellias is caused by a fungus.

A white fuzz on the underside of camellia leaves usually indicates an infestation of tea scale. Healthy plants have glossy green leaves (right).

Peony scale attacks the stems of camellias and appears either as raised, white bumps or sunken, white lesions.

Bagworms are among the worst pests of narrow-leaf evergreens such as cedar and juniper.

Some of the leaves on my camellias and azaleas are thickened and distorted. What could be wrong?

Large, thickened, distorted leaves often found on camellias and evergreen azaleas during cool, moist weather are caused by a fungus, *Exobasidium camelliae* (camellia leaf gall). The upper surface of the leaves is usually the normal color, but the underside is white and covered by a thin membrane that can be peeled off to expose the fungus spores.

The disease usually occurs in the fall or spring, when moisture and temperature conditions are ideal for development of the fungus. The fungus does not do serious or permanent damage to the plant and will disappear in the warmer weather of spring and summer. Handpicking the affected foliage is usually all that is needed to control the disease. Also, pick up any fallen diseased tissue and discard it, since it will cause a return of the disease next year if environmental conditions are right.

Some of our camellia blossoms have developed small brownish specks at the tips of the petals, and the centers of some blossoms turn soft and brown. What should we do?

The camellias are probably infected with petal blight. (*See Figure 1.*) The fungus that causes the disease lies dormant in old flowers, mulch, and soil beneath the plant. Remove old mulch and blighted flowers from the plant and ground. Spray opening flowers and the ground under the plant with zineb according to label directions. Drenching the soil with captan or Terraclor® can also help control the fungus.

Some of the leaves of my camellias have a white fuzzy coating on the underside. What is this? Will it harm the plant?

It is probably tea scale, which appears as a white, fuzzy residue on the underside of leaves. Tea scale and peony scale, which appears as white, crusty bumps or sunken white lesions on the stems, are among the most destructive insects of camellias in the South.

While both of these scales are difficult to eliminate, they can be controlled with dormant oil sprays or dimethoate. Spray plants with dormant oil in spring after blooming and in fall, before blooming. Use the spray at the rate recommended on the label, and coat stems and undersides of leaves thoroughly. Several applications at least 10 days apart may be needed for control.

When it is too warm to use dormant oil sprays, use dimethoate as a foliar spray at the rate recommended on the label. Repeat the application at monthly intervals until there are no new signs of infestation. Or, apply Di-Syston, repeating applications every 4 to 6 weeks, if necessary.

Dimethoate is also effective when applied as a soil drench, provided the camellias are actively growing. Additional applications at 8- to 10-week intervals may be necessary. If the scale infestation is severe, and most are in the South, use the soil drench in addition to a dimethoate spray program. In late spring and early summer you can use malathion, Diazinon®, carbaryl, acephate, or Isotox® to kill crawlers (young scale that are mobile until they find a permanent location on a plant).

The branches of our cedar trees have silken, needle-covered bags hanging from them. What are they? Should we do anything about them?

Your cedar trees are infested with bagworms, tiny caterpillars which spin the bags and live inside them as they move about, feeding on the foliage of pines, juniper, hemlock, arborvitae, and other evergreens. The best times to control bagworms are winter and early spring, before eggs laid in the fall can hatch.

To control bagworms, pick off all the bags you can reach and burn them. Then spray the plants with malathion, Isotox®, *Bacillus thuringiensis*, acephate, or carbaryl to ensure control. Repeat the application whenever you detect new bags. Dimethoate (Cygon®) is also an effective insecticide for bagworm control, but read the label carefully to avoid spraying plants that may be damaged by this insecticide.

For the past two years the few blooms our pink dogwood produced turned brown when about half open, then dropped off. How can I save the blossoms?

Your dogwood problem sounds like anthracnose. Flowers are stunted and covered with small, tan spots ringed with brown or purple. (*See Figure 2.*) Leaves, stems, and fruit are marked with gray and purple spots. To control this disease, you will need to spray with maneb or Fore®. Apply the fungicide when buds begin opening, when the bracts fall a month later, and again in late summer after next season's flower buds form. Pink dogwoods generally do not perform as well as the white selections and are more susceptible to problems in the landscape.

How can I tell whether borers have attacked my dogwood tree? If they have, is there anything I can do to save the tree?

The lower portion of the dogwood trunk is highly susceptible to attack by borers, especially if the bark has been nicked by a lawn mower. These ½-inch-long caterpillars feed in the cambium (inner, cell-producing layer of bark) of dogwoods. Infested areas may be up to 2 feet long and contain as many as 50 borers. Such populations can quickly girdle and kill the tree. Little can be done to save a badly infested tree.

The best protection is a monthly spray program beginning in early May. Using a solution of lindane mixed according to label directions, spray the trunk and branches to the point of runoff. Repeat in 7 to 10 days. It may be necessary to make a third application two weeks after the second.

To prevent future damage, remove grass from a 2-foot-diameter circle around the tree and mulch so that it will not be necessary to mow close to the trunk.

We have always enjoyed berry-laden branches of firethorn indoors during the Christmas season, but this year the berries turned black when they should have been turning red. The leaves also wilted and turned black. What happened?

Apparently your firethorn (pyracantha) is infected with fire blight. (*See Figure 3.*) Cut off all infected branches at least 6 inches below any sign of disease and destroy them. Disinfect pruning tools with a 10 percent solution of household bleach after each cut. If left untreated, fire blight will produce cankers on the limbs in spring; these cankers will ooze bacteria in wet spring weather, further spreading the disease.

Streptomycin will kill the bacteria that causes fire blight and is used on apple and pear trees. In some states it is also labeled for use on ornamentals. Check with your county Extension agent for this information.

The leaves on our holly tree have small lines winding through them. They are not dead, but they look bad. What is the problem and how can it be controlled?

Holly leaf miners are the problem. These larvae of a tiny black fly feed between the upper and lower surfaces of leaves. Because the insects are not exposed to a direct spray,

Fig. 2 *Blossoms on a dogwood infected with anthracnose are covered with brown and purple spots.*

Fig. 3 *Fireblight causes the leaves of firethorn to wilt and turn black.*

Winding lines scarring holly leaves are the result of holly leaf miners feeding between the upper and lower surfaces of the leaves.

Pitch tubes, created by resin that oozes from the holes where a beetle has entered the tree, are the first indication of Southern pine beetle infestation.

Sawfly damage is evident at the top of this Mugo pine, where the sawflies have stripped the plant needles.

control is difficult. In early spring, watch your holly carefully. When you see swarms of black flies around new growth, spray with Isotox® or Diazinon®. This should kill many of the adults before they can lay eggs in the new leaves.

The palm trees around our Florida home are turning yellow and dying. We have been told they have lethal yellowing. Please tell us what this is and what we can do about it.

Lethal yellowing is a highly destructive disease caused by a microorganism that lives in the sap of certain palm trees. It is spread from tree to tree by a type of sap-sucking insect. Symptoms of lethal yellowing may take six months to two years to appear after trees have been infected. There is no cure for the disease, but it can be prevented by injecting palms with tetracycline every four months.

Lethal yellowing is a relatively new problem in Florida, and the disease and its treatment are still being researched. Before you purchase palms for your landscape, consult your county Extension agent.

Southern pine beetles are a problem in our area. Is there any way to protect our trees from this pest?

Southern pine beetles are a serious pest of pine trees in the South. Old pines and those weakened by improper care are most susceptible; but when the beetles reach epidemic proportions, even the healthiest pines are not safe. Slash pines and longleaf pines resist attack better than other types.

The first sign of infestation is the presence of pitch tubes in the trunks of pines; this is where pine resin has oozed out of the bark through the entrance holes made by the beetles. Initially, the beetles attack the midsection of the tree; later, entrance holes may be found along the entire length of the trunk.

In dry weather, pitch tubes may not be present; the beetles are then indicated by sawdustlike red boring dust that collects at their entrance holes, in bark crevices, spider webs, and at the base of the tree. If you peel away the bark, you will find S-shaped galleries made by the beetles. Several other pine beetles also make galleries under the bark, but they are different patterns. Consult your county Extension agent if you are not sure about correct identification.

The final stage of infestation is the turning of the pine needles to yellow, then red, and eventually to brown as the tree dies.

Pines infested with Southern pine beetles must be cut down and removed from your property. Immediate removal is critical, since the beetles spend only three to five weeks in a tree before moving on to infest other trees. Thorough cleanup of all debris from the infested tree is also essential.

Many of the stems of my Mugo, Virginia, and white pines are naked. What could be causing this?

Your pines are probably being attacked by sawfly larvae. These caterpillarlike insects feed on pine needles in late summer and fall.

Sawfly larvae are actually the larvae of nonstinging wasps. The most common sawfly larva that attacks pines is about an inch long and green yellow, with rows of black spots down its body. The head may be red or black, depending on the species. In the Upper South, there is also a species that has longitudinal lines instead of spots running down its back. But it, too, can be distinguished as a sawfly by its seven pairs of prolegs (the stumpy legs that carry the long body) instead of the two to five pairs characteristic of true caterpillars.

To control a large population of sawflies, spray with carbaryl according to label directions. For young trees or small pines like Mugo, you can control small numbers by handpicking sawflies from the plants.

Last year I grew bedding plants from seeds. The seedlings looked good at first, but soon all of them were dead. What can I do to avoid the problem this year?

The problem was most likely caused by damping off, a common fungus problem in warm, humid conditions. Using sterilized potting soil or a sterile medium, such as vermiculite, perlite, or sphagnum moss, should prevent damping off. If you start seeds outdoors, apply Terraclor® or captan to the soil before sowing seeds. You can also dust the seeds with a protectant containing thiram. (*See Figure 4.*)

Last year all the top leaves of my cannas were twisted and rolled up together and never opened. Of course, I got no flowers. What could have been wrong?

Your cannas were infested with canna leaf rollers. The lesser canna leaf roller is an inch-long, greenish white caterpillar. This pest fastens young rolled-up leaves together, feeding on the foliage and leaving it ragged. Leaves may turn brown and die. The larger canna leaf roller is ¾ inch long and green with an orange head and narrow neck. It cuts a strip from the edge of the leaf, folds it over itself, and then eats large holes in the leaf.

To prevent an infestation of leaf rollers, spray plants with carbaryl as soon as new growth begins. It is important to apply the insecticide before leaf rollers can begin rolling the leaves. Once they are inside the leaves, they are protected from pesticides and are very difficult to control. Individual caterpillars may be killed by smashing them. The lesser canna leaf roller can also be controlled by cleaning up debris around the plants.

This year I intend to keep my roses free of black spot disease. What chemicals should I use?

Folpet is one of the most effective chemicals for control of black spot on roses. It is available as either a liquid or a dust. Make the first application just as the new leaves begin to unfold. Continue the applications weekly throughout the growing season as a preventive, not a cure. If black spot should become a problem while using folpet, switch to maneb or benomyl, and apply as recommended on the label.

You can simplify rose care by using one of the combination sprays or dusts especially formulated for roses. Most of these contain a total of three or four fungicides and insecticides to control the most common rose pests and diseases.

I am having a difficult time controlling aphids on my roses. What kind of controls do you suggest?

Spraying regularly with malathion, acephate, Di-Syston, or dimethoate should keep aphids under control. All except malathion are systemic (that is, absorbed by the plant's tissues). Aphids reproduce rapidly, so you will need to spray frequently to control them. If weekly spraying is not having an effect, spray twice a week. If rain washes the insecticide off before it dries on the foliage, reapply after it stops raining. Aphids develop resistance to some chemicals, so alternate insecticides for maximum effectiveness. Many rose sprays combine insecticides and fungicides for total pest and disease control for roses. Look for a spray containing a pesticide recommended for control of aphids.

Most needles are chewed completely back to the stem as a result of pine sawfly larvae feeding.

Inch-long, greenish yellow pine sawflies make their appearance in late summer and fall.

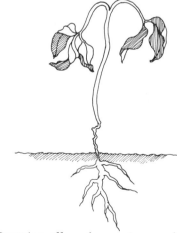

Fig. 4 *Damping off can be a serious problem for bedding plants.*

Praying mantids are the gardener's allies. They feed on aphids, beetles, flies and other insects that damage plants.

Mexican bean beetles feed on the underside of bean leaves. They can be recognized by their golden color and black spots that appear on their backs.

The bean leaf roller is easy to identify by its blue green color and large black head.

The bean leaf roller usually stays under the folded leaf when it is not feeding.

Vegetables and Fruits

I would like to keep the use of chemicals in my garden to a minimum. Can you suggest some natural ways to control pests and diseases?

The practices suggested for a productive garden will also help you to have a healthy garden. Tilling the soil between growing seasons aerates the soil and helps kill insects overwintering in the ground. Choosing disease-resistant selections helps keep problems from getting a foothold. Thinning seedlings to avoid overcrowding promotes good air circulation, which helps prevent fungus diseases. Keeping the ground free of weeds, fallen fruit, old vegetable plants, and other debris eliminates a feeding and breeding site for insects.

In addition to these practices, you have a number of animal and insect allies to help you control pests and diseases in your garden. Toads eat about 10,000 insects during a growing season. Insect-eating birds like purple martins, thrushes, warblers, swallows, wrens, and woodpeckers also help reduce insect populations. Attract them with a birdbath full of fresh water, placed out of reach of cats. Scattering nesting materials such as hair, string, and bits of cloth under trees may also encourage birds to build homes near your garden.

Perhaps your most effective natural weapons against pests are the two groups of beneficial insects. The insectivorous insects, which eat harmful pests, include dragonflies, praying mantids, ladybugs, lacewings (and their larvae, known as aphid lions), firefly grubs, ground beetles, centipedes, and larvae of syrphid flies. The parasitic insects, such as some tiny wasps and certain flies, lay their eggs on the bodies of pests. When the eggs hatch, the larvae feed on the body of the host until it is destroyed.

I have just planted several rows of beans. What kinds of pests should I watch for?

The worst pest of beans is the Mexican bean beetle. These insects chew on the underside of leaves between the veins until the leaves take on a laced appearance. The mature insect resembles a large ladybug beetle. Like the ladybug, it has brown spots; but the bean beetle is closer to copper in color and has exactly sixteen spots, while different ladybugs have varying numbers. The larvae are bright yellow, spiny, and oval shaped, and are usually found on the underside of the leaves. If not controlled, Mexican bean beetles can destroy a small planting of beans in a week or two.

To control bean beetles, spray or dust plants with carbaryl, rotenone, or malathion every four or five days until the bean beetles are gone. Be sure to cover the plant thoroughly with insecticide, especially the underside of the leaves.

Other pests to watch for are mites and bean leaf rollers. Bean leaf roller populations are usually not large enough to require control. Control mites with Kelthane® or malathion.

The leaves on my bean plants are all folded over. What could be the problem?

Your bean plants are probably infested with the bean leaf roller. Named for its habit of rolling up leaves, this yellow green caterpillar has a large black head and constricted neck, making it easy to identify.

Bean leaf rollers are the larvae of skippers, a mostly harmless insect group that exhibits characteristics of both moths and butterflies. Bean leaf rollers feed on plant leaves while hiding under a piece of leaf, which they cut and fold over to form a tentlike home. Usually they are neither serious defoliators nor present in great numbers like bean beetles. To control these pests, simply pick them off.

The foliage on my bean plants is covered with raised rust-colored spots surrounded by yellow, and the leaves are dying and falling off. What is this?

Your bean plants probably have rust. The disease may also cause spots on pods and stems. (*See Figure 5.*) The spores spread rapidly, carried on tools and clothing; they will also overwinter on trellises to infect next year's crop. Beans infected with rust may be sprayed with chlorothalonil or zineb. Or, prevent the disease by dusting plants every 5 to 7 days with maneb, beginning when the plants are small.

Most snap beans are rust tolerant. Kentucky Wonder RR pole bean is a rust-resistant selection recommended for most of the South. Dade is a rust-resistant pole bean selection for South Florida. Resistant lima bean selections include Thorogreen, Henderson's Bush, Nemagreen, Jackson Wonder, and Fordhook 242.

I have planted broccoli, brussels sprouts, cabbage, and cauliflower in my fall garden. What caterpillars should I watch for and how can I control them?

The three caterpillars most destructive to crops in the cabbage family are the cabbage looper, the imported cabbageworm, and the cross-striped cabbageworm.

Cabbage loopers are light-green worms that eat holes in leaves and loop like an inchworm when they move. Imported cabbageworms are also green but move without looping; they feed on the underside of leaves and often bore into the heads of cole crops. Cross-striped cabbageworms are gray when they first hatch; they later develop black stripes across the back and a bright-yellow stripe along each side. They riddle the heads of cabbage and nibble on tender young buds of broccoli and cauliflower.

The most effective control for these caterpillars is *Bacillus thuringiensis*. This insecticide is host-specific; that is, it kills only these and certain other caterpillars but does not affect their natural enemies. Rotenone may also be used for control.

The tips of my corn ears were gnawed and ruined this year. What could have caused this?

Your corn was probably attacked by corn earworms, 1- to 2-inch-long, green- to brown-striped caterpillars. Mature corn earworm moths lay eggs in the silks, and the larvae feed on the silks and developing ears. Their feeding on the silks interferes with pollination, and unpollinated kernels do not fill out. Kernels on which the earworms have fed are susceptible to fungus diseases.

To prevent an infestation of corn earworms, spray or dust plants with carbaryl. Begin spraying when the silks first appear, and repeat the treatment every two or three days until the silks turn brown. If you have only a small planting of corn, an effective measure for warding off corn earworms is to sprinkle a few drops of mineral oil on the silks after they begin to turn brown.

I have found something that looks like corn earworms in my tomatoes. Is this likely?

Corn earworm is the same creature as tomato fruitworm and can be very destructive to your tomato crop. The caterpillars first attack the foliage, then tunnel into the green tomatoes to feed. They move from fruit to fruit, so a small caterpillar population can

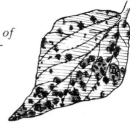

Fig. 5 *Rust causes leaves of bean plants to develop reddish brown spots surrounded by yellow. Spots may also appear on stems and pods.*

Holes in the leaves of plants in the cabbage family are often the work of cabbage loopers and imported cabbageworms.

Imported cabbageworms feed on the underside of leaves and may bore into the heads of cole crops.

The corn earworm feeds on silks and developing kernels. It can destroy the entire ear.

Tiny holes scattered all over a leaf indicate an infestation of flea beetles.

Hornworms should be removed while they are still small.

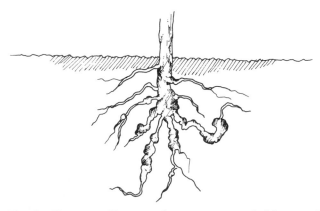

Fig. 6 *Knotty swellings on plant roots are probably caused by root-knot nematodes.*

Powdery mildew and downy mildew have a similar appearance on squash but develop under different weather conditions.

damage many tomatoes. These pests will also feed on beans, cabbage, broccoli, and lettuce. A natural parasite, the pupae of the braconid wasp, kills many caterpillars while they are on the fruit. You can also control them with carbaryl applied as soon as you see the insects or their damage.

Leaves on my eggplants are riddled with tiny holes. The damage seems to have been done by a tiny black beetle. How can I control this pest?

The pest is probably flea beetle, which makes tiny holes in leaves and jumps like a flea when disturbed. To control flea beetles, spray or dust your plants with carbaryl following label directions. Repeat as often as necessary until 7 to 14 days before harvest, depending on the pesticide used. Flea beetles will also damage potato plants, radishes, corn, and most cole crops.

I understand that hornworms can defoliate an entire tomato plant in a matter of days. Please tell me how to identify and control hornworms so I can protect my tomato plants.

In Southern gardens, two types of hornworms may be present, the tomato hornworm and the tobacco hornworm. Both are large, glossy caterpillars, up to 4 inches long, pale green with diagonal stripes, and a horn on the posterior. However, the tomato hornworm has eight diagonal stripes on its back; the tobacco hornworm has only seven. Also, the horn on the tomato hornworm is black; on the tobacco hornworm, it is red. Both species are equally willing to feed on your tomato plants, as well as on your pepper, eggplant, and potato plants.

Hornworms should be handpicked from plants or sprayed as soon as you discover them. Do not be wary of the ferocious-looking horn. Hornworms do not sting or bite. It is important to control infestations of hornworms when the worms are still small; they are increasingly difficult to kill as they grow larger.

You can also control hornworms with *Bacillus thuringiensis* sprays or with carbaryl dusts. However, do not kill caterpillars carrying oval white objects; these are cocoons of the parasitic braconid wasp, natural enemies of the hornworm.

My okra and bean plants wilted, turned yellow, and died this year. I dug some of the plants and found the roots were all knotted and covered with swellings. What caused this?

You probably have root-knot nematodes in your garden soil. (*See Figure 6.*) There are several species of these microscopic worms that feed on the roots of a wide variety of vegetable crops, ornamental trees and shrubs, annuals, and perennials. Some species may be controlled by rotating crops. In general, however, fumigating the soil before planting provides the best control. Use Vapam® following label directions carefully. Vapam® can be applied when the soil is warm and the air temperature is below 90 degrees. Wait two to three weeks after fumigating to plant.

A solid planting of French-type marigolds may also provide effective control, but you will not be able to use that area for vegetable crops that year. The selections Tangerine, Petite Gold, Petite Harmony, and Goldie give best results.

We want to plant squash this year but are not sure about disease control. What should we watch for, and what preventive measures can we take?

Diseases most destructive to squash include downy mildew, powdery mildew, bacterial wilt, squash mosaic, several leaf spots, scab, fruit rot, and belly rot. There are a few simple measures you can take to limit or prevent these diseases. These include planting disease-resistant selections, rotating crops so that squash is not planted in the same location more often than every three years, and locating the beds in well-drained soil. Here is how to control specific diseases.

—Powdery mildew appears as a white or brown mealy growth on young stems and both sides of the leaves. Downy mildew causes yellow or brownish spots on the top of leaves, and after hot weather white, gray, or black mold may appear on the underside. Powdery mildew is more widespread than downy mildew in dry, hot weather; downy mildew spreads rapidly in cool, wet weather. Both diseases cause leaves to wither, and eventually the plants die. To control downy mildew, spray plants with captan, maneb, zineb, or chlorothalonil. To control powdery mildew, spray with karathane or copper.

—Bacterial wilt is characterized by sudden wilting, followed by rapid decline of the plant. This disease is spread by cucumber beetles. To control, remove and destroy all infected plants, and spray or dust remaining plants with malathion or a commercially available maneb-carbaryl mixture to control the cucumber beetle.

—Squash mosaic, a viral disease, is spread by the cucumber beetle and aphids. Leaves are curled, deformed, and yellow between the veins. The fruit may be deformed, warty, or spotted with green. To control mosaic, remove infected plants immediately. Control aphids and cucumber beetles with malathion to limit the spread of the disease.

—Fruit rot or blossom blight commonly affects summer squash in humid, wet weather. A white fungus covers flowers and young fruit, becoming brown and then purple. A soft rot develops at the blossom end of the fruit. To control the disease, grow squash on well-drained land that was not used for cucurbits or melons the previous year. Spray plants with copper or zineb and remove infected flowers and fruit.

What kind of insects should I watch for on my squash?

Squash are subject to attack by a number of insects, especially during late summer. Of these, the squash-vine borer is the most destructive. These white worms are 1 inch long or less. They tunnel inside the stems, causing plants to wilt suddenly. The best treatment is preventive. When the plants are about 6 inches tall, dust the foliage, stems, and especially the base of the plants weekly with rotenone, carbaryl, or methoxychlor.

Other pests that can damage squash include squash beetle, striped cucumber beetle, pickleworm, and squash bug. The squash beetle, golden yellow with 14 black spots on its back, is not a major pest. The striped cucumber beetle is yellowish with three black stripes. The adult feeds on foliage and flowers, and the larva attacks plant roots.

If you see any of these pests on your squash vines, spray weekly with carbaryl. It is particularly important to apply insecticide on the underside of the leaves as well as on the upper surface. To avoid killing bees as they pollinate the plants, spray in the late afternoon when bees are less active, and avoid wetting the blossoms with the spray. In small plantings, you may prefer to handpick and destroy insects rather than apply insecticides.

What insects should I watch for around my strawberry plants?

As weather warms and strawberries ripen, plants may be threatened by spider mites, leaf rollers, spittlebugs, Japanese beetle larvae, grubworms, slugs, and ants. The most damaging pest of strawberries, however, is probably the pill bug, also called roly-poly or sow bug. This oval, ½-inch-long, dark-gray or brown insect curls into a ball when disturbed. Like its distant cousin the crayfish, the pill bug breathes through gills. It lives

Blossom-end rot will cause deformed flowers. The affected flowers will not produce fruit.

Bacterial wilt, suffered by the plants at the end of this row, causes sudden wilting and decline of plants.

Pillbugs or roly-polies are probably the most damaging pests of strawberries.

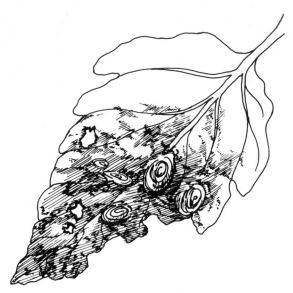

Fig. 7 *Early blight of tomato.*

Fig. 8 *Blossom-end rot appears as sunken areas on the bottom of the fruit.*

in damp, protected places, under flower pots or rotting boards, or in the soil.

Pill bugs, leaf rollers, spittlebugs, and adult Japanese beetles can be controlled by spraying with carbaryl. Malathion will control spider mites. Be sure to read label instructions, however, since application will be so close to harvesttime. Make applications of insecticide, if necessary, after each picking.

What diseases should we watch for on our tomato plants?

Some of the most common tomato disease are early blight, late blight, fusarium wilt, and verticillium wilt. Early blight first appears on the lower leaves of the plant as round, dark-brown spots with concentric rings. (*See Figure 7.*) The spots fuse, blighting most or all of the leaf. On older plants, stems may develop sunken spots or lesions, and the tomatoes have dark, leathery spots near the stem end.

Late blight appears on seedlings as small dark spots on leaves or stems, and seedlings quickly die. Older plants develop dark, water-soaked spots on leaves and large brown spots on fruit. As the disease progresses, leaves die and fruit rots. Both early and late blight may be controlled with captan, maneb, or zineb.

Fusarium wilt causes seedlings to droop, wilt, and die. Leaves of older plants turn yellow first on one side of the stem, then the other, then wither and die. The fungus enters through the roots, grows into the stem, and in severe infections, grows into the fruit and seed. Fruit usually drops, however. Fusarium wilt begins in the soil, thriving in light sandy soil and warm temperatures. Low potassium and high nitrogen make the condition worse. To prevent infections, use resistant selections, start seedlings in clean soil, and rotate tomato plantings every year.

Verticillium wilt shows symptoms similar to fusarium wilt, except that the whole plant is affected at the same time. Prevent verticillium wilt by planting resistant selections. Tomato selections recommended for the South and resistant to both verticillium and fusarium wilt include Small Fry, Heinz 1350, Tropic, Roma, Beefmaster, Better Boy, Floramerica Hybrid, Rutgers Hybrid, Sunripe, and Super Fantastic.

My tomatoes are rotting at the flower end. What kind of spray should I use to protect the oncoming tomatoes?

This condition is known as blossom-end rot. It appears as sunken spots on the blossom end of the fruit and develops into dark, leathery areas. (*See Figure 8.*) It usually occurs when the early part of the season has been wet, followed by drought. Calcium deficiency also encourages the disease. This year, spray your plants with a 1 percent calcium chloride solution and maintain an even supply of moisture in the soil by mulching and irrigating. Next year, when you prepare the beds, lime the soil to increase the supply of calcium available to the plants. And again, maintain an even moisture supply with mulch and irrigation.

Houseplants

How can I control insects on my houseplants?

Inspect all your plants regularly. Place those with any sign of insect infestation in a room away from other houseplants or outside in the shade. Insects can spread to other houseplants rapidly.

If the infestation is light, you may be able to control it by sponging the foliage with a solution of mild liquid dishwashing detergent and warm water (2 teaspoons detergent to a gallon of water). However, if the infestation is severe, you may have to use a chemical insecticide. If you must spray, do it outdoors.

A good way to ensure thorough coverage of small houseplants with insecticides is to fill a bucket or plastic wastebasket with water, add the recommended amount of concentrated insecticide (liquid or wettable powder), and dip the plant to the soil line into the solution. To keep the soil from sliding out of the pot, cover loose soil with newspaper and hold it back with your hand.

Do not exceed the manufacturer's recommended dosage in preparing insecticide solutions. And be sure not to use the container that held the insecticide solution for any other purpose. Wear gloves to protect your hands from coming in contact with pesticides.

Something that looks like small blotches of cotton has appeared on the leaves and stems of some of my houseplants. What is it?

Your plants are infested with mealybugs, insects that attack outdoor plants in warm weather and indoor plants year-round. These soft-bodied members of the scale family are about 1/16 to ¼ inch long. They usually move about in colonies, feeding on stems and leaves, preferring the junctions of leaves and stems and other tight, protected places on the plant. Mealybugs may also appear as masses of white, powdery specks which discolor the underside of leaves. The root or ground mealybug lives in the soil and feeds on the roots of African violets and other houseplants, damaging young, tender roots; plants infected with root mealybugs wilt despite watering.

If the infestation on your houseplants is not severe, try dipping a cotton swab in alcohol and swabbing the mealybugs off the plants. Heavily infested plants should be taken outdoors and sprayed with malathion according to label directions. A houseplant insecticide containing pyrethrins and rotenone will control mealybugs on African violet, philodendron, ivy, rubber plant, pothos, peperomia, begonia, gardenia, and similar plants.

I have discovered scale insects on several of my ferns. Should I spray them with an insecticide?

Although the use of insecticides on ferns is usually discouraged, if scale is present, your options are to destroy the plants or spray them. If you spray, use a weak solution of nicotine emulsion according to label directions. Before treating the entire plant, test the spray on one or two fronds to see whether damage occurs. You might also contact the nursery where you purchased the plant and ask whether they have found an insecticide that controls scale on your kind of ferns without damaging the plants.

How do I get rid of spider mites on palms?

The occurrence of spider mites is worse in warm, dry rooms with poor air circulation. Provide favorable conditions for your palms, and you will probably avoid the problem. (*See* Chapter 4, "Houseplants," for the palm's cultural requirements.)

If spider mites should develop, take the plant outdoors and wash the leaves, especially the undersides, with a mild soap solution to help dislodge the pests. Insecticides like Kelthane® and malathion are available for treatment of mite infestations. Spray the plant outdoors following label directions. A follow-up treatment is usually required to completely rid the plant of mites. Regular misting or hosing palms outdoors may help prevent infestation.

Mealybugs look like bits of cotton on the leaves and stems of plants.

Soft brown scale clusters along the stems of ferns and many other indoor plants.

Grasshoppers are usually not serious pests of home gardens unless they are present in great numbers.

Other Pests

How can I tell whether chinch bugs are the cause of yellow patches that have appeared in our St. Augustine lawn?

Hairy chinch bugs are tiny black insects with short white wings. Adults and the bright-red nymphs feed on grass blades through the summer. As a result of hairy chinch bug activity, circular patches of turf turn brown with a yellow perimeter that indicates a new feeding ground. To confirm the presence of the insects, remove the top and bottom of a tin can and force it 2 inches into the edge of a yellowing area in the turf. Fill the can with water, and wait about 10 minutes. Any chinch bugs present will float to the top. Spray the lawn with Diazinon® or carbaryl according to label directions to control the insect.

If no chinch bugs are present, the yellowing patches could be caused by brown patch of turf, a root and leaf rot. Symptoms are similar to hairy chinch bug injury. Circular areas 1 inch to 3 feet in diameter turn black, then pale brown. In warm, humid weather, the disease spreads rapidly. Brown patch can be controlled with Terraclor®, chlorothalonil, captan, or Fore®.

Recently grasshoppers have invaded our yard. What can we do?

Most species of grasshoppers are not serious pests to home gardens. They probably laid eggs in your garden last season and are now all hatching out at the same time. If the infestation is heavy and they are chewing up your vegetables or ornamentals, dust your plants with carbaryl.

Can wheel bugs sting humans?

Yes. Wheel bugs can sting you with the same long mouthparts they use to kill caterpillars and other garden insects. Identified by the wheel-like crest on their back, wheel bugs are dark-brown, long-legged insects over an inch long whose abdomen flattens out on the sides like an airfoil. They belong to a family of insects commonly known as assassin bugs, so named because they feed on other insects.

The wheel bug and related insects do not kill their prey by completely eating them; instead, they suck body juices with their long, beaklike mouthparts, part of which are folded under the head. Because of their feeding habit, wheel bugs and related insects help control caterpillars and other soft-bodied insects that damage vegetable crops and ornamental plants.

Since wheel bugs are rarely present in large numbers, they will not be a hazard to you in the garden if you do not aggravate or handle them. If they are on a plant you need to handle, shake the plant or prod them gently with an object. They are not aggressive and will fly away.

How can I control weeds in my lawn?

Weeds have little opportunity to become a problem when the lawn grass used is adapted to the area and proper attention is given to feeding, watering, and mowing. When one of these practices is ignored, the grass is weakened and weeds begin to invade the lawn.

The wheel bug is easily identified by the wheellike crest on its back.

If the infestation is light, handweeding is perhaps the most practical way to tackle the problem. Regular, frequent mowing will control many weeds. If weeds are wide-spread, the best solution is to use a herbicide, one that will kill the weeds and do the least damage to the lawn grass.

Broadleaved weeds make up the largest group of weeds that attack lawns. These include such familiar kinds as dandelion, chickweed, henbit, plantain, buckthorn, and spurge. These weeds can be controlled with materials containing 2,4-D or a combination of dicamba and 2,4-D. Follow directions on the labels very carefully, as these herbicides will injure many ornamentals and crop plants if the spray gets on the foliage. Do not use dicamba and 2,4-D on St. Augustine or centipede lawns. When used in liquid form, chemicals should be applied on a calm day.

The grassy weeds (nutgrass, crabgrass, Johnson grass, annual bluegrass, goose grass, Bahia grass, and Dallis grass) can be controlled with monosodium acid methanearsonate (MSMA). Do not use on centipede, St. Augustine, carpet, Bahia, or bent grass lawns. MSMA also controls chickweed and wood sorrel. Before applying any chemicals, be sure you have identified your weed problem correctly. Your nurseryman or county Extension agent can help you with this and advise you on the best herbicide to use.

An alternative to controlling weeds after they emerge is to use a selective preemergence herbicide, such as Dacthal® W-75 herbicide. This wettable powder kills the seeds of crabgrass, chickweed, and certain other grassy and broadleaved weeds before they germinate. Do not apply Dacthal® W-75 herbicide to a newly seeded lawn until the grass seedlings are 1 to 2 inches tall, or you will kill the turf grass seeds as well as the weeds. Follow all label directions carefully.

Fig. 9 *Florida betony.*

Every year dandelions are a nuisance in our lawn. How can we kill these weeds?

Control dandelions with a weed killer containing 2, 4-D and dicamba. Be sure to follow directions on the container label. Avoid getting the chemical on flowering shrubs or other desirable broadleaf plants because it can also kill them.

Please tell me how to get rid of Florida betony.

For postemergence control of Florida betony (*Stachys floridana*), use Purge™. Follow label instructions for application. (*See Figure 9.*)

Fig. 10 *When you apply a herbicide to poison ivy, be careful not to let the chemical drift onto desirable plants, as it will kill them as well.*

We want to keep our backyard looking as natural as possible, but a great deal of poison ivy is growing there. What is the best way to kill it?

An herbicide containing 2, 4-D is generally effective in controlling poison ivy. Be sure to follow label directions and precautions closely in applying this chemical; it will also kill desirable broadleaf plants on which it is sprayed. (*See Figure 10.*)

Our lawn is spotted with unsightly toadstools. The grass is healthy, and we have good soil in our yard. What can we do to kill the toadstools?

During humid weather, toadstools often appear on lawns growing in soil that has a high humus content. Although unsightly, toadstools do not damage grass. You can remove them by raking with the back of a rake, breaking the toadstools off at the ground.

Toadstools do not damage grass and may be removed simply by raking with the back of a rake.

Lawns & Ground Covers

St. Augustine Grass

Tall Fescue

For the homeowner, one of the important differences between lawns and ground covers is the amount of maintenance required. A well-cared-for lawn is considered the highest maintenance item in any garden. Ground covers, on the other hand, are planted to reduce or practically eliminate maintenance.

The regions of the South dictate which type of turf grass may be used. Warm-season grass does well in the Lower and most of the Middle South. Most cool-season grasses, on the other hand, cannot tolerate the warmth, humidity, and strong sunlight of the Lower South; but they may be grown in the Upper South and higher elevations of the Middle South. Tall fescue is an exception to this general rule; a cool-season grass, it may be grown in lightly shaded areas and higher elevations throughout the Middle South and in the northernmost regions of the Lower South. The critical decision for homeowners in most of the Middle South is whether you want a refined warm-season lawn that will have to be overseeded each fall with annual ryegrass to stay green all winter, or a coarse-textured turf that grows best in fall and spring but is under stress in the summer.

The style of the lawn should also be considered in choosing turf. Warm-season grass generally can provide the homeowner with either the pale-green unrefined look of Bahia or the formal dark-green look of zoysia. Cool-season grass offers the same diversity—tall

Blue Rug Juniper

English Ivy

Bugleweed and Common Periwinkle

fescue provides an unrefined, informal look while bluegrass can create a blue green carpetlike effect. The important point to remember is that the cultural requirements and care of warm-season grasses are entirely different from cool-season grasses. If your lawn is already established, be sure you know what type of turf grass you have before you attempt to care for it.

A well-kept lawn can be a homeowner's pride and joy, but there are situations in which turf grass will not work well. Steep slopes, rocky terrain, and deeply shaded areas do not support lush carpets of lawn grass and are difficult to mow. But these problem areas and others can be easily solved with ground covers.

Any plant can serve as a ground cover, but horticulturally they are classified as plants that spread or trail along the ground rather than grow upright. Their mature height rarely exceeds 2 feet. Your selection of a ground cover will depend on the plant's purpose, horticultural requirements, and appearance. If, for example, you need to stabilize a slope, choose a ground cover that spreads rapidly and roots easily, such as common periwinkle, blue fescue, or English ivy. To cover a rocky area where soil is too shallow to allow good root penetration, plant a ground cover that spreads by stems (stolons) running over the ground, like Japanese honeysuckle or carpet bugleweed.

Tall Fescue

Big Blue Liriope

Tall Fescue

The plant's horticultural requirements will also determine its suitability for your garden. Cold hardiness, heat tolerance, soil type, and watering needs must be considered. But the most important factor is the amount of sunlight the plant can tolerate. Some ground covers, such as periwinkle and mondo grass, thrive in either sun or shade. Most plants, however, have more specific requirements. Junipers require full sun for best growth; in too much shade, they will be spindly. On the other hand, plants that require deep to partial shade, like English ivy, cast-iron plant, and holly fern, may be damaged by strong sunlight.

The final consideration in selecting a ground cover is its appearance. To contribute most effectively to your garden, the ground cover's unique character should blend with the style of your other plantings. For example, the coarse texture and lustrous foliage of holly fern lends a woodsy feeling to the landscape, while English ivy's timeless, weathered look is especially suitable for traditional settings. The junipers offer a range of landscape effects, from the Andorra juniper, which is the tallest creeping selection and becomes rusty purple in winter, to the blue rug juniper, which is low-growing and distinctly bluish in color. Ground covers can provide the finishing touch that unifies your plantings into a well-planned landscape.

Tall Fescue

Zoysia Grass

Ryegrass

168

Lawns

I hear people refer to their lawns as being warm-season grasses or cool-season grasses. Can you define the terms and tell me why the difference is important to the homeowner?

The terms describe the climates to which grasses are adapted. Warm-season grasses thrive in hot weather, tolerating temperatures up to 100 degrees. These grasses begin growing in early spring and continue to grow until the first heavy frost, when they become dormant. Cool-season grasses grow best in areas with moderately warm days, cool nights, and cold winters. They grow and remain green all year.

The difference is important to homeowners choosing a type of grass for their lawn. Homeowners in the Lower South will generally have little success with cool-season grasses except as a temporary winter lawn, or in shade or higher elevations. But they can choose from a variety of warm-season grasses for a permanent lawn. Homeowners in the Middle and Upper South may grow either cool-season or warm-season grasses successfully. As a general rule, warm-season turf is faster growing and denser than cool-season turf. (*See* chart for warm- and cool-season grasses recommended for the South.)

Warm-season grasses are best adapted to the sunny, hot climate of the South; but in some parts of the region, homeowners may also grow cool-season grasses successfully.

TYPES OF LAWN TURF RECOMMENDED FOR THE SOUTH

WARM-SEASON GRASSES		COOL-SEASON GRASSES	
Bahia	LS**	Bent	US
Bermuda	US, MS, LS	Bluegrass	US, MS
Carpet	LS	Red fescue	US
Centipede	MS, LS	Tall fescue	US, MS
St. Augustine	LS	Annual rye*	US, MS, LS
Zoysia	US, MS, LS	Perennial rye	US

*Basically used for overseeding warm-season turf.
**(US) Upper South, (MS) Middle South, (LS) Lower South

How should I prepare the soil to install a lawn?

Successful lawn installation depends greatly on thorough bed preparation. Start with a soil test, then till the soil to a depth of 6 to 10 inches until it is uniformly broken up. Lime according to the soil test results, and broadcast a lawn fertilizer such as 10-6-4 (20 pounds per 1000 square feet) over the bed and cover the area with peat moss (1 bale per 100 square feet).

Next, till the fertilizer and peat into the soil to prevent recompaction of soil, to aid water retention, and to improve soil fertility. Ground pine bark, rotted leaves, and rotted sawdust are also good soil additives.

Rake the lawn bed, clearing it of rocks and soil clods. Fill a rolling drum with water and roll it over the bed when the soil is barely moist, not wet. This will level the bed and help you detect low spots. One easy method of checking the levelness of the bed is called string grading. Drive a stake into the center of the rolled bed. Attach a string to the stake at soil level. By stretching the string to the perimeters of the bed, you can check the

A well-kept lawn is an asset to any home.

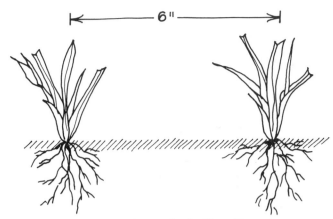

Fig. 1 *Sprigging method of installing a lawn.*

Fertilize turf grasses only when they are actively growing. To ensure even distribution of fertilizer, always apply with a spreader.

Use a vertical mower to dethatch your lawn. Vertically rotating blades slice through matted clippings and dead grass roots to improve the penetration of moisture and nutrients into the turf.

evenness of the soil at any point in the lawn bed. A thin layer of mulch after you have seeded or planted sprigs or plugs will help prevent soil erosion and weed growth. Mulch also shades tender young plants. Straw is a good mulch for new lawns.

What is the most economical method of installing a lawn other than seeding?

Sprigging is the most economical method, as well as the most tedious. Wash the soil from a strip of sod to expose the roots. Pull sprigs of grass from the strip and plant them 6 inches apart in a slightly moist prepared bed. Mulch the bed with hay. (*See Figure 1.*)

Plugging is easier and faster than sprigging but less expensive than sodding. (For more information on plugging, *see* question on establishing a zoysia lawn.)

How do the time and rate of fertilization vary between warm-season and cool-season turf?

Grasses should be fertilized only when they are actively growing. Over most of the South, warm-season grasses should receive fertilizer in March, June, and August. Fertilizing later than August may delay their going dormant and expose them to winter injury. Fertilizing earlier than March can be wasteful, since some of the fertilizer leaches from the topsoil before the roots are ready to absorb it. However, if you are applying a pre-emergence herbicide in combination with the fertilizer, February fertilization is advisable.

Cool-season grasses, on the other hand, generally require fertilizer every two months during fall, winter, and early spring. Do not fertilize during June, July, and August, when these grasses are under stress and grow slowly.

The rate of fertilization will depend on type of grass, soil type, rainfall, length of growing season, and type of fertilizer. Improved Bermuda grasses require more nitrogen than bluegrasses or St. Augustine; and zoysia, Bahia, carpet, and centipede grasses require still less. Use a complete fertilizer with a high percentage of nitrogen, such as 16-4-8 or 12-4-8.

Note: A turf fertilizer especially formulated for the type of grass you have is the safest and easiest type to apply. Always use a fertilizer spreader to apply fertilizer to your lawn. A drop-type spreader is best. Be sure to clean it after use to prevent rust.

What does "dethatching" a lawn mean?

Thatch is a layer of grass that has not decomposed. It may build up when grass is overfertilized, causing new grass to grow faster than old grass can die and break down. It may also build up from clippings left on the lawn after mowing.

As thatch builds up, roots of the new grass begin to grow in the thatch rather than in the soil. When the thatch dries out during the hot summer months, the grass dies from lack of moisture.

Dethatching is the process of removing layers of thatch by raking vigorously or by going over the lawn with a dethatching (verticut) machine. Thatch can be prevented by fertilizing the soil moderately, mowing the lawn regularly, removing clippings after mowing, and raking the lawn thoroughly and vigorously in early spring. To promote complete decomposition of dead grass, topdress the lawn annually with ¼ inch of compost or weed-free manure. This is effective on most lawns except zoysia. On zoysia, use a reel-type mower and set the bed knife at ½ to 1 inch. Use a grass catcher to prevent thatch build-up.

How high should I set the cutting height of my lawn mower?

Proper mowing height is essential to maintaining a healthy lawn. Because lawn grasses differ in their tolerance to close mowing, you need to adjust your mower to suit the grass. Some grasses, such as Bermuda and bent grass, tolerate closer cutting than others, like centipede and St. Augustine. Cutting grass at a lower height than it will tolerate will seriously weaken it and invite weeds, pests, and disease into the lawn.

One important rule is never remove more than one-third of the grass blade at a single mowing. Removing more will exhaust the grass while it tries to replace the lost foliage. Stored food reserves in the root system are depleted, and many roots may be killed. If your lawn is extremely overgrown, cut only one-third of the blade height and wait a few days before mowing to its normal height.

Centipede grass and the dwarf St. Augustine selections, such as Floratam and Floratine, should be cut to a height of ½ to 2 inches. Bermuda, bent grass, zoysia, and annual bluegrass should be cut much closer, to a height of ½ to 1 inch. Red fescue, Kentucky bluegrass, ryegrass, and carpet grass should be cut at a medium height of 1 to 2 inches.

Other grasses, like tall fescue and Bahia, require high mowing heights. Mow tall fescue and Bahia to a height of 1½ to 3 inches. Old St. Augustine selections, such as Roselawn and common St. Augustine, must be cut very high, to a height of 2 to 3 inches. (*See Figure 2.*)

What do you recommend as the best lawn grass for coastal areas?

St. Augustine grasses are the most popular for coastal areas. They perform well in acid or alkaline soils, in full sun or moderate shade, and in poorly drained as well as well-drained soils. St. Augustine grasses are the most salt tolerant and have relatively few disease and nematode problems.

The Floratam type of St. Augustine covers the ground rapidly, has good color, and has fair tolerance to downy mildew and gray leaf spot diseases. This type also has resistance to chinch bug attack and the mosaic virus, St. Augustine Decline.

Is there any way to keep my Bermuda grass lawn green all winter?

The only way to keep your Bermuda grass lawn green during the winter is to overseed in the fall with a cool-season grass (like ryegrass) that becomes established quickly.

To overseed, mow your existing lawn very closely, and rake carefully to remove as much debris as possible. Sow 10 to 20 pounds of fresh, weed-free common ryegrass seed per 1000 square feet of lawn area. For even coverage, apply half in one direction and the rest at right angles to the first application. Rake lightly to move the seeds through the old sod downward to contact the soil, then water carefully. Keep the seeds moist until they germinate, and water the young seedlings often until they get a good start. If the weather is warm, you may need to water lightly several times a day.

To prevent the ryegrass from competing with Bermuda grass in the spring, mow the ryegrass very closely and allow it to die out before applying nitrogen fertilizer.

What are some methods I could use to establish a zoysia lawn?

The most efficient method of establishing a zoysia lawn is to lay sod; that is, to cover the lawn area with sections of turf. However, this can become expensive.

Improve the health of matted turf and compacted soil with a plug aerifier. It removes small plugs of soil from established turf, improving moisture penetration and root development.

MOWING HEIGHTS FOR TURF GRASSES				
½" to 1"	1" to 2"	1½" to 2"	1½" to 3"	2" to 3"
bermuda	red fescue	centipede	tall fescue	st. augustine
bent grass	kentucky bluegrass		Bahia grass	
zoysia	rye grass			
	carpet grass			

Fig. 2

Bermuda grass forms a thick, lush, durable lawn that stays green from spring through fall.

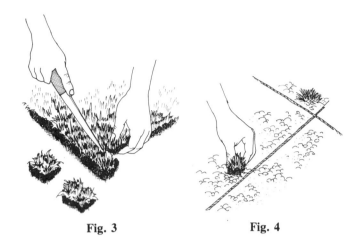

Fig. 3   Fig. 4

A more economical, although slower, method is called plugging. Purchase several strips of sod at a nursery or garden center. Good selections of zoysia grass include Meyer, Emerald, and Matrella. With a sharp knife, cut the sod into 2-inch squares. (*See Figure 3.*)

Make planting holes for the sod squares 12 inches apart in rows 12 inches apart. Plant the plugs so they are even with the surrounding soil, and firm the soil around each plug. (*See Figure 4.*) Stagger the rows to hasten coverage of the grass.

Water the lawn thoroughly after planting. If dry weather follows, water the new lawn every three to five rainless days to keep the soil continually moist but not saturated.

After signs of new growth are apparent, make a light application of nitrogen fertilizer every two weeks. Use ammonium nitrate or ammonium sulfate at the rate of $\frac{1}{4}$ to $\frac{1}{2}$ pound per 1000 square feet. Keep the area absolutely free of weeds. It is a good idea to use stakes and string to rope off the newly planted area so that no one will walk on it.

Zoysia spreads by runners; by planting early and by watering, weeding, and fertilizing judiciously, you can plan on complete coverage by the end of the growing season.

Use ground covers instead of turf grass on slopes and under small trees to eliminate difficult mowing and protect slender tree trunks from possible injury.

Plant around exposed tree trunks with a ground cover.

Ground Covers

When should a ground cover be used instead of turf grass?

Use ground covers in areas where maintaining a turf lawn would be difficult or impossible—on steep slopes, over large areas, in confined spaces, on rocky terrain, in heavily shaded areas, or even in crevices in patios. You can also underplant bulbs or cover exposed tree roots with a ground cover. Ground covers require much less maintenance than turf lawns and can solve a wide range of problems while adding variety to your landscape.

Can you suggest any new ways to use ground covers?

Ground covers were once thought of only as substitutes for lawn grasses when covering large areas, but that is no longer the case. Ground covers can also be used as accent plants to emphasize trees, shrubs, and flower borders. In this use, contrast is the key to effectiveness.

By combining ground covers that differ from other garden plants in color or texture, you can create a simple yet dramatic effect. Ground covers make superb underplantings for trees and shrubs, intensifying the form and feeling of each plant and at the same time acting as a living mulch to minimize weed growth.

Ground cover plants may also be used to accent one another. For example, an edging of carpet bugleweed (*Ajuga reptans*) along a bed of Confederate jasmine (*Trachelospermum jasminoides*) can make both plants more distinctive.

The lowest growing ground covers—carpet bugleweed, gold moss (*Sedum acre*), thyme (*Thymus sp.*), and mondo grass (*Ophiopogon japonicus*)—are excellent for accenting walkways and terraces; they are especially effective for those that are constructed of flagstone, as these plants can fill the spaces between the stones.

Can you suggest some ground covers that are heat and drought resistant?

Ground covers that tolerate heat and drought (and can survive in average or poor soil) include santolina (*Santolina chamaecyparissus, S. virens*), moss pink (*Phlox subulata*), juniper (*Juniperus sp.*), trailing lantana (*Lantana montevidensis*), cottage pinks (*Dianthus plumarius*), and wedelia (*Wedelia trilobata*). Moss pink, verbena (*Verbena sp.*), and some junipers will not grow well in southern Florida; wedelia and trailing lantana cannot tolerate the cold winter temperatures of the Upper South.

What plants could I use as ground cover near the beach?

Among the plants best suited to the dry, sandy soil and salty air of the seashore are beach wormwood (*Artemisia stellerana*), cinquefoil (*Potentilla sp.*), Hall's Japanese honeysuckle (*Lonicera japonica* Halliana), juniper, lantana, big blue liriope (*Liriope muscari*), moss sandwort (*Arenaria verna* Caespitosa), snow-in-summer (*Cerastium tomentosum*), stonecrop (*Sedum sp.*), thrift or moss pink, verbena, and woolly yarrow (*Achillea tomentosa*).

I have large cracks in my garden walkway. Are there any plants that will survive in these spaces?

A number of common ground cover plants are suited to crevice gardening, notably cinquefoil and zoysia grass.

Other suitable plants include baby's tears (*Soleirolia soleirolii*), bluet (*Hedyotis caerulea*), dichondra (*Dichondra carolinensis*), snow-in-summer, New Zealand bur (*Acaena microphylla*), and blue fescue (*Festuca ovina* Glauca).

Your choice of specific plants must also depend on the amount of light the plants will receive. All of the plants listed above are tolerant of either sun or shade except New Zealand bur, which requires full sun, and baby's tears and bluets, which should receive no direct sun.

If the walkway crevice is too narrow to permit insertion of roots, use a chisel and hammer to widen the gap to make 2-inch-square planting pockets. Cultivate the soil in the crevice or pocket with a screwdriver to loosen it; then wrap the roots of each plant with a small piece of sphagnum moss and guide them into the crevice.

When using a lawn grass like zoysia for crevice filling, cultivate the soil between the patio or paving squares to a depth of at least 4 inches. Cut strips of sod to size and lay them between the squares, firming them in place with your foot. Do not forget to water during dry weather.

For years our border of big blue liriope was attractive, but last summer it never did reach the beautiful all-green stage. We pulled out as many of the bottom brown leaves as we could, but this did not help. What do you suggest we do?

In early spring, cut big blue liriope back to just above the ground, using a pair of stout scissors, a very sharp lawn mower blade, or a nylon cord edger. Usually within several weeks after cutting, new leaves will sprout and the appearance of the plants will be remarkably improved. Cutting back also improves the quality and number of blooms that will be produced in late summer.

Do grassy ground covers like big blue liriope require much maintenance? Can you recommend some others?

Grassy evergreen ground covers not only require little maintenance, they also embellish difficult niches in the garden in a pleasing and unusual way. Some grassy

When trees with low-growing branches shade out grass, a ground cover is a good replacement. Here, English ivy grows out to the tree's drip line.

Wedelia provides a lush mat of green even in hot, dry weather.

Thrift makes a colorful ground cover in the sandy soils of beach areas.

Strips of zoysia grass planted between blocks of aggregate concrete give the illusion that the area is an extension of the surrounding lawn. This use of zoysia also helps reduce the surface temperature of the concrete area.

Big blue liriope will embellish a garden with coarse, grassy texture. Best of all, this versatile ground cover requires little maintenance.

Ferns add a woodsy feeling to the home garden. Use them as ground covers in moist soil and light shade.

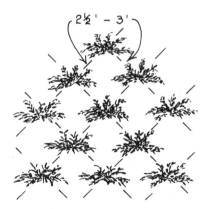

DIAMOND-GRID PATTERN

Fig. 5 *Plant junipers and other ground covers on a diamond grid pattern to fill in the planting area quickly and avoid the look of straight rows.*

ground covers, such as big blue liriope, can grow in deep shade and poor soil where no turf grass would be practical. In addition, the grassy ground covers provide a subtle contrast in texture and color with lawn grasses.

Among the best grassy ground covers are liriope, mondo grass (also called monkey grass), blue fescue, and creeping red fescue (*Festuca rubra*).

Can ferns be used as ground cover? Which species adapt well to the home garden?

Ferns can be planted as ground cover in moist, rich soil under tall shrubs or trees, where they will receive light filtered shade. Among the species recommended for cultivation in the South are: maidenhair fern, Christmas fern, marginal wood fern, Southern lady fern, New York fern, broad beech fern, ebony spleenwort, cinnamon fern, holly fern, and royal fern.

Holly fern can be grown as far inland as Shreveport, Louisiana, and Birmingham, Alabama, and as far up the Atlantic Coast as Raleigh, North Carolina. The fern is not hardy at temperatures under 15 degrees, however. Cinnamon fern is hardy everywhere in the South except the southernmost counties of Texas and Florida. Christmas fern, broad beech fern, and royal fern grow throughout most of the South to northern Florida. Marginal wood fern, maidenhair fern, Southern lady fern, New York fern, and ebony spleenwort grow in the woodlands of the Upper and Middle South.

Are there any junipers that would be suitable as ground covers?

Yes, almost all of the prostrate types are suitable; but two of the best ground covers from the juniper family are the Andorra juniper (*Juniperus horizontalis* Plumosa) and the blue rug juniper (*Juniperus horizontalis* Wiltonii). They have similar cultural requirements, but the differences in color, texture, and individual forms make them very different plants for landscape design.

Both the Andorra and blue rug junipers have a creeping habit of growth, spreading horizontally (as the botanical name would suggest) over the ground. They are tolerant of almost every soil condition and will adapt to a hot situation quite satisfactorily, except in South Florida. Junipers withstand full exposure to sun, wind, and intense cold. They have a medium to slow rate of growth, but they perform much better when given favorable soil conditions. Spacing junipers 2½ to 3 feet apart provides complete coverage of the planting area in 2 to 3 years. (*See Figure 5.*)

There is one aspect of the blue rug juniper that deserves special consideration. It is truly blue. Not robin's egg blue, of course, but a definite silvery blue with just a touch of green underneath. It is not difficult to work with, but it is not compatible with certain other shades of blue, or with plants having intense red, violet, or lavender flowers; so use it with care.

How should mondo grass and liriope be planted? Are they expensive plants to use in the landscape?

If you plant mondo grass or liriope the way you find them in the nursery (usually sold in 1-gallon cans), they can be rather expensive items in your landscape budget. It is not really necessary, however, to plant an entire clump in one location, unless you want to create a mounded or lumpy effect in the landscape.

A gallon can of mondo grass or liriope can usually be divided into 15 or 20 individual plantlets or sprigs; by planting these sprigs 4 to 6 inches apart, you can create an effect that is quite satisfying even before the planting has matured. (*See Figure 6.*)

What is the best way to use mondo grass in the landscape?

Even though mondo grass is frequently used for borders and edgings, the professional garden designer will usually insist on using it as a ground cover. This insistence, however, is based on something more than a professional whim.

Mondo grass is, by its very nature, a ground cover plant. Spreading by means of shallow underground rhizomes similar to those of St. Augustine, centipede, and Bermuda grass, mondo grass will form a low, irregular mass that becomes increasingly dense as the planting matures.

The most successful uses of mondo grass take advantage of its characteristic color, texture, and adaptability. Mondo grass can withstand all sorts of physical abuse with an amazing amount of stamina. Prolonged periods of drought and periodic inundations seem to have no serious effects on its performance. This makes it a particularly useful plant for areas that receive irregular amounts of rainfall or occasional periods of standing water—under eaves, on steep banks, or in secondary drainage ways.

Mondo grass can even tolerate a certain amount of trampling, a quality that makes it desirable for areas of heavy traffic such as entrance courts, service yards, and the space between the sidewalk and a curb.

In addition to its extreme durability, the color and texture of mondo grass make it an effective substitute lawn where traditional lawn grass would be difficult or impossible to maintain. In areas of irregular topography, dense shade, steep slopes, or heavy root competition from surface-feeding trees like beeches and magnolias, mondo grass may be the only solution when the effect of a lawn is required.

Please give me some information about using pachysandra as a ground cover.

In shaded situations, Japanese spurge (*Pachysandra terminalis*) will perform well as an evergreen ground cover in the South. The plant spreads rapidly by stolons and thrives in full shade or semishade in fertile soil with medium moisture.

The leaves of Japanese spurge are dark green; small spikes of greenish white flowers appear in May, followed by white berries in the fall. A selection with white variegated leaves is also available.

The best plantingtime in the South is from January to March. Space plants grown in 2¼-inch pots about 6 to 12 inches apart, depending on how fast you want coverage. Feed with an all-purpose fertilizer, such as 5-10-10, after new growth begins; feed again in midsummer.

What is the best way to plant periwinkle?

Common periwinkle (*Vinca minor*) can tolerate full sun but prefers shade or partial shade, attaining its best growth in the filtered light under a tree canopy. This plant will grow in clay soil but prefers a rich, sandy loam that is high in organic matter; so till the planting bed well, and work in bark and peat moss.

Plant the clumps, then spread the runners out in a circle. Follow the runners until you find a section of stem where there are either leaves or roots. Bend the stem at that point, and bury the leaves or roots in the soil. This small section will produce roots and establish a new plant, helping to fill in the bed quickly.

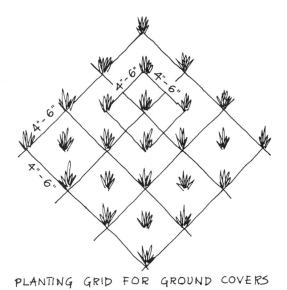

PLANTING GRID FOR GROUND COVERS

Fig. 6 *Spaced 4 to 6 inches apart, sprigs of mondo grass or liriope will give an even coverage in about two years.*

Japanese spurge provides year-round green, with a bonus of whitish flowers in spring and white berries in fall.

Trees & Shrubs

Hybrid Rhododendrons

Trees and shrubs are the backbone of any garden. Large trees form the canopy that gives the garden a sense of overhead enclosure. Small trees provide seasonal color and blend the large trees with the rest of the elements in the garden. Shrubs can enclose or accent the garden, or provide the background for other garden plants. A good gardener should classify plants according to the way they are used—for example, function, space, and general aesthetics—and despite the varied soil types, topography, and climates of the South, it is possible to choose a shrub or tree that satisfies both the horticultural and design objectives of any gardening situation.

Before you plant a tree or shrub, you should know how it grows and what conditions it needs for maximum growth. Until you know about the plant's character, it is difficult to determine whether it is the plant you need for a particular location in your garden. Also, the effect the seasons have on your trees and shrubs is important. For instance, the foliage of evergreen nandina (heavenly bamboo) is green most of the year but becomes bronzy purple in winter. And of course, deciduous plants change completely from one

Beautyberry

Native Azalea

Winged Euonymus

Chaste Tree

Viburnum

American Holly

season to the next. When you select a tree or shrub for a particular location, be sure its seasonal color changes will complement and not clash with your other plantings.

Once the design and location considerations are settled, it is important to follow the proper planting procedures. The old saying that you need to dig a $40 hole for a $5 plant is true. And planting is not just a matter of digging a big hole and putting the plant in it. It is important to know at what level the new plant's root ball should be placed in the ground. For instance, if the plant is grafted, you should always keep the graft above the soil line. Azalea, camellia, and hybrid rhododendron must be planted with the top of the soil ball slightly above the soil line.

Correctly installing the plant is just the beginning of your work. Postplanting care will determine the ultimate success or failure of keeping the plant healthy over the years. During the first years of establishment, most plants should be watered at least every 7 to 10 rainless days. Water thoroughly to induce a deep root system. Trees and shrubs also need proper fertilization (generally twice a year), control of pests and diseases that may

Japanese Quince

Border Forsythia

Indian Azalea

Oakleaf Hydrangea

Banana Shrub

Gardenia

179

Mountain Laurel

infest them, and corrective pruning. Generally, trees and shrubs should be pruned only as a means of guiding them to grow into their natural form and size. Even then, pruning should be minor and selective. Young trees and shrubs usually receive an initial pruning before you buy them. When this has not been done, the pruning is up to you. For example, a maple tree should have only one straight leader, and others that develop need to be removed. On the other hand, a border forsythia or showy jasmine with just one or two leaders needs to be pruned back to encourage more stem growth. As they develop their natural forms, trees and shrubs will provide the framework that helps define the unique character of your garden.

Florist's Hydrangea

Canadian Hemlock

Wax Myrtle

Palm

Sargent Crabapple

Fruitland Elaeagnus

General Recommendations

What trees are good for screens?

Red cedar (*Juniperus virginiana*), Virginia pine (*Pinus virginiana*), and white pine (*Pinus strobus*) are excellent trees for screens. Red cedar maintains a tight sheared look for years, then becomes shaggy and weathered looking. A drawback is its comparatively slow rate of growth. Virginia and white pines should be planted 10 feet apart. They will then fill in to provide a dense, visually impenetrable barrier. These trees offer an excellent backdrop for deciduous plantings, too.

Please advise me on the fastest growing shrub I can use as a screen. I want to hide an unsightly view.

Waxleaf privet (*Ligustrum japonicum*), thorny elaeagnus (*Elaeagnus pungens*), and Fraser photinia (*Photinia* x *fraseri*) are fast growing and reach a sizable height in a relatively short time. These evergreens require basic care; proper feeding, watering, and mulching will encourage rapid growth.

An entrance planting of white pine and Pfitzer juniper makes an impenetrable screen. Note the soft texture the needles give the tree.

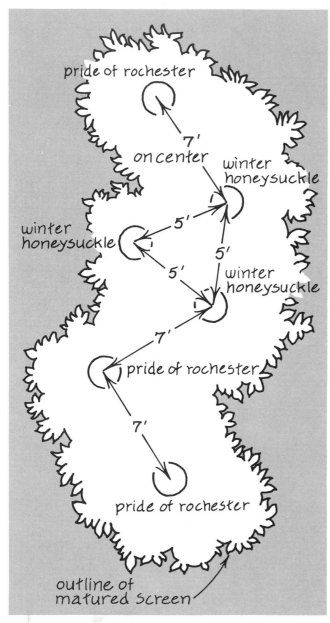

Yaupon is grown as a small tree or large shrub. These yaupons accent an entry and are kept compact by occasional shearing.

What are some deciduous (rather than evergreen) shrubs I could use for a screen in an area that receives full sun?

Japanese quince (*Chaenomeles speciosa*) and Pride of Rochester (*Deutzia scabra*) make good screens in areas exposed to full sun. Winter honeysuckle (*Lonicera fragrantissima*) also makes a dense large-scale screen. Pruned to tree form, it provides enclosure without entirely blocking the view. Crepe myrtle (*Lagerstroemia indica*) can be used in a similar way and offers a bonus of brilliantly colored flowers throughout the summer. (*See Figure 1.*)

I want to plant a screen in a partially shaded location. What shrubs would you recommend?

Rhododendron (*Rhododendron sp.*), mountain laurel (*Kalmia latifolia*), Florida leucothöe (*Leucothöe populifolia*), and sasanqua camellia (*Camellia sasanqua*) can be massed to form informal screens. They require little pruning and are ideal for gardens where shrubs are allowed to grow to their natural shape and size.

Can you recommend some trees and shrubs that are heat and drought resistant?

There are a number of attractive trees and shrubs that can tolerate heat and drought. Yaupon holly (*Ilex vomitoria*), live oak (*Quercus virginiana*), Chinese tallow tree (*Sapium sebiferum*), Eastern redbud (*Cercis canadensis*), and wax myrtle (*Myrica cerifera*) can be planted in full sun and in nearly any kind of soil. Honey mesquite (*Prosopis glandulosa*) has a wide-ranging root system that enables it to survive dry periods, but it is seldom found east of the Mississippi. Flowering quince (*Chaenomeles sp.*), firethorn (*Pyracantha sp.*), heavenly bamboo or nandina (*Nandina domestica*), glossy abelia (*Abelia* x *grandiflora*), and Japanese pittosporum (*Pittosporum tobira*) also tolerate full sun and dry conditions. Gold-dust aucuba (*Aucuba japonica* Variegata), once established, can withstand heat and drought but not direct sunlight.

Live oak is imposing even when young, but its character increases with age.

Chinese tallow tree is one of the most pest-free trees in cultivation. It is hardy in the Lower and Middle South.

Native to the South, wax myrtle can be grown as a large evergreen shrub or a small multistemmed tree.

Honey mesquite gives a light, airy feeling to the garden and casts a small amount of shade.

Trees & Shrubs   183

Wax myrtle and yaupon holly are natural choices for a beach home. Shore juniper, a rampant-growing ground cover, will protect dunes from wind erosion.

Threadleaf Japanese maple is noted not only for its softly mounded weeping form, but also for its delicate, deeply dissected leaves.

Weeping cherry merits a special place in the landscape because of its distinctive shape and summer foliage, as well as its springtime veil of shell pink flowers.

We have just bought a beach house. Can you suggest some shrubs that will tolerate the salt spray and sandy soil?

Wax myrtle, red cedar, yaupon, Indian hawthorn (*Raphiolepis indica*), and oleander (*Nerium oleander*) are good choices.

An area of our garden drains poorly, so the soil is moist most of the time. Can you suggest some trees and ornamental shrubs that will grow there?

Deciduous trees that you might plant are bald cypress (*Taxodium distichum*), sycamore (*Platanus occidentalis*), red or swamp maple (*Acer sp.*), sweet gum (*Liquidambar styraciflua*), and river birch (*Betula nigra*). Evergreen trees recommended for such sites include Southern magnolia (*Magnolia grandiflora*), sweet bay magnolia (*Magnolia virginiana*), Southern cherry laurel (*Prunus caroliniana*), and American holly (*Ilex opaca*). Some shrubs that you could use there include buttonbush (*Cephalanthus occidentalis*), red chokeberry (*Aronia arbutifolia*), American elder (*Sambucus canadensis*), swamp azalea (*Azalea viscosum*), swamp rose (*Rosa palustris*), sweet pepperbush (*Clethra alnifolia*), common sweet shrub (*Calycanthus floridus*), pussy willow (*Salix discolor*), selections of American arborvitae (*Thuja occidentalis*), and drooping leucothöe (*Leucothöe fontanesiana*).

Our soil is slightly alkaline. Can you suggest some trees or shrubs that we could grow in this soil?

While very few plants do well in strongly alkaline soil, the following will tolerate slightly alkaline soil (pH 7.0 to 7.5): American elm (*Ulmus americana*), bigleaf hydrangea (*Hydrangea macrophylla*), American linden (*Tilia americana*), maple, white oak (*Quercus alba*), red cedar, lesser flowering quince (*Chaenomeles japonica*), honey mesquite, and weeping willow (*Salix babylonica*).

I would like to plant an unusual tree in my yard, one that is weeping or twisted. What do you recommend?

Both corkscrew willow (*Salix matsudana* Tortuosa) and the weeping type of Japanese maple (*Acer palmatum*) have an exotic appearance. The corkscrew willow is relatively fast growing and may reach as much as 25 feet in height at maturity. It prefers full sun and requires large amounts of water. The Japanese maple needs good soil and partial shade to reach its mature height of 15 to 20 feet.

Two other plants to consider are weeping cherry (*Prunus subhirtella* Pendula) and weeping crabapple (*Malus* x Red Jade). Each is effective as a single specimen in a prominent location. They can tolerate full sun or partial shade.

We are tired of pruning fast-growing privet hedges that must be clipped regularly. Please suggest some plants to replace them.

The choice depends on factors such as height and growth characteristics. For instance, if the maximum height desired is 5 feet, choose a stable, 4- to 6-foot plant such as Hetz holly (*Ilex crenata* Hetzii); for an 8-foot hedge, glossy abelia and Dwarf Burford holly (*I. cornuta* Dwarf Burford) can be maintained with little pruning. Azalea selections (*Azalea sp.*) vary considerably in height and growth characteristics, and you may find one of them to suit your needs.

Japanese yew (*Podocarpus macrophyllus*) is relatively drought tolerant and pest resistant (for Lower South only), and its slow growth means that it requires little pruning. Deciduous barberry (*Berberis sp.*) and dwarf yaupon (*I. vomitoria* Nana) also need little pruning and make good low hedges (less than 3 feet). For a naturalistic hedge, try wax myrtle or winged euonymus (*Euonymus alata*). For a more formal setting, consider Mugo pine (*Pinus mugo*).

Can you give me some tips to help me identify trees by their twigs?

Identifying deciduous trees by their twigs is a challenging game for a winter outing. You will need a small magnifying glass and a twig key guide (field guide). Be sure you select a simple guide with good illustrations, understandable definitions of botanical terms, and a simple, readable key to leafless trees.

Here are some tips to help your investigation.

—Instead of collecting twigs for later identification, try to do the keying in the field. Bark and fallen leaves (although you cannot always tell which tree they came from) could be a help.

—If you should take a specimen for later work, do not cut it from a deformed or misshapen limb.

—Twigs used for identification should be taken from the end of a main branch rather than from the stubby branches known as spur branches. (*See Figure 2.*)

—If you are uncertain about your identification, mark the tree with twine or ribbon; that way, you can return to the tree to check it when it leafs out.

Can you make some suggestions on planning for fall color?

With a little planning, you can orchestrate a grand fall foliage display. The following are some guidelines you should consider.

—If you have a heavily wooded lot or one with a substantial number of shade trees, it is likely that you will look for smaller understory ornamental trees to complement the color show of the existing canopy. For instance, a lot canopied predominantly with hickory (*Carya sp.*) and tulip trees (*Liriodendron tulipfera*), which have yellow fall coloration, would be an excellent backdrop for displaying the lucid orange of sassafras (*Sassafras albidum*) or Franklin trees (*Franklinia alatamaha*).

—A natural backdrop, such as a lot full of pines, offers unlimited choices, from the maroon red of dogwood (*Cornus florida*) to the scarlet of sourwood (*Oxydendrum arboreum*). Even a seemingly random color selection can work well beneath the green shelter of pines.

—Color problems can be planted out. A red-brick house dominated by a white oak, which has a rust red fall color, needs another color as an accent. Planting a brighter colored tree closer to the street, such as a sugar maple (*Acer saccharum*), which will turn brilliant yellow orange, will capture the eye and mask the clash of the white oak and the house.

—If you are shopping for your first few trees to install on a treeless lot, select shade trees that complement the basic color of the facade. For example, red brick needs a yellow fall color. By contrast, an ocher or more earth-tone brick can be an effective neutral display for the intense red of a red maple or a black gum (*Nyssa sylvatica*).

—If the initial planting is to be the fast-growing shade trees that will canopy the house, pick a single species, such as tulip trees, to give a dominant color. Then play against this color when selecting ornamental trees and slower-growing medium-size shade trees, which may provide more brilliant color.

—Drift trees in a color pattern. Careful selection of trees will allow a sweep of color

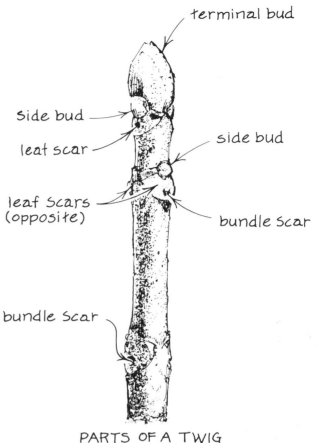

PARTS OF A TWIG

Fig. 2

from bright yellow to brilliant red to purple. Such a planting could include a tulip tree, maidenhair tree (*Ginkgo biloba*), sugar maple, red maple, black gum, and sweet gum.

—Along a straight drive or in a formal planting, alternating colors can be effective. For example, alternate sugar maple and American linden (yellow) or maidenhair tree and red maple. Or you can alternate shade and ornamental trees: sugar maple and redbud (yellow); red maple and sassafras.

Can you suggest some trees and shrubs that will bloom in the fall?

The Franklin tree begins blooming in early fall and continues to produce showy, white flowers through October. Its orange red fall color is also quite spectacular. Among the best fall-blooming woody ornamentals are sweet olive (*Osmanthus fragrans*) and thorny elaeagnus; both are large evergreen shrubs with fragrant flowers. Other attractive fall-blooming shrubs include orange-eye butterfly bush (*Buddleia davidii*), loquat (*Eriobotrya japonica*), and sasanqua camellias. In much of the South common oleander will continue to bloom into November.

In addition to these, many species and hybrids of hibiscus (*Hibiscus sp.*) can continue to bloom into October, especially if the plants are properly fed and watered. Yellow sage (*Lantana camara*) and flowery senna (*Cassia corymbosa*) also tend to hold their bloom into fall, as do the everblooming selections of floribunda roses.

We would like to plant several small trees that provide fall color. Please recommend some.

Sassafras, crepe myrtle, Chinese tallow tree, dogwood, maidenhair tree, redbud, persimmon (*Diospyros virginiana*), and sugar maple should provide a colorful display.

Maidenhair tree is a good choice for fall color. Its butter yellow leaves will remain colorful for about two weeks.

Franklin tree is famous for its dramatic fall showing of flowers as well as its fall color. The leaves turn a vivid orange red that rivals that of sourwood or red maple.

Care

What kind of care should mail-order plants receive after they arrive?

Plants ordered through the mail should be planted as soon as they arrive. Being packaged for shipment places stress on plants, and recovery will be hampered if plants are subjected to further stress by remaining out of the ground for any length of time. Prepare the plant bed in advance by working plenty of organic matter into the soil. When the plants arrive, water them at once. If they have been shipped in the soil in which they were growing, inspect the clumps to determine which side is up, and discard any rotted portions.

Can you give me some tips on selecting healthy plants?

If you are unfamiliar with the characteristic form and color of the plant you want, visit several nurseries to compare their specimens before making your purchase. Carefully inspect the plant. Examine trees and shrubs for weak branches, scarring, girdling at the soil line, split bark, pruning cuts that are not flush with the trunk or branch, dead wood, holes, or other disfigurations. Healthy foliage is not distorted in shape or size. Examine leaf texture and color; it should be characteristic of the plant. Leaves should not be chlorotic (unnaturally yellowed or faded), bruised, or injured. Look for signs of disease such as browned areas, leaf spots, and soft, mushy areas on the leaves or stems. And examine the entire plant for pests; look in the tight areas between leaves and stems, on the underside of leaves, and on leaf stems. Check the foliage for signs of pest damage.

Container-grown plants should not be excessively root bound. Nor should the roots be growing out of the container. Remove the plant from the container to make sure that roots are not matted into a tight mass. Check for signs of browning or weak, stringy roots that look rotted.

One of my trees is leaning badly. How can I prop it up and not detract from the appearance of my garden?

Follow the example of the Japanese. Instead of using rusty metal poles or wooden 2 × 4s that detract from the garden's appearance, they employ natural materials and treat the prop as sculpture. Fashioned from a dead branch, a handsome forked support can cradle the limb of a leaning tree and share the weight with the trunk. The prop should give the visual impression that it will adequately bear the weight to which it is subjected; a skinny stick may be sufficient for the weight but might look too feeble. Neatly saw the top and bottom of the prop. These finishing touches impart to your garden's visitors a sense of care and pride. You may leave the bark of the prop intact, but strip it away if it becomes shaggy. With the bark removed, the prop will weather to a neutral light gray and dissolve visually into the garden setting.

We live on a hillside where high winds are quite a problem. What trees would you recommend planting for a windbreak?

Virginia pine would be a reliable, fast-growing tree for you. Plant young pines 10 feet apart in a staggered grid. Other good choices would be red pine (*Pinus densiflora*) or Scotch pine (*P. sylvestris*), spruce pine (*P. glabra*), red cedar, hemlock (*Tsuga sp.*), or arborvitae (*Thuja sp.*).

Remove all packaging on mail-order plants immediately so they can receive necessary air and light.

Compare the poor shape and sparse growth of the boxwood on the right to the healthy characteristics of the boxwood on the left.

Since it is often a permanent fixture in the garden, a prop for a leaning tree should be aesthetically pleasing as well as functional.

Cold-tender plants can benefit from a fresh application of mulch every fall.

The easiest way to remove faded azalea blossoms is to sweep them off the plants. Be sure to rake up and dispose of the fallen blossoms.

How can I protect my tender plants from frost damage?

A little protection goes a long way toward avoiding frost damage to tender plants such as gardenia (*Gardenia jasminoides*) and hibiscus. First, when freezing temperatures are forecast in your area, mulch plants heavily with 4 to 6 inches of wood chips, ground bark, shredded leaves, or pine straw. The mulch stabilizes soil temperature and insulates the roots against cold air. It also reduces the danger of frost heaves, a side effect of temperature fluctuation in the soil. Severe frost heaves can force plants out of the ground, damaging roots and impairing the plant's ability to conduct moisture and oxygen.

Second, water all plants thoroughly, especially young ones. Once the ground freezes, very little moisture is available to the roots. Plants that have been well watered when they enter a period of drought will fare better than those that have not. This is especially important for broad-leaved evergreens, such as aucuba (*Aucuba sp.*) and rhododendron, since they tend to lose moisture more rapidly than evergreens with smaller leaves. During prolonged freezes, it is also beneficial to mist the entire plant lightly with a garden hose. The coating of ice that forms on the leaves will help prevent dehydration.

How can I tell if my trees and shrubs have suffered freeze damage? Is there anything I can do?

Freeze damage is easily recognized: the plant foliage will be brown or black. In most cases, damaged leaves will remain on the plants in a withered condition, and the stems will have the same parched look. Wait until late April to be sure you know exactly how much of the plant is damaged. By then, the new growth will be apparent and you can prune without cutting off living tissue. To rejuvenate the plant, prune off the damaged foliage. If the bark splits, prune below the damaged portion.

What kind of care do azaleas and rhododendrons need?

If planted properly, azaleas and rhododendrons need little annual care, other than fertilizing and renewing the mulch. They require moist soil and excellent drainage and will signal a lack of water by drooping or losing their leaves. Water them thoroughly every 10 to 14 rainless days (every 3 to 5 rainless days during the growing season). Always be sure the bed is draining properly, as waterlogged soil kills many azaleas and rhododendrons. If the leaves turn brittle and brown from the edges to the middle during winter, it indicates the plant is suffering windburn. This is a signal to water, even if the ground is frozen. The water in the ground is not available to the plant and its broad leaves make it susceptible to dehydration.

Mulching these plants heavily will help keep moisture around the roots and will serve as insulation in the winter, protecting the roots from severe cold. Mulch also helps maintain the proper soil pH as it decomposes. Many mulches will work, but pine straw and pine bark are recommended.

After azaleas and rhododendrons have bloomed, remove faded blossoms by sweeping the plants with a broom. Be sure to remove the fallen flowers from around the base of the plant to discourage disease organisms. Remove old mulch to the compost pile and apply new mulch to further reduce the possibility of disease and to limit weeds. Avoid digging around the plants; azaleas and rhododendrons are shallow-rooted, and you may damage the root system.

How can I prevent snow from damaging my boxwoods and gardenias?

Shrubs like boxwood (*Buxus sempervirens*) and gardenia need special attention in the snowy regions of the Upper South. Slow-growing Truedwarf boxwood (*B. sempervirens* Suffruticosa) is particularly susceptible to severe damage from heavy wet snows. Both falling snow and the sheets of accumulated snow that slide off roofs can easily crush and ruin a boxwood planting.

One way to protect shrubs is to erect a simple platform that spans the width of the shrub. Drive four supports into the ground, place a platform on top, and secure it to the supports with wire. (*See Figure 3.*) In the case of gardenias, the frame should not touch any of the foliage and should be covered with plastic or cloth. Another preventive measure for boxwoods is to construct a triangular frame around the plant; then wrap the frame in heavy burlap to form a cone.

Our camellias are healthy and develop a nice crop of buds, but we often lose most of the blooms to cold just as they begin to open. Is there a solution?

Plant selections of common camellia (*Camellia japonica*) that have shown good flower bud resistance to cold. These include Flame (red), Blood of China (red), Professor C. S. Sargent (red), Ville de Nantes (variegated red), Lady Clare (rose pink), Berenice Boddy (pink), Dr. Tinsley (pale pink, shading to a deeper pink toward edges), Winifred Womack (white), and Purity (white).

Could you give me some tips for caring for dogwoods?

—Do not overfertilize dogwoods. Planted in partial or deep shade and loose, moist, well-drained soil, they will grow well with little or no fertilizer. Dogwoods are slow growers by nature, and attempting to induce rapid growth by fertilizing heavily is likely to burn the shallow roots, especially on young trees, and to delay flowering. If your soil is poor and fertilization is a must, then use composted cow manure or azalea-camellia fertilizer according to the label directions.

—Water dogwoods frequently when dry weather persists, about twice a week during rainless periods. Do not be fooled by light showers; a sprinkling actually does more harm than good, forcing new feeder roots to stay near the surface. A heavy rain that soaks the soil more than 10 or 12 inches deep encourages roots to penetrate into the subsoil where moisture is retained longer. Bear this in mind when watering artificially. You can simulate heavy rain by letting a hose run slowly for about one hour around the base of each tree.

—Mulching increases the effectiveness of your watering efforts, as it helps retain soil moisture. Excellent mulches for dogwoods include pine straw, rotted leaves, and wood chips, particularly those made from pine waste. Mulching dogwoods also eliminates the need for mowing close to them. Dogwoods are susceptible to damage caused by nicks in the bark made by mowers and other tools. Even minor wounds become entry points for dogwood borers and other pests and diseases. So always exercise caution when using mowers or edgers (especially nylon cord trimmers) around your dogwoods.

—Dogwoods do not usually require pruning except to remove an occasional dead twig or branch. But if pruning becomes necessary, be sure to cut all parts back to healthy wood. Use sharp pruning tools of adequate size and strength to make clean cuts. Dogwoods are brittle, especially when dry, and hand shears may not be strong enough to cut branches that are only ½ inch in diameter. Use loppers when hand shears are inadequate.

Fig. 3 *A simple wood frame shields this boxwood from possible snow damage.*

During dry periods, dogwoods require deep and frequent waterings.

Leaf scorch on gold-dust plants (aucuba) results from exposure to direct sun or strong winds.

For a number of years I have transplanted young dogwood trees from the wild. They live and put on new growth each year but do not bloom. What can I do?

The dogwoods you have were grown from seeds; such plants will vary considerably in the amount of bloom they produce and at what age they bloom. Trees sold commercially are normally grafted from heavily flowering stock plants. Continue caring for the trees as recommended in the previous question. If, after a few more years, you are still not getting satisfactory flowering, consider replacing a few of them with purchased plants.

My gardenia was blooming when purchased, but it has not bloomed since. It seems to be a healthy plant and is growing well. What can I do to make it bloom?

Several things could be responsible for keeping your gardenia from blooming. The plant might be getting too much nitrogen fertilizer, the shade could be too dense for the plant, or it may not be receiving enough summer heat to do well.

The leaves on my gardenia have been yellow for some time. Could this be caused by too much water?

Yes, overwatering could cause the leaves to yellow. When roots are too wet for a long period, they cannot function properly to take up necessary nutrients. Therefore, deficiencies may occur and cause the foliage to turn yellow. Also, the soil may not be sufficiently acid. Do not use lime. Spray the foliage with chelated iron (*see* "Pests & Diseases" chapter for more information).

Occasionally the leaf margins of my gold-dust plants turn brown and die. Eventually the browning extends down the stalk and some of the plants die. Those in sunlight suffer the most. I have treated them for nematodes and fungus, and this has not helped.

The problem is not uncommon. Move your gold-dust plants (aucuba) to a location where they will get filtered partial shade and protection from the wind.

My heavenly bamboo grows beautifully and blooms profusely, but the berries never seem to stay on. Do you have any suggestions?

The plant may get too dry during hot summer weather, or you may be using too much nitrogen fertilizer. Water the shrub during dry weather and reduce the amount of nitrogen fertilizer. You should get a good crop of berries that persist well into winter.

Our holly tree is about 5 years old, 8 feet tall, and appears to be in good health, but it has never produced berries. We have been told that this may be a male tree, in which case it will never bear fruit. Is this true?

If your holly tree is male, it will not produce berries. For most selections of holly it is necessary for a male and a female plant to grow near enough to each other for cross-pollination. A healthy female holly tree, cross-pollinated in bloom, should bear fruit within two or three years after it is transplanted into the home landscape.

All of the privets in our privacy screen are dying. I wonder if the nylon cord trimmer I have been using to trim around the plants is responsible. Is this likely?

Yes. If the line of the weeding implement consistently hits the trunks of tender shrubs or young trees, it can cause cuts that may girdle the trunks. Complete girdling of the trunks can cause the plants to die. Before you replace the shrubs, weed the bed; then mulch with 3 or 4 inches of pine straw, crushed bark, or bark nuggets. Mulching will help control grass and weeds, and you will not need to trim so close to the trunks.

How do I propagate shrubs from cuttings?

Take stem cuttings 4 to 8 inches long and strip the leaves from the bottom half of the stems. Dip each cutting in a root-inducing hormone powder (available in most garden supply centers) to speed rooting. In a flat or other shallow container, prepare the planting medium. Sand is a good rooting medium, but a mixture of peat and perlite or peat and potting soil will also work. Moisten the medium and make a hole for each cutting. Insert the cuttings and firm the medium around them.

Place the flat where it will receive indirect light, and keep the medium moist until roots have formed. Pot rooted cuttings in individual containers; after several years, transplant them to their permanent location.

How do I go about ground layering a shrub?

Ground layering is one of the easiest methods of propagating many shrubs. First, make a shallow cut on the underside of a low-growing branch. Then firmly press that part of the branch into the ground, and secure it with a brick. (*See Figure 4.*) Depending on the plant, roots should form at the site of the cut in one to four months. Do not be shy about looking under the brick from time to time to check the progress of the layer. After roots have formed, cut the rooted branch away from the parent and plant it.

Start the layers early in March, before new growth begins on the plants you wish to propagate. An early start will allow new roots to develop in time for you to plant the rooted layers in the fall.

Planting

When should I plant ornamental trees and shrubs?

Planting at the correct time is essential for any tree or shrub. In the South, that means during the dormant season (fall and winter) for most specimens; dormant planting is always recommended for deciduous plants. Ornamentals set out during the dormant season are easier to establish, as there is time enough for new roots to develop before young leaves appear in the spring. And since dormant-planted trees and shrubs will be well on their way to being established before warm weather, they will be less subject to the stresses of summer—heat, drought, and severe sunscald.

Keep plants watered to avoid cold damage during freezing weather and stake them firmly to prevent damage from high winds. Mulch generously with hay, dried grass clippings, or leaves to protect roots against extreme temperature changes and to help retain moisture. Withhold fertilizer until after the first growing season.

How should I care for my newly planted trees this winter?

Without adequate protection and anchorage, newly planted or transplanted trees and shrubs may have difficulty surviving their first winter. This is particularly true in areas subjected to high winds and hot sun. Large trees require as much protection as small

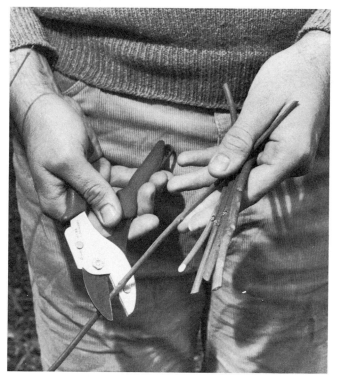

To make hardwood cuttings, take cuttings 4 to 8 inches long from healthy wood, making a slanting cut just above a node or joint in the twig.

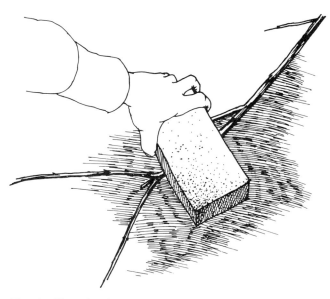

Fig. 4 *Use a brick to secure the branch to be ground layered. The cut underside of the branch must be in constant contact with the soil for roots to form.*

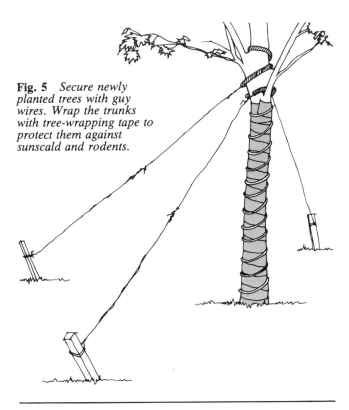

Fig. 5 *Secure newly planted trees with guy wires. Wrap the trunks with tree-wrapping tape to protect them against sunscald and rodents.*

Fig. 6 *Many ornamentals are grafted. Be certain that the graft union, usually a small bulge near the base of the stem, is a few inches above the soil level.*

ones, so do not be deceived by the size of your tree. Until new roots have become established and the tree is firmly anchored in its new location, take measures to minimize the shock of planting.

Top-heavy trees and shrubs from 3 to 20 feet in height should be staked to prevent wind damage. One or two strong stakes, 6 to 8 feet tall, are recommended. Carefully drive the stakes 2 feet into the ground, 6 to 12 inches from the trunk. This is usually easier if done before the planting hole is completely filled and also results in less root injury. Depending on the number of stakes used, thread a length of wire through a piece of garden hose; twist it in a figure eight around the tree, being sure no bare wire touches the trunk. Fasten the wire to the stake so the trunk is held firmly in place. The hose is essential for protecting tender bark; bare wire may girdle or scrape newly established plants, providing an entryway for pests and diseases. (*See Figure 5.*)

Trees, especially larger specimens, may also be supported by cabling or guying. This should be avoided in high-traffic areas if possible, however, as the wire is often difficult to see and may be dangerous to passersby. Drive three 6- to 8-foot-tall sturdy stakes into the ground in an equilateral triangle around the plant. Using three lengths of wire, thread each through a piece of hosing; loop each around the plant, halfway up the trunk; then secure a length of wire to each stake. Periodically check all wires wrapped around plants to be sure no girdling or other damage has taken place. Wires that seem tight should be loosened to prevent damage. Staked or guyed plants should be allowed to remain undisturbed for one to two years; then remove the supports.

Can you give me some tips for watering established trees and shrubs?

Trees and shrubs need supplemental watering, especially during periods of drought and hot weather and after planting. The most important principle in watering woody plants is to water deeply and thoroughly. Repeated light sprinklings do nothing but encourage shallow root growth, which is usually inefficient and may even reduce the ability of plants to withstand strong winds.

As a general rule, you should water established plants when the top inch of soil is dry, being sure to check often during periods of sparse rainfall. And although it is essential to water plants thoroughly, it is equally important to allow them to dry out slightly before rewatering. The length of time between waterings will depend on the temperature, wind, humidity, rainfall, and soil type in your area. Under normal conditions, clay soils dry out in about 20 days; loam, 15 days; sand, 7 to 9 days. But if you do not water deeply and thoroughly, the soil will dry out more quickly.

Proper watering of ornamentals means soaking the soil to a depth of 1½ to 2 feet. This will take about 60 gallons of water for a 50-square-foot area of sandy soil, about 100 gallons for loam, and around 175 gallons for heavy clay. At normal volume and pressure, a common garden hose produces about 5 gallons of water per minute, so it will take about 15 minutes to water thoroughly a sandy area 50 feet square, 20 minutes for loam, and about 40 minutes in an area of clay.

Do I have to take special precautions when planting grafted plants?

When you plant grafted nursery stock, especially roses, dogwoods, weeping Higan cherries, and fruit trees, be sure to keep the graft union at least 1 inch above the soil level. (*See Figure 6.*) If buried, the scion (grafted portion) will root and overgrow the rootstock. A rootstock is usually chosen for its vigor, resistance to disease, dwarfing effect, or some other specific quality; if overgrown, the rootstock will be ineffective.

How should bare-root trees and shrubs be planted?

For best results, soak the roots in cool water for 24 hours before planting. Then, using a garden spade, dig a well-rounded hole that is deep and wide enough to accommodate the root system without crowding. A hole about 12 inches deeper than the length of the root system is recommended. (*See Figure 7.*)

Thoroughly mix peat moss, finely ground pine bark, or compost into the backfill, especially in heavy clay soils. Bone meal or superphosphate may also be added to the backfill; these are slow acting and safely stimulate the growth of new roots. Use at the rate of ¼ pound for a 4- to 6-foot plant, ½ pound for an 8- to 10-foot specimen, and ¾ pound for larger ones. (Do not use inorganic, high-nitrogen fertilizers at plantingtime, as they can easily burn young roots.)

Place 6 inches of amended backfill into the prepared hole, thoroughly tamping it down; over this, form a firm cone of soil to adjust the plant to the correct height. (*See Figure 8.*) After trimming away any broken roots, position the roots of the plant over the soil cone, spreading them evenly so that none are crowded.

At this point, check to be sure the plant will be set at the same depth it grew in the nursery; a dark-brown line on the lower trunk indicates its original planting depth. Planting too deep is one of the major causes of decline in newly established ornamentals.

Holding the trunk of the plant steady, lightly sprinkle backfill over and around the roots, filling the hole to within 3 to 4 inches of the soil line. Periodically shake the plant gently to eliminate any air pockets that may have formed in the soil. Water the plant thoroughly before completely filling in the planting hole, and allow it to drain; then use the remainder of the backfill to fashion a berm or rim around the planting hole. Such a berm creates a basin, directing rainwater into the root zone. (*See Figure 9.*) Water again to eliminate air pockets. Mulch with a 4- to 6-inch layer of pine straw or other organic matter.

Remove one-third of the branches of a newly planted bare-root ornamental at plantingtime. Do not simply lop off the top third of the plant; carefully prune away individual branches, selecting weak or poorly placed limbs first. Never cut out the main stem or leader, as the plant's form may be destroyed.

Do balled-and-burlapped plants need special planting treatment?

With few exceptions, balled-and-burlapped specimens should be planted much like bare-root plants. As the name implies, balled-and-burlapped plants are dug from the nursery with a ball of soil around the roots, then wrapped in burlap. (*See Figure 10.*) Immediate planting is also recommended for balled-and-burlapped ornamentals, although it is not quite as critical as with bare-root plants. If there is a delay, wrap the root balls with damp towels, tarps, or moist mulch until the plants can be set in the ground.

Dig the planting hole twice as wide and 12 inches deeper than the root ball. Amend backfill with peat moss and bone meal or superphosphate as recommended in bare-root planting; then add enough backfill to the planting hole to make the hole as deep as the root ball. Like bare-root ornamentals, plant most balled-and-burlapped specimens at the same depth they grew at the nursery. When properly planted, the top of the root ball should be at ground level. (Azaleas, rhododendrons, and camellias should be planted slightly higher.) Gently set the plant into the prepared hole, grasping it by the root ball rather than the trunk; otherwise, you may break small feeder roots growing close to the soil surface.

Fig. 7

Fig. 8 *To check for correct planting depth, place the shovel across the planting hole to make sure the dark line on the lower trunk is level with the ground surface.*

Fig. 9

Fig. 10

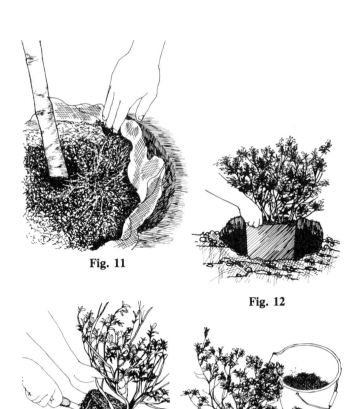

Fig. 11

Fig. 12

Fig. 13

Fig. 14 *Mix soil removed from the planting hole with an equal portion of organic matter. Add to the hole to adjust the height of plant; then fill in around the root ball, and firm the soil.*

Fig. 15

Break away the top rim of the peat pot to prevent it from acting as a wick.

Untie the cord from the burlap, and discard it; fold the burlap back from the root ball (do not remove it); gradually fill the hole three-fourths full of soil. (*See Figure 11.*) Water the soil thoroughly several times during the filling process to remove any air pockets, and allow the water to drain; then finish filling the hole, bringing it up even with ground level. Selectively prune one-third of the top growth of newly planted specimens in the manner described for bare-root plants. Also apply mulch as you would for bare-root plants.

Can you give me some guidelines on setting out container-grown plants?

Container-grown plants are generally available in vinyl, metal, or plantable pots in sizes that range from 1 gallon up to as large as 7 gallons. With the exception of plantable pots, always remove the container prior to planting. Turn the plant upside down, and give the edge of the container a sharp rap to loosen most of the root system; then carefully remove the container. If your plant is in a metal container, be sure to have the nurseryman slit the sides of the can and tie it together with twine, or you will have difficulty removing the plant without damaging it.

Plantable pots are thick, cardboardlike containers made of papier-mâché or compressed peat and may be planted right along with the root system. Check with the nurseryman to make sure the containers are plantable and biodegradable; if not and you plant them, the plants will soon be potbound or choked by girdling roots. Remember to bury plantable pots completely; any exposed portion will act as a wick and draw valuable water away from the plant roots.

Dig a planting hole twice as wide and deep as the container holding the plant. (*See Figure 12.*) Mix the soil you have removed with an equal portion of peat moss, ground pine bark, compost, leaf mold, or other organic matter. Where soil is predominantly alkaline, such as in Texas, azaleas and other acid-loving plants should be planted in a backfill of ½ peat and ½ sand.

Remove the plant from its container and inspect the roots that can be seen on the soil ball. Slice firmly through the soil ball with a sharp knife to loosen any roots that may have matted around the soil ball. (*See Figure 13.*) Use mixed backfill to adjust the plant to the correct height in the hole. (*See Figure 14.*) In heavy soils, the top of the root ball should be about 2 inches above the level of surrounding soil. In sandy, rapidly draining soils, make a slight depression or basin around the plant, but be sure you do not submerge the top of the root ball below the ground line. Always make sure the top of the root ball is at the ground line or slightly above. Fill in around the plant with backfill soil and pack it with your foot. Water the plant thoroughly, and mulch. (*See Figure 15.*)

Will it hurt my transplants to leave them in the peat pots when I plant them?

Peat pots decay and therefore need not be removed. In fact, they protect tender roots during the planting. However, if allowed to protrude above the soil level, the rim of the pots act as a wick, drawing moisture away from the transplants. To prevent this, break away at least the uppermost rim of the pots before planting; also make sure the pots are completely covered with soil.

When is the best time to transplant trees?

If you have been waiting for the dormant season to do needed transplanting of shrubs and young trees, prepare to do so when deciduous plants have lost their leaves. You may also transplant evergreens during the cool months. In the Upper South, ornamentals are most successfully transplanted from November 1 through March 15; in the Middle South, from December 15 to March 1; and in the Lower South, from December 31 to February 15. Avoid planting or transplanting on bright or windy days when roots may be exposed to the direct rays of the sun or drying winds.

We want to move some small native trees and shrubs from our property in the country in order to have colorful autumn foliage in our home yard. Can this be done in the fall?

Autumn is the time to note and mark specimens with the best fall coloring; but wait until February, just before the plants break dormancy, to transplant them. Look especially for plants with vivid coloring, such as maple, hickory, sour gum, sweet gum, scarlet oak, sumac (*Rhus sp.*), sourwood, and oakleaf hydrangea (*Hydrangea quercifolia*).

As soon as you can after marking a plant, prune the roots near the soil surface by forcing a spade into the soil as far as possible to form a circle. The circle should be about 18 inches in diameter around the trunk of smaller plants and 2 to 3 feet in diameter around larger ones. New feeder roots will develop where established roots are severed. When transplanted, these new roots will aid the tree or shrub in getting a good start in its new location.

I have a plant in my garden that would make a wonderful accent plant. Can you give me some suggestions for moving it?

Specimen-quality plants (plants that have matured and developed the shape and form that exemplify the species) should be placed in a location where they will contribute to the overall landscape design. Whatever plant you want to move, proper digging is a must. Here is how to move the plant and help ensure its survival.

—Make sure the cultural requirements of the plant match the conditions of the new location. For example, do not move a shade-loving plant to a full-sun location.

—If possible, move the plant during the dormant season. This will increase the chance of its surviving the shock of the move.

—Always measure before you move. If the plant is too large for the new location, severe pruning may be required, and this could destroy the character of the plant.

—Prepare the new hole before digging the plant; this reduces the time the plant spends out of the ground. (*See Figure 16.*)

—To remove the plant, turn the digging spade toward you and dig straight down, circling the plant. Make the first cut at least 2 feet away from the plant all the way around. (*See Figure 17.*)

—Cut away soil on the outside of the initial cut; this will begin to form the root ball. (*See Figure 18.*)

—With the shovel tip, carefully shave the ball underneath. Avoid cutting into the top 8 inches of soil. (*See Figure 19.*)

—Pry the plant loose with the shovel and lift onto a blanket or cloth. (*See Figure 20.*)

—Set the plant so that the root ball is about 2 inches above ground level. Mound loose soil against the root ball, and press soil firmly into place.

—After the plant is moved, thin the crown of the plant to compensate for root loss.

—Soak the plant for at least one hour or until the ground around it is saturated. Then cover the root ball with a 3-inch mulch.

Fig. 16 *Prepare the new hole first. Dig the hole at least twice as wide and deep as the size of the root ball. Work in organic matter, such as finely ground bark or compost; backfill with the prepared soil.*

Fig. 17

Fig. 18

Fig. 19

Fig. 20

Before planting azaleas or rhododendrons, make three shallow, vertical cuts around the root ball of the plant.

A shallow, dish-shaped excavation is all that is necessary for azaleas and rhododendrons, as they will be smothered if planted too deeply.

Mound the loose soil in the bed carefully around the root ball of the azalea and press gently into place.

When is the best time to transplant pine seedlings?

For best results, transplant pine seedlings in February, when they are generally dormant. The smaller the plant, the better results you are likely to have.

Could you please give me some guidelines for purchasing and planting azaleas and rhododendrons?

When you select azaleas and rhododendrons, look for well-branched, full plants. Limbs should be close to the ground and the foliage bright and healthy looking. The leaves should be turned upward, not drooping.

When purchasing young azaleas or rhododendrons for planting, do not be fooled by their shape. Because they are nursery grown, they will be stiff and upright and may seem too rigid and ungainly. But as plants mature, they spread out and the foliage weeps slightly. Bear in mind that it will take a few years for the shrubs to loosen up and achieve their characteristic growth habit.

To plant, choose a partially shaded site with good drainage. Proper bed preparation is also extremely important for these plants. This means tilling a bed 4 or 5 feet wider than the size of the root ball or container. It is preferable to do this the season before you plant to allow time for the soil to weather and break up. Here are the basic steps for bed preparation and planting.

—Till the soil in the bed vigorously, a minimum of 12 inches deep. Break up all soil, leaving no clods. Check the quality of the soil by squeezing a handful. If it clumps together in a claylike mass, it needs extensive work. Bring in sand and finely shredded or ground bark, and till it in until the soil is loose and friable (workable). But if the soil spills out of your hand like sand, a combination of equal parts topsoil and fine bark will need to be worked in to provide a good growing medium.

—In almost every instance (unless other azaleas or rhododendrons grow naturally nearby), plan to work finely ground bark into the soil at the specific location of each plant, in addition to any bark tilled into the original bed. This will ensure a porous soil for good drainage, provide a highly organic growing medium that is naturally acid, and help keep sufficient moisture around the roots to keep them from drying out.

—Before planting, lightly make three vertical cuts around the root ball of the plant. This cuts the roots near the surface, stimulating formation of new feeder roots.

—If planted too deep, azaleas and rhododendrons may smother and die. So when planting, do not dig a hole in the prepared bed. Instead, make a shallow dish-shaped excavation with your hands; then set the plant in the center of the dish. The top of the root ball should be 3 to 5 inches above the level of the bed. Carefully mound the loose soil in the bed around the root ball, and press it gently into place. Planting in this fashion will facilitate drainage as well as allow the plant to spread its surface root system downward into the bed.

—After planting, mulch the plant with 4 to 5 inches of loose pine straw; then soak the bed thoroughly.

How should I plant my camellias?

Adequate planting holes and good soil preparation are crucial with camellias. Dig the hole at least 1½ times the size of the root ball. Like azaleas, camellias prefer moist, well-drained acid soil (ideal pH is 5.5 to 6). However, they are somewhat more drought tolerant than azaleas when established. If the soil is predominantly alkaline in your area, mix a generous amount of peat moss, compost, leaf mold, or well-decayed pine straw with the backfill soil. If the soil is high in clay, dig the planting hole at least twice the size of the root ball; backfill with soil mixed with a generous amount of organic matter such as peat moss, compost, or leaf mold. Regardless of the soil type, incorporate ½ cup azalea-camellia fertilizer into the backfill of each planting hole.

What is the best method for planting dogwoods?

Although these popular trees are native to the South, they can be temperamental in the home garden. First, purchase a healthy tree from a reputable nursery rather than trying to transplant a tree from the wild. Once you have purchased a tree, do not delay planting it. Select a planting site that is partially shaded, especially from afternoon sun.

Dig a planting hole twice as wide and deep as the root ball. Dogwoods are more particular about drainage than they are about soil, but you can improve both soil structure and drainage if you dig the hole about 18 inches deep and mix leaf mold, pine bark, or peat moss into the backfill soil. On extremely heavy soils, break up existing hardpan before attempting to grow a dogwood.

On balled-and-burlapped plants, unfasten the burlap from around the trunk, but do not remove it from the root ball. On container-grown plants, loosen the roots if they have become matted around the soil ball.

Begin to refill the planting hole, firming the soil to adjust the plant to the correct height. The top of the root ball should be slightly above the soil surrounding the planting hole. Lay the handle of a shovel or a rake on the ground to check the level of the root ball; then firm backfill soil around the roots. Water thoroughly to settle the soil, and add more backfill if necessary. The first year in the ground is crucial for a dogwood, so be sure to water during rainless weather.

Please tell me how to plant oakleaf hydrangeas. Do they need special care?

Oakleaf hydrangeas will need protection from direct summer and winter winds. Since the branches are rather brittle, heavy accumulations of snow will need to be shaken off to avoid breakage. Also be sure to keep plants well watered during dry periods.

Oakleaf hydrangeas should be set out during autumn or early spring. Choose a shady location, and plant in rich, well-drained, slightly acid soil. Dig a planting hole at least twice the size of the root ball; mix backfill soil with a generous amount of compost, peat, or other organic matter. Water thoroughly, and apply a 4- to 5-inch layer of mulch.

What is the best method for planting palms and when is the best time?

Since a large palm is also heavy, you might not be able to handle it without assistance. If you must have the plant delivered to your home, you might as well have the retailer install the plant as well. Although the installation service will increase the cost, most nurserymen and landscape installation contractors guarantee any plant they install themselves for the first year it is in the ground.

If you do the planting yourself, select a site with the proper lighting conditions for your plant. Dig a hole at least twice as deep and wide as the container the plant is in, and backfill with plenty of sand and organic matter to ensure adequate drainage. Be sure the plant is set at the same depth it grew at the nursery.

Since the roots of palms become established rapidly during warm weather, early summer is the best time to plant palms.

When you plant a dogwood, be sure the top of the root ball is slightly higher than ground level. Mound backfill soil into the hole and firm it around the roots.

Oakleaf hydrangea is one of the South's finest native shrubs. In the Upper South, however, it may need some winter protection.

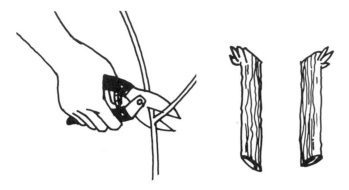

Fig. 21 *Prune back to a branch or bud. The direction the bud points will be the direction of new growth.*

Fig. 22 *Cut halfway through the underside of the limb. Make another cut on the upper side of the limb, about 1 inch away.*

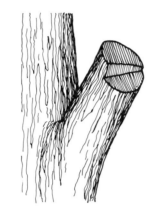

Fig. 23 *The limb will fall under its own weight, but it will not break or strip the bark.*

Fig. 24 *Remove the stub flush with the trunk.*

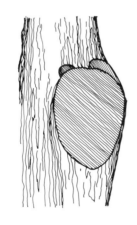

Fig. 25 *Seal the wound with shellac.*

Pruning

Can you give me some tips on how to prune trees and shrubs?

Use a clean, sharp pruning tool to make smooth cuts back to a bud or flush with a branch or with the main trunk. Pruning cuts made to a bud should be at a 45-degree angle, slanting downward just above the bud. (*See Figure 21.*) Cup-shaped cuts will hold water and may cause rotting. Also avoid leaving any stubs, as they will rot and may provide an entrance for pests and diseases. To seal pruning cuts and protect from pests and diseases, paint cuts wider than an inch with orange shellac. When you remove diseased branches, disinfect the pruning tool by dipping the blades in alcohol between cuts; this helps prevent spreading the disease to healthy branches.

Limbs more than 4 to 6 inches in diameter and high up in a tree could be dangerous to remove and should be taken down by a professional arborist. To remove smaller limbs, make a cut from the underside of the limb about a foot from the main trunk, cutting halfway through. Make the second cut about an inch up from the first on the opposite side of the limb. The wood between the cuts will break under the weight of the limb. Cut the stub back flush with the trunk, and seal with shellac. (*See Figures 22–25.*)

When should I prune shrubs that flower in early spring?

Shrubs which flower in early spring, such as forsythia (*Forsythia* x *intermedia*), azaleas, camellias, oakleaf and bigleaf hydrangeas, and privet, should be pruned after flowering. As these plants produce flower buds on the previous year's growth, early pruning would remove the buds.

Azaleas should be pruned only to remove dead or diseased wood and wayward shoots. When pruning is required, cut back branches to their point of origin; this may stimulate new growth and will help maintain a uniform appearance without giving the plants an unnaturally rounded or square look.

Late spring is the time to revive overgrown forsythia and bigleaf hydrangea by removing the oldest branches at the point of origin. To keep plants like camellias, mountain laurel, and hibiscus compact and bushy, pinch off the end buds in the early summer, after blossoms have fallen.

When is the best time to prune summer-flowering shrubs?

March, April, and May are important pruning months in the South. Summer-flowering shrubs and trees which form flower buds on the current year's growth can be

Glossy abelia will produce new flower-bearing branches when the old wood is cut back close to the ground.

pruned in late winter or early spring, while the plant is dormant and before new buds have formed. This will stimulate the growth of new flower-bearing branches on plants such as glossy abelia, chaste tree (*Vitex agnus-castus*), pomegranate (*Punica granatum*), orange-eye butterfly bush, and peegee hydrangea (*Hydrangea paniculata* Grandiflora). Shrubs with extended blooming periods, like Chinese hibiscus (*Hibiscus rosa-sinensis*), oleander, lantana, banana shrub (*Michelia figo*), and cape plumbago, will also benefit from occasional tip pruning during the summer.

Rejuvenate overgrown oleander in the spring by cutting the entire plant back to 6 inches from the ground. Cape plumbago and glossy abelia can be revived at this time by removing the oldest branches at their points of origin.

We have some overgrown shrubs in our yard. Is there any way I can prune them to make them interesting landscape features?

A little artistic pruning can transform an overgrown shrub into a striking landscape feature. By removing the lower branches to sculpt the shrub into tree form, you can develop an accent specimen, a shade plant, or if using more than one, a screen or miniature allée. Besides having handsome stems, most species suggested for this treatment are evergreen plants and provide a steady look all year.

What kinds of shrubs do well pruned into tree form?

When you choose shrubs to prune into tree form, consider their hardiness and rate of growth, eventual height, and character of foliage and stems. Shrubs which do well pruned into tree form include Burford holly, Japan cleyera (*Ternstroemia gymnanthera*), Japanese pittosporum, rosebay (*Rhododendron maximum*), sasanqua camellia, sweet olive, waxleaf privet, wax myrtle, and yaupon. These reach heights of 15 to 35 feet after 20 years of normal growth and tolerate a variety of adverse conditions.

How should hedges be pruned?

A properly shaped hedge or shrub is narrower at the top than at the base. This allows sunlight to reach the lower branches, which helps keep the hedge dense from top to bottom. Otherwise, the top of the hedge would shade the lower part, causing the lower branches to become spindly and shed leaves. (*See Figure 26.*)

When clipping shrubs and hedges, stretch a cord or string along the upper edge to help guide you in making a neat edge and to maintain a uniform height and width. Attach the cord to a tall stake placed at the end of the hedge or attach it to a corner branch of the hedge itself. Later, move the cord to the bottom of the hedge to guide your

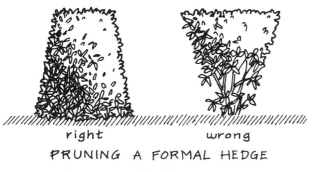

right   wrong

PRUNING A FORMAL HEDGE

Fig. 26

Waxleaf privet, pruned to tree form, is a superb specimen.

Instead of waging a continual battle against the surging growth of these Burford hollies, the owners let them grow and pruned them to tree form. Now they shade the terrace.

Filling in old boxwoods with young ones will keep the planting looking full and bushy.

Fig. 27

clipping there. Shape the hedge so that the top width is three-fourths the width of the bottom.

Always use high-quality pruning tools. Hand-held hook-and-blade shears are recommended for pruning. A good pair of heavy, sharp-bladed shears will make clean cuts and leave no hangnail wood.

How often should hedges be pruned?

The frequency of pruning depends on the growth rate of the plant and its growing conditions. Faster-growing shrubs, such as privet, require more frequent pruning than slow-growing hedges, such as Japanese yew or common boxwood. In the Lower South, where the growing season is longer, you may have to prune more often than in the Upper South. A good general rule is to prune shrubs and hedges when new growth is 2 or 3 inches long, or when the new growth causes the plant to look shaggy and unkempt and disturbs the desired shape. Pruning should be done at least twice a year in most of the South.

Some large old boxwoods that line my driveway have become somewhat unkempt. Can I prune them back safely to make them bush out?

Unfortunately, established boxwoods usually will not fill out well if cut back. Few growth buds are found on old wood. It might be best to put out some small shrubs to replace the old plants gradually.

Our firethorn shrubs need extensive pruning. When can we prune them without hindering the development of berries?

Since firethorns (pyracanthas) flower and produce berries on the previous year's growth, anytime you prune you are going to reduce the number of berries the following year. Most people prefer to prune while the branches are loaded with berries so they can be used for indoor decoration during the holiday season. However, pruning at any season is not likely to harm the plants.

Should I prune my heavenly bamboo?

Heavenly bamboo or nandina does not have to be pruned, but it will be more attractive if carefully shaped this winter. Pruning also encourages berry production.

Since heavenly bamboo characteristically bears most of its leaves at the top of the canes, the key to proper pruning lies in cutting back canes at staggered heights. This will create a layered effect when new foliage appears. Leave some tall canes at the rear of the plant, but cut excessively leggy canes back to the ground. Cut the remaining canes back to heights ranging from 2 to 3 feet to create the staggered effect; be sure to make cuts above a leaf scar (bulge on the stem where an old leaf was attached). Plan to leave some canes with foliage so the plant will not be bare all winter. (*See Figure 27.*)

Our 6-foot-tall mountain laurel is growing in front of a low window. Could I cut it back about 18 inches without losing too many future blooms?

That much pruning would remove most of the flower buds that have formed, and buds do not form readily on old mountain laurel wood. Sometimes it is necessary to cut the shrub back to the ground and grow a new top. It might be best to move the plant this fall or winter to a location where it can develop normally.

Our hybrid rhododendrons have become leggy and unattractive. What can I do to encourage compact, sturdy growth?

The best way is to cut all the stems back to within 4 to 8 inches of the ground before new growth begins. New growth will sprout from the base and develop into shapely new plants in a few years. If you cannot bring yourself to prune this severely, cut one-third of the canes back the same way each year for three years. In early spring, spread ½ cup of 5-10-10 on the soil around each plant and water thoroughly.

Some of my ornamental trees need severe pruning. Can you give me some pointers on how to make them look their best?

The first step in pruning deciduous trees and shrubs like flowering quince, forsythia, and dogwood is to remove all dead, diseased, or injured branches. Next, remove branches that cross each other or that would become entangled by strong winds. If the tree still looks too thick, remove some of the older branches and any that are distinctly different from the rest of the tree. Cut back excessively long growth to a bud that is 4 to 6 inches below the average branch length. If you need to reduce the length of all the branches, be sure to cut back close to a bud or side twig.

My 10-foot crepe myrtle tree has never been pruned. How much and when can I safely prune it?

While major pruning is not necessary, tip pruning (carefully removing the flower clusters after bloom) is recommended for crepe myrtle. This encourages bloom the following season without inhibiting the plant's natural form. Just nip the old clusters off with hand shears or lopping shears. (*See Figure 28.*) Any additional pruning underneath the canopy to remove twiggy growth will keep the trunks clean and allow free air circulation that will help prevent mildew.

Stump pruning is a more drastic alternative to tip pruning. It involves cutting the plant back to a few main trunks, either to eye level or almost all the way to the ground. This forces the plant to produce an abundance of twiggy growth that will bloom heavily, but it makes the plant lose one of its most desirable characteristics—its sculptural form. February is the best time to do this kind of pruning, before new growth begins. Being pruned so severely, the crepe myrtle will probably have few flowers the first season. By the second year, flower production should be normal.

What is the correct way to prune a hemlock?

Hemlocks are beautiful and stately enough in their natural form that pruning is recommended only to remove dead wood. If your hemlock has some dead wood or very spindly limbs, you can remove an entire limb with a pruning saw or loppers; tip prune dead or damaged ends of branches with hand shears. Always try to keep the natural shape when pruning; do not shear the tree into a hedge.

How can I make my hemlock screen more dense? The trees, 40 to 60 feet tall, are getting sparse at ground level and for several feet above. Will cutting off the tops thicken the growth of lower branches?

There is no way to greatly increase the density of such old trees. If the trees were younger, late spring or early summer pruning would make the tips branch more, but

When the branches of a tree touch and rub against each other, they should be removed.

Fig. 28 *Crepe myrtle needs little pruning, but keeping the trunks free of twiggy growth improves air circulation, which helps prevent mildew.*

The punch-bar method is an alternative to the use of tree spikes. It is, however, a rather lengthy process.

such pruning would do little good at this stage. You might consider planting a backup screen to fill in the empty spaces in the trees. Mountain laurel, rhododendron, and leucothöe are good choices.

Fertilizing

How do I fertilize trees and shrubs?

To fertilize shrubs, broadcast the fertilizer evenly beneath the plant at the rate recommended by the manufacturer; water well to wash fertilizer into the soil. Do not try to work the fertilizer into the soil with a hoe or rake, because you may damage the shallow root system. Neither should you let the fertilizer come into direct contact with the plant.

Fertilize small trees just as you would shrubs. For large trees, there are two ways to fertilize. Trees growing in the open ground (no vegetation beneath) may be fed by broadcasting fertilizer under the tree canopy; apply to within 1 foot of the trunk, and water thoroughly. This type of fertilization encourages roots to grow near the soil surface, which may interfere with mowing and makes the tree more susceptible to drought stress during dry periods.

The best way to fertilize large trees in most areas is by the punch-bar method. This involves punching deep holes into the ground in the area of the tree roots and filling them with fertilizer. Using a crowbar or hammer and stake, make 2-inch-wide holes 18 inches deep (at a slant toward the tree) 2 feet apart in the region of the tree's feeder roots. In general, the feeder roots are located in a circle that extends two-thirds of the way from slightly outside the canopy to near the tree trunk. Make 10 to 20 holes for each inch of trunk diameter; then evenly distribute the recommended amount of fertilizer among the holes, and refill with peat moss, soil, or manure.

The punch-bar method is a lengthy process, but much of the work can be eliminated by using tree spike fertilizer. These fertilizer spikes are driven directly into the ground so there are no holes to fill or refill.

When should I fertilize my ornamental trees and shrubs?

Early spring (just before growth starts) is the time to fertilize all trees and shrubs. Use a low-nitrogen formulation, such as 5-10-10 or 6-12-12. For shrubs and young trees, summer fertilization is equally important. Again, use a low-nitrogen formulation. Roses, French hydrangea, hibiscus, oleander, and other plants that grow rapidly, that produce an abundance of foliage, or that flower in a short time should be fertilized every six to eight weeks during the growing season if adequate moisture is available.

In extreme South Texas and South Florida, plants that are not dormant during winter and are growing in sandy soils should be fertilized bimonthly with a low-nitrogen fertilizer, such as 6-12-12.

I have not had my soil tested. Are there some general guidelines I can follow for fertilizing my trees and shrubs?

Generally, you can fertilize newly planted trees and shrubs with ½ cup 5-10-10, 6-12-12, or similar analysis applied three times per year (March, May, and July). Always make sure adequate moisture is available.

Established or mature shrubs can benefit from 1 cup of 5-10-10, 6-12-12, or similar analysis applied two times per year (March and July). Established trees can be fertilized with the same analysis as shrubs, applied each spring at a rate of 1 cup per inch of trunk diameter.

How do I know whether to use an acid-forming fertilizer?

Some favorite ornamentals grown in the South prefer an acid soil (that is, soil in which the pH is lower than 7). Among the more familiar acid-loving plants are azaleas, camellias, gardenias, viburnums (*Viburnum sp.*), dogwoods, magnolias, and blueberries (*Vaccinium sp.*).

Whether you should use an acid fertilizer on these plants depends entirely on the soil in your garden. A soil test is the surest way to find out exactly what the pH of your soil is. In most of the South, the soil is sufficiently acid to promote good growth on azaleas, camellias, and other acid-loving plants, and a special fertilizer is not required. In fact, azaleas respond poorly to soil that is too acid. If this is the case, it may be necessary to lime the soil to raise the pH to the optimum range of 5 to 6.

In coastal areas, particularly in the Carolinas and along the Gulf, soil pH may need to be adjusted downward, and an acid fertilizer may help. In parts of Texas and Florida where soil is notoriously alkaline, growing azaleas may be too difficult because of the high soil pH. You can try adding sulfur, aluminum sulfate, iron sulfate, or ammonium sulfate to acidify the soil. However, it is probably best to select other plants that you know will grow well in your area.

Our azaleas are growing beneath oak trees. Are the fallen oak leaves harmful or beneficial to the azaleas?

Oak leaves have an acid pH, making them beneficial to azaleas. However, be sure that you do not allow large accumulations of leaves to remain around the plants, as they may smother the shallow root system of azaleas.

What kind of feeding do azaleas and rhododendrons require?

Azaleas, rhododendrons and other such acid-loving plants rarely require heavy feeding. For general fertilizing, however, you can use a slow-acting organic fertilizer such as cottonseed meal or soybean meal. Or you can apply a fast-acting commercial "azalea-rhododendron-camellia" fertilizer which includes ammonium sulfate. Superphosphate applied in late winter or early spring ensures bud set and promotes intensity of color.

Should I fertilize my camellias in the fall?

You can prepare your camellias for winter and improve the blooms by feeding in September with a nitrogen-free fertilizer, such as 0-12-12. Nitrogen applied in the fall will stimulate new vegetative growth which is too tender to withstand low winter temperatures. Sasanqua camellias can benefit from a light application of a concentrated liquid houseplant fertilizer, such as 20-20-20, mixed at ½ the concentration suggested on the label. Do not overfertilize, however.

How do I fertilize my heavenly bamboo?

Heavenly bamboo (or nandina) is generally fertilized in early spring and again in midsummer with a complete fertilizer like 5-10-10.

When fertilizing shrubs, broadcast the fertilizer evenly around the plant at the rate recommended in the manufacturer's directions.

Wildflowers

Queen Anne's Lace

Bloodroots

In some ways, wildflowers are taken for granted along the roadways of the South—buttercups in spring, Queen Anne's lace in summer, and goldenrod in fall. But when we stop and realize that they are really nature's specialty, we begin not only to appreciate these plants but to admire them as well. Wildflowers are hardy, surviving and adapting to every type of climatic situation and soil condition. For this and other reasons, people have become more and more interested in the cultivation of wildflowers.

Along with the development of a home wildflower garden, however, comes a responsibility. You cannot just go roaming the woods and dig up that beautiful trillium you see in bloom. In the first place, it could be illegal. Secondly, the plants often will not survive. Sometimes, however, wooded areas marked for development may be dug for wildflowers, provided you obtain permission first. Usually wildflower societies or state and planning commissions sponsor and organize the digs. There are even organizations like the Plant Rescue Volunteers at the North Carolina Botanical Gardens in Chapel Hill, which collect rare and endangered plants from condemned areas and propagate plants from these specimens. Whether it is a group like this or a reputable wildflower

Black-Eyed Susans

Texas Bluebonnets

Yellow Lady's Slipper Orchids

nursery (*see* our list on page 210), be sure to obtain the wildflowers you need from a legal source.

Another way to start your wildflower garden is to collect the seeds and grow them yourself. Fall is the best time to germinate wildflowers, but collect the seeds all season as they mature. If you collect them from the wild, start them in soil dug from the area where the parent plant grew. If you have to mix your own soil, use 1 part sand to 1 part compost, leaf mold, or peat moss. Sow seeds in flats or pots with good drainage, planting each seed no deeper than three times its diameter. Small, dustlike seeds may be sprinkled on the soil's surface. Dust sphagnum moss over the surface. Leave flats outside over the winter, but be sure not to let the soil dry out. Most plants will be ready to transplant when the first true leaves appear, usually about midspring. Seedlings grow at different rates, and some may be ready to transplant to a permanent location.

When you transplant wildflowers, be sure to match as nearly as possible the growing conditions of each plant's natural environment. This means reproducing the amount of sunlight, shade, and moisture available and the content, pH, and porosity of the soil of

Bee Balm

Jack-in-the-Pulpit

Butterfly Weed

Jack-in-the-Pulpit

Tickseed

Virginia Bluebells

the original habitat. Some wildflowers require the deep shade and acid soil of a coniferous forest; others flourish in the filtered shade and less-acid soil of a deciduous forest or the full sun and drier soil of an open field.

Those that grow in fields and meadows can grow in the same soil as your other garden plants—a rich loam consisting of clay, silt, sand, and organic matter. Forest-type flowers require a soil improved with decayed leaves or peat moss worked in to a depth of about 1 foot. Try to use a leaf mold with the same degree of acidity to which the wildflowers are adapted. Leaves or needles of pine, spruce, hemlock, oak, azalea, and rhododendron will produce very acid leaf mold; red maple, moderately acid; hickory, tulip, poplar, dogwood, and red cedar, slightly acid. Since you probably will not be able to duplicate exactly the wildflowers' natural environment, keep the wildflower beds well watered and mulched to help them adapt to a less-than-ideal environment. Once established, a wildflower garden can be one of the least demanding plantings in your landscape. And with careful planning, you can enjoy a garden that takes on a new character with each season.

Atamasco Lilies

Rue Anemone

Bird's-Foot Violet

Sweet Beth Trillium

General Recommendations

Please give me some guidelines for planting a wildflower garden.

First, determine what kind of environment you can provide. This will guide you in choosing which wildflowers to plant. To decide on their placement in the garden, consider the colors, time and length of blooming seasons, and heights of the flowers. Choose one or more focal points—a tree, a group of shrubs, or some rock outcroppings, for example—and arrange the plantings around them. Develop a layered effect with wildflowers of different heights; after the blooming season ends, the levels of foliage will continue to provide visual interest and variety. Extend the blooming season by planting later-blooming wildflowers along with the spring-blooming ones.

Mulch is essential to a wildflower garden. Duplicate the mulch of the forest floor with fallen leaves or pine needles; or use stones or rocks to enhance the natural setting and conserve moisture. Hay can be used to mulch wildflowers growing in a field or meadowlike environment. Because wildflowers cannot grow in compacted soil, paths or stepping-stones should also be included in your garden plan. This will allow you to work in and enjoy your garden without walking on the flower beds.

I would like to start a wildflower garden. Where should I get the wildflowers?

It is always best to buy nursery-grown plants, as they are more adaptable to variations in the soil and will suffer less cultural shock than a plant transplanted from the wild. Another advantage to nursery-grown plants is that you can often obtain planting and cultural information when you buy the plants. Buy from a reputable nursery specializing in wildflowers and make sure the wildflowers are grown there and not collected from the woods. Some species are becoming rare and perhaps endangered because of overcollecting from the wild by nurseries. If you have to order by mail, be sure to use the scientific name to avoid mistakes.

Do not dig wildflowers in the woods because it upsets the balance of nature. It is against the law to dig certain plants. Often, however, wooded areas marked for

A rock outcropping makes a good focal point for a wild-flower garden.

When a wooded area is slated for development, local wildflower societies or planning commissions may open the area to the public so that wild plants may be dug. This is the only time you should try to obtain wildflowers from the woods.

After planting a wildflower garden, be sure to mulch plants well. A mulch of pine straw and fallen leaves enhances the natural feel of the garden and conserves moisture.

To collect wildflower seeds, tie a piece of stocking or muslin over the flower while it is still in bloom. Seeds will collect in the covering in a few weeks.

development may be dug for wildflowers, provided you obtain permission from the proper authorities. Information about digs—situations in which the public is invited to dig wild plants—can usually be obtained from local wildflower societies, from city and state planning commissions, and from regional Federal offices or wildflower departments. Check also with the Department of Soil Conservation in your state to find out if any wildflower species are endangered in your area. Avoid digging them. If you go to a dig, try to transplant the wildflowers within 24 hours.

Many people propagate their own wildflowers from seeds and cuttings. This method is fascinating but time-consuming, because some plants could take several years to bloom from seed.

Where can we order wildflower seeds, root stock, or transplants? We cannot find them in our local nursery.

There are a number of nurseries that offer wildflowers. Here are a few of them that you might wish to write for catalogs.

Lloyd Tate
Beersheba Wildflower Gardens
Beersheba Springs, TN 37305

Ruth Hardy's Wildflower Nursery
Route 7—South Canaan Road
Falls Village, CT 06031

Carroll Abbott's Green Horizons
400 Thompson Drive
Kerrville, TX 78029

The Three Laurels
Route 3, Box 15
Marshall, NC 28753

Charles H. Meuller
River Road
New Hope, PA 18938

Van Bourgondien Brothers
Box A
Babylon, NY 11702

Environmental Seed Producers, Inc.
P. O. Box 5904
El Monte, CA 91734

Vick's Wildgardens, Inc.
Box 115
Gladwyne, PA 19035

George W. Park Seed Company
Box 31
Greenwood, SC 29647

Wayside Gardens
Hodges, SC 29695

Jackson & Perkins Company
Medford, OR 97501

Winder's Wildflower Nursery
2925 Peoria Road
Springfield, IL 62701

Mellinger's Nursery
2310 West South Range
North Lima, OH 44452

I have ordered some wildflowers in the mail. What kind of care should I give them when they arrive?

Prepare the soil in the garden bed before your wildflowers arrive. If the plants arrive bare-rooted, soak the roots in water for at least two hours before planting. If they arrive with soil balls or in containers, set them directly in the garden, observing any special instructions that come with them. Water thoroughly. For about a week after planting, protect them from the sun and keep them moist.

Can you give me some hints on gathering wildflower seeds?

While the flower is still in bloom, cut a piece of muslin or nylon stocking large enough to fit over the flower head. Secure it over the flower with a twist tie around the stem. In a couple of weeks, the seeds should have dropped from the flower and collected in the cloth cover. Shake a few seeds on the ground to help nature replenish its stock, and put the remaining seeds in an envelope. To avoid mixing the seeds, use a separate envelope for each plant. On the envelope, note the name of the plant, light and soil conditions in the area, and other important information about the plant's environment. If possible, collect some soil from around the parent plant; seeds usually germinate more readily if sown in the original soil.

Seeds should be sown in flats at once; if you must wait, spread the seeds out on sheets of paper to dry. Then clean them by gently rubbing off the husks or soaking them in water overnight. Allow them to dry on a fine mesh screen; then store them in a cool, dry place until you are ready to plant.

What wildflowers can I plant for an extended season of bloom in my wildflower garden? It is a woodlands type of environment.

Start with some of early spring's favorites: purple blue bird's-foot violet (*Viola pedata*); tiny round-lobed hepatica (*Hepatica americana*) blooming in blue, white, or purple; 6-inch-tall dwarf iris (*Iris verna*) with orange- or yellow-banded violet flowers; and the delicate white rue anemone (*Anemonella thalictroides*). The white blossoms of bloodroot (*Sanguinaria canadensis*) and May apple (*Podophylum peltatum*) appear in spring. Move from late spring into early summer with the exotic red and yellow flowers of columbine (*Aquilegia canadensis*), Jack-in-the-pulpit (*Arisaema triphyllum*), the blue flowers of Virginia spiderwort (*Tradescantia virginiana*) and Jacob's ladder (*Polemonium reptans*), and the white blossoms of Canada violet (*Viola canadensis*).

From early to midsummer, low-growing partridgeberry (*Mitchella repens*) produces ½-inch waxy, fragrant white or pink flowers, while Canada lily (*Lilium canadense*) sends up 2- to 6-foot stems topped by brown-spotted orange yellow flowers. In summer and early fall, the brilliant red blossoms of bee balm (*Monarda didyma*) and cardinal flower (*Lobelia cardinalis*), the delicate pink of wild bleeding heart (*Dicentra eximia*), and the purple or pink of wild asters (*Aster sp.*) will splash your woodlands garden with color.

All of these wildflowers should be grown in light shade and moist, well-drained, humus-rich soil with a pH of 6.0. Jacob's ladder, bee balm, and asters may also be planted in full sun. Dwarf iris may thrive in a sandier, more acidic soil than the other plants will tolerate.

Plant nursery stock in the spring, except bleeding heart, which should be planted in the fall. Most of these wildflowers may also be propagated by dividing roots or clumps in early spring. Some will grow well from seed; sow Virginia spiderwort in late summer and

Jack-in-the-pulpit's unusual striped green flower appears in late spring or early summer.

Wild ginger thrives in the shade or filtered sun. In mid-spring, tiny flowers appear beneath the leaves.

Orange butterfly weed can provide brilliant summer color in a sunny area with moist moderately acid soil.

Jacob's ladder, Canada violet, bee balm, and asters in fall. (*See* pages 216, 213 for specific information on planting hepatica, cardinal flower, and Jack-in-the-pulpit. *See* page 55 for information on planting iris.)

Can you recommend some wildflowers that will grow well in the shade?

A shady forest is home for many wildflowers and ferns, including trillium (*Trillium sp.*), snakeroot (*Cimicifuga racemosa*), Dutchman's-breeches (*Dicentra cucullaria*), maidenhair fern (*Adiantum sp.*), Indian pink (*Spigelia marilandica*), and wild ginger (*Asarum canadense*). These will grow well in your garden, in filtered sun or shade, as will any of the wildflowers suggested for an extended season of bloom in a woodlands type of garden (*see* previous question).

We have a sunny, open area that we would like to plant in wildflowers. Would it be possible to have flowers blooming there from spring to fall?

You can have color from spring through fall in your sunny area by planting wildflowers with successive blooming seasons. If the soil is sandy, rich in humus, well drained, and slightly acid to neutral (6.0 to 7.0), try California poppies (*Eschscholzia californica*) and shooting stars (*Dodecatheon meadia*) for early spring bloom. To follow these into early summer, plant Queen Anne's lace (*Daucus carota*) and red gilia (*Ipomopsis rubra*). In summer, fill your open field with the color of coreopsis (*Coreopsis lanceolata*), blanketflower (*Gaillardia aristata*), black-eyed Susan (*Rudbeckia hirta*), oxeye daisy (*Chrysanthemum leucanthemum*), and orange butterfly weed (*Asclepias tuberosa*). Then from midsummer into fall you can enjoy purple coneflower (*Echinacea purpurea*), hardy ageratum (*Eupatorium coelestinum*), wild bergamot (*Monarda fistulosa*), blazing star (*Liatris sp.*), and goldenrod (*Solidago sp.*).

If your clearing has a moderately acid (5.5 to 6.5), moist, rich soil like that of a woodlands environment, plant marsh marigolds (*Caltha palustris*), bluets (*Hedyotis caerulea*), common golden star grass (*Hypoxis hirsuta*), fire pinks (*Silene virginica*), and wild pinks (*S. caroliniana*) for spring color. For summer bloom, plant Carolina lupine (*Thermopsis caroliniana*), common sundrop (*Oenothera fruticosa*), common blue-eyed grass (*Sisyrinchium angustifolium*), and orange butterfly weed. Bonesets (*Eupatorium perfoliatum*), ageratum, goldenrod, asters, sneezeweed (*Helenium sp.*), and narrow-leaved sunflower (*Helianthus sp.*) will provide color from summer to fall.

Can you recommend some wildflowers that will give some blue color to my garden?

Try mass plantings of blue flag iris (*Iris virginica*), common blue-eyed grass, hairy spiderwort (*Tradescantia hirsuticaulis*), dayflower (*Commelina sp.*), skullcap (*Scutellaria integrifolia*), spiderwort, stoke's aster (*Stokesia laevis*), or sundial lupine (*Lupinus perennis*) for a sweep of blue in your garden.

Popular Wildflowers

I have a collection of azaleas and rhododendrons. Are there any wildflowers that will grow well in their shade in that moist, acid soil?

There are many wildflowers that will thrive in that environment. Partridgeberry, trout lily or common fawnlily (*Erythronium americanum*), round-lobed hepatica, creeping phlox (*Phlox stolonifera*), galax (*Galax urceolata*), and trillium are a few.

Do you recommend growing bloodroot from seeds or from rhizomes?

Bloodroot, a spring-blooming perennial, may be grown from seeds sown in late summer, but plants will not bloom for two or three years. To start from seed, sow in a mixture of leaf mold, sand, and sphagnum moss and place in a cold frame. Seedlings will appear in the spring; transplant them to the garden when the leaves are 1 inch wide.

To get blooms the first or second year, plant rhizomes in the fall. Divide established plants or purchase nursery stock and set the rhizomes ½ to 1 inch deep and 6 inches apart, with the bud end pointing up. Plant bloodroot in moist, humus-rich, moderately acid soil (pH 5.5 to 6.5), and protect it from strong winds. Bloodroot grows well under deciduous trees, as it requires sunlight in spring, and shade in summer. It bears single white flowers on a 6- to 9-inch stem. After the flowers die, the deeply lobed foliage unfolds to form a thick, green carpet which lasts until late summer.

Can you give me some tips for growing bluebonnets from seeds?

Texas bluebonnets (*Lupinus texensis*) are easy to grow in your garden from seeds. To have bluebonnets blooming in the spring, sow the seeds in late summer or early fall. They need cool weather to germinate, and planting early will allow time for the plants to become established over the winter months.

The key to successful germination is good penetration of the seed coat. Before planting, soak bluebonnet seeds in warm water for three or four days, changing the water daily. Even those gardeners who plant as late as December may have successful germination with the following seed treatment—place the seeds in the freezer for two days; then remove and cover them with boiling water. Soak them for two days, draining and adding more hot water daily.

Sow the treated seeds ½ inch deep in a well-prepared bed; in large planting areas, scatter them over slightly loosened soil. Cover the seeds lightly but firmly, as bluebonnets must have darkness to germinate. Water thoroughly after planting, maintaining even soil moisture until germination has occurred. Although adequate water is essential, never allow the soil to become waterlogged. Like many other wildflowers, bluebonnets do best when lightly mulched with pine straw, leaves, or other organic matter.

In mid-February when flower buds begin to form, pinch out the first flowering stalk of each plant as soon as it develops. This forces the plant to produce additional flower spikes, which increases the number of blooms and may extend flowering up to a month.

Can you suggest how and where I might use Texas bluebonnets in my garden?

Texas bluebonnets adapt well to many situations in the home landscape, provided they are grown in a sunny location and well-drained soil. Perhaps the most spectacular use is in a mass planting, as the bright-blue drifts in early spring create an effect reminiscent of a Texas hillside. But bluebonnets are also handsome in planting beds either alone or in combination with annuals and perennials such as pansies, columbine, cottage pinks, and sweet William.

What conditions does cardinal flower need to grow in a wildflower garden?

The cardinal flower can be found along stream beds and other low, wet places in the

Try underplanting azaleas and rhododendrons with galax. In spring and summer, stalks of white flowers tower above the glossy, evergreen leaves.

To enjoy bluebonnets in the spring, sow the seeds in late summer or early fall.

Cardinal flower provides a splash of vivid red in the wild-flower garden.

Wild columbine is native to every Southern state.

The yellow flowers of common fawnlily will reappear every year.

wild, but it is also a favorite plant for the cultivated garden. A perennial, it usually grows from 2 to 4 feet tall. In late summer, it bears brilliant red flowers that attract hummingbirds.

Cardinal flower does well in partial shade or full sun. It needs a moist, slightly acid, well-drained soil rich in humus. When planting, add peat moss to improve the soil, and mulch to keep the soil cool and moist.

I planted some columbine in my wildflower garden, but it only produced foliage and no flowers. What did I do wrong?

Columbine is one of the easiest wildflowers to cultivate; but if the soil is too rich, the plants will produce lush foliage and no flowers. Plant columbine in partial shade in moist, well-drained, sandy, slightly acid soil.

The best way to start this spring-blooming perennial is to set out nursery-grown plants in the early spring or fall. Established plants have long roots and are hard to transplant. Columbine may also be started easily from ripened seeds. Sow the seeds outdoors in early spring or summer, or indoors in flats in winter. When grown from seed, the plants should produce their small, graceful, red and yellow blossoms the second year.

Please tell me how to grow common fawnlily. Will I have to replant it every year?

The common fawnlily, also called trout lily, yellow adder's tongue, and dogtooth violet, is a favorite for the wildflower garden. It grows from slender, deeply buried corms and bears solitary ½-inch yellow blossoms on top of 4- to 10-inch stems in the spring. Its mottled green and purplish brown foliage dies back in midsummer.

The fawnlily prefers light shade and moist, humus-rich, acid soil. To grow fawnlily, plant corms in the fall or summer, about 6 inches deep and 4 to 6 inches apart. The fawnlily will perpetuate itself but can be propagated in summer or fall from small offsets. It can also be grown from seed but may take many years to reach flowering size.

Can you recommend some native ferns that we can plant in our garden?

Hardy native ferns that will grow well in gardens as far south as northern Florida include Christmas fern (*Polystichum acrostichoides*), cinnamon fern (*Osmunda cinnamomea*), broad beech fern (*Thelypteris hexagonoptera*), blunt-lobed woodsia (*Woodsia obtusa*), rattlesnake fern (*Botrychium virginianum*), purple cliff-brake (*Pellaea atropurpurea*), Virginia chain fern (*Woodwardia virginica*), and netted chain fern (*W. areolata*). All of these ferns require deep, humus-rich, moist soil with good drainage.

The Christmas fern, among the first to send up its fiddleheads in the spring, grows easily in deep shade and requires a heavy mulch of leaves. It can tolerate sunlight if soil is consistently moist. Its evergreen leaves may grow up to 3 feet long and 5 inches wide.

Cinnamon fern will grow in either shade or partial sun, provided it is planted in acid, constantly damp soil. The sterile leaves grow 24 to 36 inches long. Cinnamon fern also produces erect, fertile leaves which look like cinnamon sticks because of the brown, tightly clustered spore cases. The fern spreads slowly.

Broad beech fern, also commonly called Southern beech fern, requires partial shade and an acid soil. The broad, triangular leaves reach 10 to 24 inches in length, and the fern spreads rapidly.

The blunt-lobed woodsia is easy to grow in open to medium shade and neutral soil. Its narrow leaf (about 3 inches wide) grows 12 to 16 inches long.

The rattlesnake fern prefers light shade and a neutral or slightly acid soil. Unlike most ferns, the rattlesnake fern forms its leaves underground in late winter. Before the fiddleheads of other ferns emerge, this fern's leaves push upward through the soil and open, fully developed, when completely above ground. It grows from 6 to 30 inches in height.

The purple cliff-brake grows in limestone crevices. You can grow it in your garden by piling several rocks together and planting the fern in the openings between them, where it can reach moist soil. Purple cliff-brake fern tolerates sun but must be watered in dry weather. Its small leaves (6 to 8 inches long) remain evergreen in the Lower South.

Virginia chain fern and netted chain fern will tolerate full sun if planted in moist, acid soil. These ferns spread rapidly and require large areas in which to grow. They will reach heights of 36 to 48 inches.

In addition to these ferns, gardeners in the Upper and Middle South can plant hay scented fern (*Dennstaedtia punctilobula*), silvery glade fern (*Athyrium thelypteroides*), intermediate shield fern (*Dryopteris intermedia*), marginal shield fern (*D. marginalis*), common maidenhair, ebony spleenwort (*Asplenium platyneuron*), maidenhair spleenwort (*A. trichomanes*), hairy lip fern (*Cheilanthes lanosa*), New York fern (*Thelypteris noveboracensis*), and Southern lady fern (*Athyrium asplenioides*).

The hay scented fern will grow in almost any soil. It can tolerate prolonged wet or dry weather and deep shade or full sun. It grows best, however, in slightly acid, damp woodland soil. Hay scented fern adapts readily to home gardens and spreads rapidly. Its feathery leaves grow 20 to 32 inches long and 11 inches wide.

The silvery glade fern will thrive in a soil mixture of rotted leaves, sand, and garden soil. It tolerates sunlight if the soil is constantly damp. Also called silvery spleenwort, the silvery glade fern produces graceful fronds that grow 3 feet tall and 7 inches wide.

Intermediate and marginal shield ferns require full to light shade and a neutral to slightly acid soil. Keep soil moist during the summer. The evergreen leaves of intermediate shield fern grow 30 inches long and 10 inches wide. Marginal shield fern, also evergreen, is slightly smaller. Its leaves reach 15 to 20 inches in length and 5 to 8 inches in width. Neither fern spreads.

The common maidenhair requires constant moisture to remain green from spring to fall. It grows 12 to 26 inches tall and bears its pinnae or leaflets in a distinctive fan shape parallel to the ground.

Ebony spleenwort grows well in rock gardens and can tolerate short dry spells. Its sterile, narrow leaves grow from 6 to 20 inches long and are evergreen.

Maidenhair spleenwort should be planted like purple cliff-brake fern, in a rock crevice. Plant it in humus-rich soil mixed with small pieces of limestone, and keep the soil moist. Maidenhair spleenwort is small (6 inches long) and evergreen.

Hairy lip fern prefers protected areas but is not particular about soil. During dry weather, water the fern to keep its 6- to 8-inch-long leaves green.

New York fern and Southern lady fern prefer moist, shady areas like their native swamps and woodlands. If kept moist, however, New York fern can tolerate bright light. New York fern grows 12 to 24 inches tall, while Southern lady fern reaches heights of 16 to 40 inches.

Can I grow wild ginger in my home garden?

Wild ginger can be grown in the home garden very successfully. It grows close to the ground, producing a pair of heart-shaped leaves, each up to 7 inches across. In the spring

Broad beech fern may grow up to 2 feet tall and will spread rapidly if planted in a suitable environment.

Common maidenhair fern is a favorite for wildflower gardens because of its distinctive shape and soft texture.

Hay-scented fern makes a good ground cover for slopes.

In early spring, croziers or fiddleheads push up through the earth and begin to uncoil and grow. The color of the fiddlehead usually does not match the color of the full-grown fern.

The mottled, heart-shaped foliage of wild ginger makes a thick ground cover for wildflower gardens.

Hepatica's pink, white, or lavender blossoms are among the first flowers of spring.

Atamasco lily can be expected to grow in home gardens throughout the South.

The speckled, orange red petals of Carolina lily curl back to touch the base of the flower.

Yellow lady's slipper is a popular native orchid.

it bears small, brownish, urn-shaped flowers in the axil of the leaves. Its name comes from the fact that its rhizome has a spicy, gingerlike smell.

Wild ginger needs shade and a slightly acid, moist, humus-rich soil. Plant in the spring or fall by burying the rhizome about ½ inch deep, with the tip just reaching the soil level. Be sure to mulch as the rhizomes must be kept moist. Wild ginger will seed itself and sometimes has a tendency to spread.

What kind of care does sharp-lobed hepatica require?

Sharp-lobed hepatica (*Hepatica acutiloba*), one of the first flowers to appear in the early spring, thrives in rocky, humus-rich, well-drained soil. It grows best on a hilly location. To bear its small white, pink, or lavender flowers, hepatica requires some direct light, but it does best in a shady location. It will put out new leaves after it blooms. The leathery three-lobed leaves will remain through the winter and should be covered with a light mulch before the first frost. Sharp-lobed hepatica can be propagated by seed or by division in spring after blooming.

Jack-in-the-pulpit is such an unusual-looking plant. Is it difficult to grow?

Jack-in-the-pulpit is a favorite wildflower that is often used in the garden. Its name comes from its green and brown flower with a spadix (flower spike in a fleshy, succulent axis) that appears to be standing in the pulpit.

Jack-in-the-pulpit grows 1 to 3 feet tall and prefers moist, humus-rich, acid soil and partial shade. It requires constant dampness or it will be stunted. Sow seeds in flats in the fall and transplant the next summer. The plant will bloom the second year after the seeds are sown.

Will Atamasco lily naturalize easily in the home garden?

Atamasco lily or zephyr lily (*Zephyranthes atamasco*) is an excellent bulbous perennial for naturalizing in the garden. Solitary white to light-pink flowers are borne erect on 4- to 10-inch stems during March and April. This woodland plant requires moist, peaty soil and partial shade. Native to the Lower Piedmont and Coastal Plains, atamasco lily can be expected to grow well throughout the South. In the landscape, naturalize atamasco lilies with crocus and jonquils in a shaded, preferably wooded, area.

Where will Carolina lilies grow?

Carolina lilies (*Lilium michauxii*) are native to the hillsides and mountains of the Piedmont and can be found from northern Florida and Georgia to Virginia and West Virginia. These plants prefer sun but may tolerate partial shade if soil and other factors are favorable. They must be staked if wind is a problem. The speckled, orange red flowers, drooping from 1- to 4-foot stems, bloom in August and September in groups of one to six.

Are there any native orchids that I can grow in my wildflower garden?

Try yellow lady's slipper (*Cypripedium calceolus*). It may be found in boggy deciduous woodlands as far south as Georgia and North Alabama. *C. calceolus* Pubescens has larger flowers than the parviflorum type; pubescens grows from 18 inches to 36 inches tall, bearing one to three blossoms on each stalk.

Purchase yellow lady's slippers from a reputable wildflower nursery. If you dig specimens in the wild, dig only those growing in a field in full sun. Lady's slippers growing in shade transplant poorly. Plant them in rotted hardwood, setting the rhizomes 1 to 1½ inches deep. Give them plenty of water and mulch lightly. Yellow lady's slippers will grow best if left in a permanent location.

Maypop passionflower is so exotic looking. Can I grow it in my garden?

Maypop passionflower (*Passiflora incarnata*) grows easily in gardens from Virginia and Kentucky south to Texas and Florida. In early summer, the light-purple flowers unfold and the vine becomes a delight, despite its tendency to become a weed. Stems grow 10 to 25 feet and climb by means of tendrils. This perennial is not particular about soil but must have full sun. Grow the vines on arbors, fences, walls, mailbox posts, lampposts, or anywhere a climbing vine can be displayed to full advantage.

Where can I obtain seeds for Queen Anne's lace? I cannot find it listed in garden catalogs.

Although easily grown from seeds, Queen Anne's lace is rarely found in garden catalogs. The easiest way to obtain seeds is to make a note of where you see the plants in bloom in June, and return during July or August to collect seeds from the dried stems.

Seeds are mature when they turn a deep gray. As they fall to the ground, many are caught in the center of the "nest" where you will find them tangled in their own spines. Put the seeds in an envelope and keep refrigerated until you are ready to sow them.

When should Queen Anne's lace be planted? Can you give me some tips on how to plant it?

Seeds may be sown outdoors in March or April. But for a headstart, sow them indoors three months before the last expected frost. Because germinating seedlings will compete and become stunted, the seeds need to be sown thinly; allow at least ¼ inch between each. Sprinkle the seeds on the surface of a loose medium such as equal parts peat, sand, and vermiculite. Sift another layer of medium over the seeds so they are about ⅛ inch deep. Germination will occur in one to two weeks.

When the seedlings reach 1 inch tall, transplant them into 3-inch pots and place in full sun. Plant them in the garden after danger of frost has passed. Because the plants are biennials, you can expect blooms the second season.

As evidenced by the profusion of flowers along roadsides, Queen Anne's lace is not particular about soil. It only needs to be well drained. But with any plant, a little care will ensure not only survival, but larger, more abundant flowers. So for best growth and flowering, work a generous amount of organic matter into the planting site.

Would wild sweet William be suitable for a small woodland garden?

Wild sweet William (*Phlox divaricata*) would be very suitable for a small woodland garden. This spring-blooming perennial, bearing clusters of blue to purple flowers on 8- to 18-inch stems, does best in a woodland-type environment. It needs moist, humus-rich soil with a moderately acid to neutral pH and partial shade like that supplied by deciduous trees. Wild sweet William will sow itself by seeds but can also be propagated by stem cuttings.

Can you suggest some trilliums for my garden?

There are dozens of species of this spring-blooming woodland perennial. Three

Maypop passionflower grows readily in the home garden, climbing on arbors, fences, or lampposts.

The best way to get seeds of Queen Anne's lace is to collect them from the dried stems in July or August.

Sow seeds of Queen Anne's lace in early spring to enjoy a profusion of blossoms in early summer.

Once established in a woodlands garden, wild sweet William will propagate itself by seeds.

The best way to start trilliums is from rhizomes planted in the fall. Plants started from seed will not be large enough to flower for several years.

White trillium changes from white to rose pink as the flowers age.

Toadshade's mottled leaves and purple brown flowers make a striking spring show in the wildflower garden.

favorites for the home garden are: white trillium (*Trillium grandiflorum*), bearing a white flower up to 6 inches wide that turns to a rose color as it ages; purple trillium (*T. erectum*), with a smaller, maroon-colored flower; and prairie trillium (*T. recurvatum*). Unlike the other trilliums, prairie trillium is often grown for its silver and green foliage. It also bears a small flower with erect, brown maroon petals. Similar species include the narrow-leaved trillium (*T. lancifolium*) and toadshade trillium (*T. cuneatum*). Some of these have green or yellow flowers.

What conditions do trilliums need?

Trilliums do best in partial shade with moist, humus-rich, slightly acid soil. Because they grow from rhizomes, they should not be picked. The rhizomes need the foliage to replenish nutrients for next year's blooms.

What is the best way to start trilliums for the garden?

Trilliums can be started from seed, but it may be several years before they are large enough to flower. Most are grown from rhizomes planted in the fall. Plant the rhizomes 2 to 4 inches deep and be sure the eyes are facing upward.

Can I grow Virginia bluebells in my home garden?

Virginia bluebells (*Mertensia virginica*) are easy to grow and will do well in the home garden. These natives of Virginia have arching stems 1 to 3 feet high that bear clusters of small blue "bells" in the spring.

Virginia bluebells prefer partial shade, but they will grow in full sun. They need humus-rich, slightly acid soil, and must be kept moist in the spring. If spring weather is dry, mulch Virginia bluebells well and water them frequently. In the summer, when the foliage dies back and the plants go dormant, they can tolerate some dryness. Be sure to plant later-blooming flowers around Virginia bluebells to avoid having a bare spot in your garden when the bluebells die back.

What is the best way to propagate Virginia bluebells?

To propagate Virginia bluebells, divide the young roots in the summer, after the foliage has died. You can also propagate them from seeds sown in spring, summer, or fall. One drawback to propagation from seeds is that the plants will not flower until the third year.

After blooming in the spring, Virginia bluebells will go dormant and the foliage will die back.

Index

DECORATING & CRAFT IDEAS — The Nation's Leading Craft Magazine ... and a PLUS for the creative person.

DECORATING & CRAFT IDEAS is about ...

The craft favorites — from stenciling, miniatures and woodworking, to tole painting, nature crafts and holiday decorations.

Fashion needlecrafts — for the home or wardrobe. We cover crochet, knitting, needlepoint, quilting, cross stitch, and more.

Decorating — and how to make your home more inviting. The monthly features detail simple, yet effective ideas on making the most of what you have, plus incorporating completed craft projects into your decor.

Creative cooking — and how to channel your craft talents into the kitchen. For special times or everyday, our food editors show you how meals can have creative eye-appeal as well as fantastic flavor.

Fashion sewing — and how simple it can be to expand a wardrobe and choose the perfect accessories for that "finished look." Plus tips to make your sewing easier.

To find out how you can receive DECORATING & CRAFT IDEAS every month, simply write to: DECORATING & CRAFT IDEAS, P. O. Box C-30, Birmingham, AL 35283